'A heartening book, confronting the hardest questions with wide knowledge and deep wisdom.'

John Carey, Emeritus Merton Professor of English Literature, University of Oxford, and Chief Literary Reviewer, Sunday Times

'In a world so blatantly imperfect and bearing no obvious hallmarks of purpose, the challenges facing Christianity are severe. Richard Harries is one of those who realize that and takes the challenges seriously. Those of us who are not in the end persuaded by his Christian defence can nonetheless appreciate the sensitivity and intelligence with which it is mounted. It is the best case that could be made.'

Andrew Copson, Director, British Humanist Association

'Mingling intellectual rigour with spiritual wisdom, Harries helps his readers to grasp the relevance of the insights at the core of the Christian faith.'

Alister E. McGrath, Andreas Idreos Professor of Science and Religion, University of Oxford

'*The Beauty and the Horror* is the most compelling exploration of suffering in the world that I have ever read . . . Written with grace and clarity, this is a book of rare power – such that, once you have finished it, you know you have been changed.'

Ian S. Markham, Dean and President, Virginia Theological Seminary

'With all his characteristic clarity of thought, Richard Harries probes how we can find God in suffering and horror, as well as beauty . . . The result is a profound statement of what it means to have faith in the living tradition of Christianity, guided by hope and love.'

Jane Shaw, Dean for Religious Life and Professor of Religious Studies, Stanford University

'What has the Bishop to say to Ivan Karamazov or Albert Camus? They posed the most formidable cases against belief in God in the past 150 years. But is there Beauty as well as Horror? Richard Harries offers us the fruit of a lifetime's deep reflection on this question in a book that will help many, both believer and non-believer, to reach beyond the shallow assumptions of atheistic rationalism.'

Lord Sutherland of Houndwood, former Professor of the History and Philosophy of Religion, King's College, London, and Vice Chancellor, University of Edinburgh

THE BEAUTY AND THE HORROR

RICHARD HARRIES

SPCK

First published in Great Britain in 2016

Society for Promoting Christian Knowledge
36 Causton Street
London SW1P 4ST
www.spck.org.uk

British Library Cataloguing-in-Publication Data
A catalogue record for this book is available from the British Library

ISBN 978–0–281–07693–2
eBook ISBN 978–0–281–07694–9

Typeset by Graphicraft Limited, Hong Kong
First printed in Great Britain by TJ International
Subsequently digitally reprinted in Great Britain

eBook produced by Graphicraft Limited, Hong Kong

Produced on paper from sustainable forests

For Luke, Toby, Ben and Sophie

I am extremely grateful to those who have read this book, or part of it, and kindly offered me their thoughts and suggestions: John Barton, John Carey, Andrew Copson, Andrew St George, Stewart Sutherland and Philip Law.

Contents

1

Life – so astonishing and so appalling

The beauty

One evening I arrived a little early for a speaking engagement at the 'Words on Water' literary festival in the theatre at Keswick. With half an hour to spare I walked along the edge of Derwentwater to Friar's Crag and looked out over the lake and mountains. Above the hills on the horizon a pale sun shone through the mist. I stood still, reluctant to move or avert my gaze, so transfixed was I by the beauty and stillness of the scene. 'How can anyone bear not to live here all the time?' was the thought in my mind. It is a very unusual person who has not had some such experience, perhaps looking at a landscape, a flower in the garden or a newborn baby. In these moments we are moved in a way that only poets seem to be able to convey. There is a sense of wonder, even awe, so that we want simply to shut off the chattering mind and be still. There is also an elusiveness about such experiences. We cannot quite grasp the scene or the moment, or its meaning. Strangely, we want to pass into it and become part of it, but we can't. The poet Edward Thomas wrote about this experience in his poem 'Glory', which contains the line 'I cannot bite the day to the core.'[1]

There is too sometimes a sense of poignancy, for this like all moments will pass. We are brought short before the passingness of things, the brevity of life, and at the same time the continuity of life without us. A friend writes of walking along with his wife one day before breakfast and seeing the sight of their shadows holding hands on the cobbles. He asked her if she would promise to bring back their grandchildren to see their shadows holding her hand. He sees experiences like this as spiritual moments. It is a moment that combines beauty, tenderness, poignancy within an overall sense of mystery, the mystery of life itself.

What I saw over Derwentwater from Friar's Crag was Ruskin's favourite view. Not surprisingly he and many others have interpreted such experiences in specifically religious terms, and carved on the monument to Ruskin on that spot are the words:

> The Spirit of God is around you in the air you breathe.
> His glory in the light you see and in the fruitfulness of
>   the earth and the joy of his creatures.
> He has written for you day by day his revelation as he
>   has granted you day by day your daily bread.

However the problem with religion, for many people, is that it seems to tie such experiences up too neatly in human words. It wants to contain them in a way their very elusiveness denies. We know that anything pat simply does not do them justice. As the painter de Chirico wrote, 'There is much more mystery in the shadow of a man walking on a sunny day than in all the religions of the world.'[2]

As will be stressed later, a sense of ultimate mystery is fundamental to any true religion, but the point now is that you don't have to be formally religious to sense this.

A magical moment for me is a familiar walk on the coastal path from New Quay to Llangrannog in Ceredigion. As the sun sets in the west the sea becomes a sheen of silver and the glory of the last light of the day almost overwhelming. Whatever difficulties some philosophers might find with it, the old word 'beauty' comes to mind, a beauty that at once draws us and escapes us, lures and eludes. That is a scene of dramatic light and colour, but a similar sense of wonder can be aroused by the sheer existence of something, however apparently ordinary. Still-life paintings are not fashionable at the moment but the best of them have a capacity to evoke a sense of the sheer 'isness' of some particular thing in its unique individuality. On a bookshelf I have a postcard of a painting by Francisco de Zurbarán, *A Cup of Water and a Rose*. It shows a pottery cup on a silver plate beside a small rose, all in delicate greys and pink – an ordinary household scene, but the objects confront the viewer with their sheer existence. They might not be, but they are. That is cause for wonder enough. But this is not just existence in general. The cup and plate and rose stand before the viewer in their unique particularity. Anything can have this effect on us, a leaf on a tree, a shell on the shore or a living being. Most of us go about our daily business taking things for granted. But some people seem to live with an extraordinary intensity, almost bowled over by the reality of the world about them – Thomas Traherne, William Blake, Walt Whitman and Stanley Spencer, to take just a few examples of very different people who shared this intensity.

Duns Scotus was a philosopher who, unusually, focused not on great universal truths but on particulars in their individuality; not just their 'thisness' in general but their 'thisness' as this or that unique object, their *haecitas*. The philosophy of Scotus found poetic expression particularly in the work of Gerard Manley Hopkins, whose language breaks all the usual bounds in order to convey something of this effect on him. The artist Stanley Spencer was another person almost overwhelmed by the strength of his astonishment. He wrote:

> When I lived in Cookham I was disturbed by a feeling of everything being meaningless. Quite suddenly I became aware that everything was full of special meaning, and this made everything holy. The instinct of Moses to take his shoes off when he saw the burning bush was very similar to my feelings. I saw many burning bushes in Cookham. I observed the sacred quality in the most unexpected quarters.[3]

The intensity of his feelings can be gauged by a remark he once made, probably about his friends the Slessors.

> I remember having some friends I was always meeting in the evenings and did not see anything special about them until one day I went to have breakfast with them, and seeing them at breakfast gave me wonderful feelings about them. I was so overcome that I could not eat my breakfast, not even bread and butter.[4]

The beauty referred to in the title of this book is above all the kind of beauty people like Hopkins and Spencer and other artists have tried to convey. It is the beauty of existence as such, the fact that something might not have existed, or might have existed differently, but there it is, as uniquely itself. The experience is also one of wonder and awe, but I use the word 'beauty' because this implies an evaluative element. In such experiences, we respond to that which we recognize as having value; it is worthwhile in itself for itself, and this both excites and draws us to it.

The horror

However this joy in being alive, this exultation in existence as such, coexists with another very different reaction. In the small hours of a morning in 1961, Samuel Beckett was sitting over a drink in a Paris café with his fellow playwright Harold Pinter. Pinter suggested that Beckett's work was an attempt to impose order and form on the wretched mess mankind had made of the world, but Beckett disagreed.

> If you must insist on finding form, I'll describe it for you. I was in hospital once. There was a man in another ward dying of throat cancer. In the silence, I could hear the screams continually. That's the only kind of form my work has.[5]

Advances in palliative care since then have made such a scene much less likely in the West. Strong painkilling drugs administered at the correct intervals can control almost all forms of physical pain. But that does not alter the fundamental point that in so many ways and in so many places the screams of sufferers continue to cry out.

'Don't kill me, Mum.' These were the last words of an eight-year-old boy as his mother pushed him under the water in the bath and killed him. Some years before she had killed her two young babies but it was thought, tragically, that she was now in her right mind and her older boy was safe.

On 24 March 2015, Andreas Lubitz deliberately flew the plane of which he was the co-pilot into a mountain, killing all 150 people on board. That was horror enough. But the horror is intensified at the thought that as he went on board he greeted his colleagues in the usual way. Yet behind his 'Good morning' was not just a depressed mind but one fixed on bringing about the deaths of everyone on board. Many people suffer from depression, but planning and executing the deaths of others in such a way is something very different. What goes on behind the facades we put up? What is going on the in the minds of those who commit terrorist atrocities or child abuse? Such questions strip away all that we take for granted about what is normal, the assumptions we work on day by day.

These are just examples of the kinds of story one can read or hear about through the media every day, from many different parts of the world. Recently it has been the horror of whole families of refugees being drowned in flimsy rubber boats. The cries are unceasing, the horror unending. One that has haunted me all my life dates from the time when I was working as a curate in Hampstead. I used to visit a lady who had a cancer that had spread and eaten up her face. It was partly hollowed out so that you saw straight into the back of the mouth and throat. What was particularly terrible is that rather than seeking medical help at an early stage of the illness she had been persuaded that if only she had faith enough, God would heal her. Her sense of isolation was total.

That is horror enough but there is horror of a more fundamental kind involved in the very fact of being human. In the modern world, it is above all Samuel Beckett who has expressed this. I have been fortunate enough to see two great performances of his play *Happy Days*, the first with Peggy Ashcroft in the starring role, the second with Billie Whitelaw. In the play Winnie, the main character, sits in the centre of stage in a pile of sand. In the first part of the play, the sand is up to her waist, in the second up to her neck, with a fierce light blazing down from above. At the edge of the heap of sand is her husband, Willie, trying, but not able, to crawl forward. There is a revolver he might be able to reach. The rising pile of sand is an obvious but powerful symbol of our mortality, as is the revolver of the latent violence in so many of our close relationships. But the genius of the play is in the poignant monologue of Winnie as she tries to keep her spirits up. She fiddles with the objects in her handbag and tells herself little sayings and prayers, always trying to look on the bright side of things. In one way, the play superbly depicts a view of life, partly philosophical and partly religious, that has been very common in history, namely that we are essentially souls imprisoned in bodies, longing for our release. That is not a view most of us share today because we know that body and mind are a unity, that we are a psychosomatic whole, that what we do physically to the brain affects the way we think and feel. We are embodied selves, to use the current jargon. But this does not take away from the fact that our conscious self can feel very vulnerable to the way we are at the mercy of the physical side of our nature, our genetic inheritance and the extraordinarily complex organisms that make up each one of us. We can think wonderful thoughts but all the time we are dependent on the millions of operations going on in our genes, which are the product of billions of years of evolution, an evolution at least partly dictated by the struggle to eat and avoid being eaten.

I think it was this kind of nameless horror that was behind some of Beckett's more challenging plays, not just the horror of decrepit old age as in *Endgame* but something else, as in *Not I*, which consists of a large illuminated mouth on stage uttering a loud, non-stop monologue of increasing anxiety. Again, I was fortunate enough to see a powerful performance by Billie Whitelaw, and such was the intensity that at one point my wife and I just had to put our heads down and stop looking.

It is, I suspect, this more fundamental fear that lies behind one of the most famous utterances in modern literature, the last words of Kurtz in Joseph Conrad's novella, *Heart of Darkness*: 'The horror! The horror'.[6] It is not surprising that these words were referred to by T. S. Eliot in the epigraph to his poem 'The Hollow Men', a poem written at a time when his personal life was bleak but that also reflected the breakdown of spirit and the sense of total meaningless felt by so many in the aftermath of the First World War. A similar nameless horror is expressed in Edvard Munch's painting *The Scream*, which became one of the iconic images of the twentieth century, with its portrayal of a person on a bridge whose scream seems to fill the whole universe.

'Joy and woe are woven fine'

Life has its wonderful moments. The English scholar John Carey, having won an open scholarship to Oxford University from his small Surrey grammar school and waiting to start his studies, describes his first visit to France with a few friends in 1952.

> On our last night we stopped on our way back from dinner, lay on the sweet, dry grass – a bit drunk, I suppose – and talked dreamily of all the things we had seen. I gazed up at a sky full of stars and thought that life was unfathomably wonderful.[7]

Unfathomably wonderful, yes. But also, at times, unbearable. Indeed one recent argument is that it is so unbearable we can get by only with palliatives such as drugs or drink. This view holds that religion, though untrue, is like art and love a useful palliative provided we know it is an illusion.[8]

The beauty of life and the horror of life; the sheer wonder and awesomeness of being alive, together with an acute awareness of the prevalence of cruelty and evil in the world and the sense of nameless horror that can sometimes come over us as we become aware of ourselves as a thinking being bound up with a vulnerable body. That is the theme of this book, together with the question of whether we can find God in such a contradictory world. If life were all beauty and goodness there would be no problem. We would live our lives as an instinctive paean of praise. If life were all horror, again there would be no problem. It is difficult to see what reason there would be not to commit suicide. But the almost universal experience of humanity is that it consists of both. As William Blake put it in his poem 'Auguries of Innocence', 'joy and woe are woven fine'. There is the puzzle.

One example of how closely woven they are is experienced when we watch some of the wonderful nature programmes on television, especially those by Sir David Attenborough. We might be admiring a tiger in all its grace and beauty, as well as its skill as it hunts its prey. Then it pounces and we may have to watch a gazelle, an equally beautiful animal, being torn to pieces. No less telling are the more positive examples that can emerge out of human cruelty and suffering. A Somali terrorist group attacked a bus in northern Kenya, spraying it with bullets before demanding that all passengers get off. Muslims were to go on one side and Christians on the other, so that the former could be spared and the latter killed. However the passengers refused to split into two groups and the Christians were given some Muslim attire to hide them better among the other passengers. As one of the Muslims said, 'The militants threatened to shoot us but we still refused and protected our brothers and sisters. Finally they gave up and left.'[9] A heroic and beautiful act in the midst of terror.

Terri Roberts heard that there had been an atrocity near her home. That was bad enough. Then she learnt that it had been carried out by her son. He had gone into an Amish school, ordered the boys to leave and then shot ten girls, killing five and injuring five, one of whom was left with permanent brain damage. He then turned the gun on himself. It is difficult to imagine anything more appalling to live with. Then at the funeral she found that members of the Amish community not only came up to her to sympathize with her for the loss of her son but surrounded her in order to shield her from the press. Their care for her has continued, including welcoming her help in feeding the badly damaged child at mealtimes.[10] A beautiful community response in the midst of horror. The horror is not lessened, the suffering remains, nothing is resolved. But there is something else to put beside it. Perhaps we can all bring to mind experiences or scenes in which this is the case. A friend recalls the image of a wounded American soldier on a stretcher being loaded on to a helicopter and his sergeant holding his hand and kissing his forehead.

Dante begins his great work *The Divine Comedy*: 'In the middle of life I found myself lost in a dark wood.'[11] You do not have to be in the middle of life to find yourself in that wood. You can wake up to it when young and be conscious of it in your dying days. The mystery remains. But this book sets out on a journey to explore one particular perspective on that mystery. Can we find God in a suffering world? This does not take away the contradiction between the beauty and the horror but seeks to offer a framework in which we can live, and live better, with it. It is a book that tries to avoid cheap polemics and easy answers, taking seriously all the time the very understandable objections that might be made against the perspective from which it is written.

2

Asking the right questions

Giving our own meaning to life

Some of the people I much admire have no religious belief. They care for their families and work to alleviate suffering or protect the human rights of others just because it seems to them the right thing to do. It is obvious that you do not have to be religious in order to possess admirable qualities. Courage, integrity, idealism and generosity are shown by people of all kinds of belief and non-belief. It is arguable that the real heroine of George Eliot's novel *Middlemarch* is not Dorothea but Mary Garth. Eliot writes of her:

> Mary was fond of her own thoughts, and could amuse herself well sitting in twilight with her hands in her lap; for, having early had strong reason to believe that things were not likely to be arranged for her peculiar satisfaction, she wasted no time in astonishment and annoyance at that fact. And she had already come to take life very much as a comedy in which she had a proud, nay, a generous resolution not to act the mean or treacherous part. Mary might have become cynical if she had not had parents whom she honoured, and a well of affectionate gratitude within her, which was all the fuller because she had learned to make no unreasonable claims.[1]

What is interesting about this description of Mary's stance on life is that it makes no reference either to religion or a moral philosophy. Rather it is part of her proper pride in herself that she chooses not to be mean or treacherous. She simply does not want to be that kind of person. What is also interesting is that her stance on life might have slipped into cynicism had she not been formed by loving parents whom she honoured.

People give a variety of reasons for the values they regard as important but very often it will be as it was for Mary Garth: they want to be a particular kind of person. Furthermore what is in fact decisive is not so much any consciously chosen religion or philosophy that we might adopt but the shaping influence of our parents or those who provided the environment in which we grew up and first learnt to relate to others.

So you do not have to possess any thought-out philosophy to exhibit the kind of truthful no-nonsense love Mary Garth showed for the feckless Fred who wanted to marry her.[2] More widely, you do not need to have any religion or system of beliefs to find meaning in your life. People find meaning in many ways. Anthony Storr, the psychiatrist and author, said for example that it was music above all that gave meaning to his life. Many today would say something similar, if not about music then about one of the other art forms. When I was Dean of King's College, London, a student who was going to be ordained lost his faith. It was a traumatic experience for him but he told me later it was reading Shakespeare for a month or two afterwards that had helped him through. For others, the meaning of their life is found through doing what they can to make the world a less cruel place. For very many, the meaning is found in their family life, especially bringing up their children and enjoying their grandchildren, or their work.

In all these instances, the meaning of life is in the meaning we attribute to it. A powerful academic justification of this view is provided by the eminent legal philosopher Ronald Dworkin. In his book *Justice for Hedgehogs*, he argues that moral values are objective, existing in their own right, and that they can be neither undermined by science nor justified by any theological or metaphysical belief. He further argues that it is important for all human beings not just to recognize these values but consciously to live life well in their light. In this way, our life takes on meaning. He recognizes that there is something mysterious about wanting to live well – that is, to live a life we can take pride in – in a way that there is not about, for example, wanting to eat and drink well. He writes:

> We are charged to live well by the bare fact of our existence as self-conscious creatures with lives to lead . . . It is *important* that we live well; not important just to us or to anyone else, but just important.[3]

For him, this living well is integrally related to the value of having a critically good life; that is, one in which the human dignity of others is fully acknowledged and taken into account.[4]

This meaning had, on his view, no religious underpinning or rationale but it claimed him with something of the force of religion, hence the title of another book he wrote shortly before he died, *Religion without God*. There he spelt out the implication of his earlier book in which he had written:

> The justice we have imagined begins in what seems like an unchallengeable proposition: that government must treat those under its dominion with equal concern and respect . . . It is drawn from dignity and aims at dignity. It makes it easier and more likely for each of us to live a good life well. Remember, too, that the stakes are more than mortal. Without dignity our lives are only blinks of duration. But if we manage to live a good life well, we create something more. We write a subscript to our mortality. We make our lives tiny diamonds in the cosmic sands.[5]

That is a noble ideal. As the Nobel prize-winning physicist Steven Weinberg put it: 'There is a nobility in proceeding as if there were a purpose prescribed for us but knowing there isn't.'[6] But there is an alternative.[7] It is that life has a given meaning that we can discover and to which we can respond. So the question arises as to whether it does or does not have this meaning waiting to be discovered. It may not. Whether it does or not, as already stated, it is possible to live well, in Dworkin's sense, and therefore to invest one's life with meaning. Nevertheless it remains a genuine question as to whether life has only the meaning we attribute to it or whether there is a given meaning waiting to be recognized.

Discovering a given meaning

There is an analogy in early learning with children. They are given pieces of cardboard in different shapes and of different colours. The children begin to play with them, trying to fit one shape to another or one on top of another or one colour with another. They enjoy what they are doing, finding meaning in it. In fact the exercise has been designed to help their identification of different colours. In time they realize this. In terms of the argument in this chapter, there was a meaning in the exercise when they did it but they discovered what this was only at a later stage. The point of this analogy is to suggest that whether there is a given meaning to life that we can come to recognize is a valid and important question. The answer might still be that there is none. There are moments in the life of most of us when life seems to be getting nowhere and achieving nothing. We go on in the same dreary routine and wonder what it all adds up to. It is a mood that afflicted the writer of the book of Ecclesiastes in the Bible and in a more philosophical form has led others to assert that life is absurd. The writer Albert Camus, for example, drew on the myth of Sisyphus, who spent his whole time rolling a great stone up and down a hill; a futile activity, achieving nothing. But though we may sometimes feel that life is like that, it could be that there is a greater purpose to be discerned and a larger meaning to be glimpsed.

Yet something further arises. Is the question whether life has a larger, given meaning the right question to ask? We know that so often what we ask is decisive in shaping the kind of answer that will emerge. It may be that questions about the meaning of life are misconceived from the outset. One person who thought they were was Karl Marx. In a famous and moving passage, he wrote:

> *Religious* suffering is, at one and the same time, the *expression* of real suffering and a protest against real suffering. Religion is the sigh of the oppressed creature, the heart of a heartless world, and the soul of soulless conditions. It is the *opium* of the people.[8]

He believed that when a true society had been achieved, one no longer divided between the exploiter and the exploited, between the victors and their victims, one in which everyone contributed according to their ability and received according to their need, then religion would simply drop away. He believed we should concentrate on working for such a society and not allow ourselves to be drugged with the misplaced, illusory hope of religion.

It is difficult to deny the truth in what Marx said, that religion has too often been used by the powers that be to numb the sense of outrage and anger that would otherwise be directed against those who thwart efforts that aim at fundamentally changing an unjust world. Yet few have been finally persuaded by Marx's prediction that if such a society were achieved on earth, religion would simply die out. First, because death would remain part of our human condition. However much science might improve the length and quality of our lives, I do not see it enabling us to live for ever, even if that were desirable. Second, for the kind of society Marx envisaged to come into existence, it would require a radical overcoming of our clamant egos and our innate drive to pursue our own interests even when to do so is clearly at the expense of others. And although it might be true that we ourselves begin to change as individuals as we work to change society for the better, as Marxists like James Klugman used to argue, I suspect that even this would not be enough. It would not bring about that complete self-transcendence, that deeply rooted desire for the good of others, that perfection would entail.

On Marx's grave in Highgate Cemetery are inscribed his words: 'The philosophers have only interpreted the world in various ways. The point however is to change it.' But interpreting and changing are not mutually exclusive alternatives. There is a desperate need to change the manifestly unjust world in which we live today, and it is understandable if someone decides to give their energies to this while sitting somewhat light to questions of philosophy and religion. But if we are working for a different world, we will need to have some kind of idea of what world it is desirable to work for and what, given the way we are, might be possible means of bringing it about; and that will depend on our overall reading of human existence. For example, whether we are working to bring about a revolutionary socialism, a democratic socialism or an unfettered free market will depend in significant measure on our understanding of what it means to be a human being and how society works. So the question of how society can be changed for the better is a crucially important one, but it does not rule out, and for some people it entails, a prior question about what kind of beings we humans are; and this can raise the wider question of whether life has a meaning that we can discover. If it has no given meaning then that too is a significant fact that will influence the kind of world we want to achieve and the way we might try to bring it about. If it has no given meaning it will still be necessary to make some assessment of the relative strengths of altruism and self-interest in the human person, for this will affect the kind of humanism we adopt, the kind of society we think might be possible and the means that will be necessary to bring it about.

Buddhism could not be more different from Marxism but it has this in common, in that it too thinks the question about life's meaning is not the right one to ask. The historic Buddha witnessed various forms of human suffering and came to the conclusion that there are four fundamental – or what he called 'noble' – truths in life. Suffering is universal. At the root of the problem is the fact that we are driven by desire or craving. If this desire could be eliminated it would lead to detachment and enlightenment. The way to this enlightenment is by following eight fundamental principles that he set out. This path will give us true inner peace. The first of these principles is 'right understanding' and this includes a refusal to consider unprofitable questions. Such unprofitable questions include whether or not there is a God and whether there is a universal meaning to life into which we can enter. To use an analogy attributed to the Buddha, if a house is on fire we don't stop to ask what caused it. We try to put the fire out. In short, what is needed is a practical answer to the craving that drives us. Theoretical questions have no use – or as a Buddhist writing puts it:

> Suppose . . . a man were wounded by an arrow thickly smeared with poison, and his friends and companions, his kinsmen and relatives, brought a surgeon to treat him. The man would say 'I will not let the surgeon pull out the arrow until I know whether the man who wounded me was a noble or a Brahmin or a merchant or a worker.' And he

would say: 'I will not let the surgeon pull out this arrow until I know the name and clan of the man who wounded me . . . whether the man who wounded me was short or of middle height . . . was dark or brown or golden-skinned.'[9]

And so he goes on wanting to know endless details before letting the surgeon operate. 'All this would still not be known to that man and meanwhile he would die.'[10] The first point being made is that while people are arguing about metaphysical questions, 'there is birth, there is ageing, there is death, there are sorrow, lamentation, pain, grief, and despair, the destruction of which I prescribe here and now.'[11]

The prescription for these ills is to follow the four noble truths that lead to inner liberation. This means not allowing oneself to be distracted by metaphysical questions about the origin and nature of the universe. However it could well be argued that the real question is not how to achieve an inner liberation from the woes of the world but how to lessen the misery of others by improving their material circumstances or bringing them companionship in their affliction.

Second, when putting out a fire, it does in fact matter what caused it. Some ways of putting out a fire only make matters worse. Similarly it may not matter who shot the arrow but it does matter to know if the arrow has been poisoned or whether it has a barbed tip, for this will decisively affect how one goes about the practical task of operating and saving the person's life.

Most fundamental of all, we can question whether it is really desire that is at the root of the problem. From a Christian point of view, desire is a fundamental part of our human nature, which has been created good. Desire goes wrong only when it becomes distorted or inordinate. For someone like the seventeenth-century poet and mystic Thomas Traherne, the problem is not desire itself but that our desires are not ambitious enough. We are content with riches or fame or power, when the whole universe could be ours. The task is not to eliminate desire but to expand it to receive undreamt-of riches. From this point of view, our deepest desire is for God, and what goes wrong is not the existence of desire itself but that it becomes focused on lesser goods.

None of the above points should be taken as a criticism of Buddhism in itself and it is indeed true that there is a great deal of useless metaphysical speculation that can be a distraction from more fundamental truths. It is just that what appears to be the very down-to-earth, practical approach of Buddhism in fact turns out to raise a whole shelf of questions, all of which suggest that we cannot avoid exploring whether or not life has a meaning not of our making.

Behind Buddhism there is a proper concern to find an inner calm and stability and a proper rejection of inordinate desire. That is why some people find it appealing or they look to yoga and various forms of meditation to help them lessen the strains of modern living. This is all very understandable but it is different from our human capacity to respond sympathetically or empathetically to the pain of others. From a Christian point of view, the capacity to be afflicted by the affliction of others is fundamental, whereas Buddhism has a rather different rationale for encouraging its own emphasis on loving kindness.

A friend of mine, a highly intelligent, good person but someone who is I think a non-believer, urged me with great enthusiasm to read *How to Live: A Life of Montaigne in One Question and Twenty Attempts at an Answer* by Sarah Bakewell. It is a lively read but as I read on I found the character of the sixteenth-century philosopher Michel de Montaigne, as sketched by the author, more and more irritating. He seemed to have opted out of so much of life, leaving his wife to manage his estate for example, while he went into his isolated room in his tower to ruminate and write. The reason for my irritation became clear in the chapter when Sarah Bakewell considers Montaigne in relation to the mathematician and philosopher Blaise Pascal. Pascal agonizes about the big questions of life while Montaigne leaves them alone. Sarah Bakewell wrote: 'Pascal must always be at one extreme or another. He is either sunk in despair or transported by euphoria . . . It makes for exciting reading, but after a few pages one craves a dose of Montaigne's easygoing humanism.'[12]

That alleged 'easygoing humanism' has made Montaigne a favourite author of atheists and agnostics. But there is a paradox here. Montaigne was in fact an observant Catholic who urged people to submit to the authority of the Roman Catholic Church. This was not just a matter of outward conformity and a desire to keep his head down at a time of fierce religious conflict. For what has recently been shown is that the much-loved ruminations by Montaigne on this, that and the other are in fact suffused with a spiritual quality.[13] The reason why people have tended to think of him as indifferent to religion is because Pascal saw him as a threat. What infuriated Pascal was the laid-back attitude revealed in the essays, the view that nothing really mattered anyway so let's get on and relish the everyday happenings of life. But Pascal was misled by this attitude.

Clearly we all have different temperaments; some are closer to Montaigne in outlook, others to Pascal. There are also major cultural differences. You can no more imagine Jane Austen writing *The Brothers Karamazov* than you can image Dostoyevsky writing *Pride and Prejudice*. Both writers were serious Christians but Dostoyevsky needed to explore the heights and depths of human existence whereas Jane Austen expresses her Christian faith in a more hidden way through the kind of values that matter in civilized living. Dostoyevsky reflects a particular strand in the Russian temperament that is restless until it gets to the heart of things, which is unembarrassed to explore this publicly and can veer wildly from adoration to suicide. Jane Austen's underlying seriousness finds expression in restraint, perceptive characterization, wit and gentle satire.

Pascal believed that it really mattered whether or not there is a God. He explores the utter misery of humanity without God and the glorious splendour of humanity with God. The stakes could not be higher. Montaigne gives the impression that such matters are not worth troubling oneself over. Yet here we have to be careful. It is well known that humorists and cartoonists can often be people who are deeply disturbed by the horrors of existence. Being disturbed they make a conscious decision to live with as much humour as possible. There is in fact a world of difference between heavy portentousness and genuine seriousness. Genuine seriousness can often mask itself with light-heartedness or humour. Ponderous agonizing can sometimes reflect a lack of real seriousness. A relaxed, amused style can be very attractive and it is not for nothing that Montaigne has been called 'the great seducer' as well as 'the great antagonist'. It is akin to the upper-class Englishman going bravely into battle with insouciance and understatement. Such a style can be enticing. But it should not be taken at face value. It could just be the expression of a shallow mind. Or it could be the way someone has consciously chosen to live, having fully measured the depths and heights. Pascal is surely right that the question of whether or not there is a wise and loving power behind the universe is a crucial question; and how one answers it makes a huge difference to how one views humanity. But though Pascal is right, it does not follow that this is a question to be agonized over the whole time. Life is full of interest and challenge as well as travail and woe, and there is much to relish and enjoy. That said, it is a strange person who does not at one time or another put themselves into a Pascal mood. No doubt if we are living comfortably and things are going well with us we are content to go along without bothering too much. But as the famous First World War padre Geoffrey Studdert-Kennedy (known as 'Woodbine Willy') used to say at the beginning of sermons at that terrible time, 'There comes a time in every man's life when he wonders what the hell it's all about.'

Finally, it might be argued that questions of ultimate meaning simply do not arise in our postmodern culture. In his book *Culture and the Death of God*, the literary critic Terry Eagleton traces the alleged death of God from the rationalism of the Enlightenment through idealism and Romanticism to the philosopher Friedrich Nietzsche.[14] It is only with Nietzsche, he argues, that we have something like a true atheist; that is, someone able to face up to the full consequences of a world without God. Before then, and indeed in so many ways now, people find a substitute for the deity in nationalism or culture or try to uphold meaning in ethics and even religion as personal consolation for the poor or as a bond of social cohesion.

But with Nietzsche we are forced to face the full horror of a life without meaning and an ethics in which the new kind of human, the superman, takes charge of his or her life in disregard of everything else. Modernism, as we see it in people like the writers Samuel Beckett and Franz Kafka, was still haunted by the death of God, but our postmodern world is not; 'There is no phantom limb syndrome.'[15] Eagleton argues that it is in late capitalism that we really see that God has been put to death. God can survive a view of man as producer; 'Not even he, however, can survive the advent of Man the Eternal Consumer.'[16] But this has come with a price: the lack of depth and a great deal else of value. As he writes: 'If postmodern culture is depthless, anti-tragic, non-linear, anti-numinous, non-foundational and anti-universalist, suspicious of absolutes and averse to interiority, one might claim that it is genuinely post-religious as modernism most certainly is not.'[17]

Eagleton does not deny that some individuals still look for spiritual consolation. Indeed all the way through his survey of culture from the Enlightenment to our own time he points up the multiple ways people have invented substitutes for the God whom they think they have put aside – in culture, nationalism or spirituality, for example; anything rather than the inconvenience of believing in a living God who might actually make a difference to their lives. 'So it is that those who cannot conceive of an end of Wall Street are perfectly capable of believing in Kabbalah . . . the point of spirituality is to cater for needs that one's stylist or stockbroker cannot fulfil.'[18] But this kind of spirituality makes no difference to the culture that now shapes our lives, one driven by late capitalism.

At a more mundane level there are now multiple ways people can fill their lives with interesting and enjoyable things to do. The golden older generation still living who took early retirement on final-salary pensions, whom advanced health care keeps well and who find they have 20 or more years for enjoying themselves, do just that, moving from one holiday to another. I recognize, of course, the very different life that so many older people do in fact live – in poverty, loneliness and ill health. Nevertheless there is a tranche of people, a golden generation of those who for the first time in history have money, time and health. This is a remarkable phenomenon of our times, one that is unlikely to recur and is symptomatic of our culture as one in which ultimate questions are not only not pressing, they are hardly on the agenda in the way they were for previous generations.

Even at the highest level, the secular assumptions in our culture, though they may be stark, are scarcely noticed by most people. For example, at the 2014 Hay Festival there was an excellent interview with the conductor Sir John Eliot Gardiner about his book on Bach. He shared his knowledge and passion for Bach, and said that though he was an agnostic he found in the music of Bach much inspiration and consolation. The interviewer then suggested that Bach 'transcended faith'. By this she meant, I am sure, something entirely valid, namely that Bach's music can resonate with people whether they have a religious faith or not. But it did not seem to occur to her that it might have that resonance just because Bach's music was deeply rooted in his Christian faith. As is well known, Bach dedicated all his music to the greater glory of God. The assumptions in our society, at least among the cultural elite, are seriously secular in that religion is either treated as a private affair that makes no difference in the real world or taken over and used in relation to another purpose, social stability or personal consolation. Very rarely is it treated in its own right as that which makes troubling claims.

Though this is a marked feature of our time it is not a new phenomenon. The correspondence of the poets Gerard Manley Hopkins and his friend Robert Bridges is interesting in this regard. Hopkins argued that 'a kind of touchstone of the highest or most living art is seriousness; not gravity but the being in earnest with your subject.'[19] He then suggested that some of the most famous works of art were not in fact serious in that sense. Some modern artists and critics are definitely 'in earnest' about their subject but others may be open to the kind of complaint Hopkins made in another letter to Bridges when he wrote: 'It is long since such things had any significance for you. But what is strange and unpleasant is that you sometimes speak as if they had in reality none for me.'[20] Interestingly the philosophers Ludwig Wittgenstein and Bertrand Russell fell out because Wittgenstein felt Russell was not fundamentally serious even about mathematical logic.[21]

It may be true that this postmodern generation is not haunted by the death of God, that our lives are shaped by the secular assumptions of late capitalism and that we can fill them with interesting and amusing things without troubling our heads with big questions about life's meaning. Nevertheless such questions remain valid, and it would seem to be a normal feature of any thoughtful person's life that he or she should from time to time wonder what it is all about. Indeed there would seem to be something curiously deficient about a mind that never raised that question. A recent book goes further and argues that our brains are hardwired to search for meaning in the world. Evolution has favoured this adaptation, our development in this way, because it helps us maintain order in society. For a great many people, it is in the crises of life that they first seriously ask questions about meaning – when they are struck by illness, bereavement or failure in a relationship. It is possible to view this cynically as people looking to religion when all else fails. But those who find themselves in such situations are often suddenly aware that they have previously been living on the surface of life, and it is their present situation that has brought them up against the depths of things – a situation that for the billions of poor in the world is a daily reality.

There are many important questions to ask, not least how we can change the world for the better or how we can achieve an inner stability, but our approach to all of them will be affected one way or another by the answer we give to the question of whether life has a given meaning we can discover or whether it has only the meaning we choose to give it. However we answer, it remains of crucial importance because it will shape not only how we begin to answer other questions but the whole way we think and try to act.

3

Knowing and unknowing

Claims about the mystery

Our universe is some 13.8 billion years old. For the past 4.6 billion years, the earth has been circling round the sun and during this time has given rise to a great variety of life forms, of which we are one. The earth is but a small star in a vast galaxy, and our galaxy is only one among millions of others in a universe still rapidly expanding. This universe may not be the only one. It is possible there are others and we are part of a multiverse. When we turn our minds away from the macrocosm to the microcosm, to the subatomic level of quarks, what is revealed is equally mysterious and complex.

Whether we are looking out at the stars through a giant telescope or examining the evidence produced by the Hadron collider, our minds literally boggle. Our day-by-day imagination cannot cope and words fail. What is there can be explored only by physics at the highest level and stated in mathematical formulae.

If we then wonder what if anything might lie behind, beyond and within the scientific world mapped out by mathematical physics, then it is even more apparent that words must fail. The failure of words must be not only the starting point for the rest of the book but kept in mind throughout.

Maximus the Confessor (580–662), the great defender of Christian orthodoxy, wrote: 'The perfect mind is one that through genuine faith supremely knows in supreme ignorance the supremely unknowable.'[1] It is only in paradoxical statements like this that we can begin to understand the nature of faith. God is 'the supremely unknowable' and we know 'in supreme ignorance', yet still it is possible to have faith. Maximus is not alone in emphasizing our starting point in the unknown. As John of Damascus put it, 'It is plain, then, that there is a God. But what he is in his essence and nature is absolutely incomprehensible and unknowable.'[2] It is not of course plain to all that there is a God, but if there is a God, the second part of his statement must be true, that he is incomprehensible and unknowable in his essence and nature. However, if this were all there is to be said we might as well stop and shut up, following the famous seventh proposition and last line of Ludwig Wittgenstein's *Tractatus Logico-Philosophicus*, 'Whereof one cannot speak, thereof one must be silent.' Yet all religious views of the world share a conviction that however deep the mystery that lies behind things, that mystery can, in some sense and however limited a way, be known and therefore talked about in ordinary human words. Indeed Maximus goes on in the same sentence to affirm that we can know God's providence in the world 'as far as allowable to men'.

It is of great importance, however, not only to start with but to stress throughout our 'supreme ignorance', not simply because this is true in itself but because it is a vital and healthy antidote to the tendency of religious people inadvertently to convey through the way they talk that they have it all off pat, all tied up. This is partly the result of a misplaced certainty but also of the casual way Christians tend to talk and pray, as though gossiping to a next-door neighbour. Now, it is true that from a Christian point of view God has indeed made himself accessible to humanity, and Jesus in St John's Gospel explicitly calls his followers his friends (John 15.15). But what it is easy to forget is that the one who calls us friends is, from a Christian point of view, also one in being with the fount and origin of the universe, and in the word 'Jesus' there is always an abyss of mystery. When the author of the last book of the Bible, the Revelation of John, encountered this mystery he recorded that he fell down as though dead and then heard the words 'I am the first and the last, and I am the living One; I was dead and now I am alive for evermore, and hold the keys of death and Hades' (Revelation 1.17–18). Those are spine-tingling words.

Whatever the limits of words when it comes to questions of ultimate meaning, words are all we have, so some understanding of the nature of religious language, what words can and cannot do, is crucial. When I was studying the Philosophy of Religion at Cambridge University from 1958 to 1961, the heyday of logical positivism had passed. The assumption behind that particular philosophical fashion was that if we uttered a proposition, it could only have meaning if in some way it could be verified. There did not seem to be any way in which religious claims could be verified, therefore they were termed meaningless. Among the various criticisms of this approach was the obvious one that the verification principle itself could not be verified. So when I was studying it was in the more nuanced intellectual climate of linguistic analysis. Nevertheless some of the assumptions behind logical positivism still lingered in the claim that for a sentence to be meaningful there must be some way it could be falsified. The challenge was put particularly sharply by Antony Flew. He said that a bold claim such as 'God loves the world' seems to be compatible with so much evidence to the contrary it makes us doubt whether the word 'love' is applicable to God at all. Christians tend to qualify their claim about what is meant by divine love until it loses all meaning and there is 'death by a thousand qualifications'. So our generation often felt that basic Christian claims were slipping through our fingers into nothing.[3]

Since then a range of different approaches have been taken on the issue of religious language. One, associated with the philosopher and theologian John Hick, proposed the idea of 'eschatological verification'. This is an asymmetrical view, allowing for verification but not falsification. For, if our beliefs are true, they will be revealed as such. That is, they will be verified when we die; if they are false it will not be possible to know this. On this view a sceptic might find a particular religious claim totally unbelievable but can in principle grasp that a claim is being made; that something is being asserted that will turn out to be either true or false.

Others have shied away from factual claims altogether, believing, for example, that religious language provides a self-enclosed world of metaphors, maxims, rules and virtues and has a validity in itself as supporting a way of life. This is a view associated particularly with Wittgenstein but well illustrated by an anecdote about the philosopher R. B. Braithwaite, who was baptized as an adult in the chapel of King's College, Cambridge. At the baptism he is alleged to have said, sotto voce, 'I will behave as if . . .' before proclaiming 'I believe . . .'. There is of course a great deal of truth in a view of religious language as expressing commitment to a way of life, and this will be affirmed in later chapters. To become a Christian is to begin to inhabit a living tradition with its specialist language, liturgy, virtues and aspirations. That living tradition is there to undergird and nourish a recognizable way of life. But is it possible to inhabit that tradition while sitting light to its central claims? The distinguished cosmologist and astrophysicist, Astronomer Royal and former President of the Royal Society, Lord Rees of Ludlow, enjoys Anglican worship and describes himself as a 'cultural Christian'. He does not share the beliefs but identifies himself with the culture and way of life. He is not alone. While this stance is understandable and will be discussed further in the next chapter, a distinction has to be made between belonging to a culture with a code of behaviour and consciously adhering to a living tradition. At the heart of a living tradition are claims that can be either believed or disbelieved.

Another approach, closely related to some of the above, is to suggest that religions offer a particular stance on life, a perspective in which one sees and interprets experience and on the basis of which one lives. This account does not make factual claims about the world. It offers a perspective, a way of seeing things. But most people would take the view that their perspective on existence does depend significantly on what they believe about it, whether it is Macbeth's 'tale told by an idiot, full of sound and fury, signifying nothing', for example, or what Keats in a letter referred to as a 'vale of soul making'.[4] The one offers a tragic view; the other, without denying a tragic dimension, suggests there is worthwhile purpose. They are both perspectives on existence but each one is rooted in a claim that is either true or false.

Students of the Philosophy of Religion in Cambridge in the 1960s, not least Rowan Williams, were heavily influenced by the philosopher Donald MacKinnon. First of all MacKinnon never let his students forget that the real world is full of horrors. He refused to allow people to avoid this by any kind of escapist fantasy. Though not a Marxist his sympathies lay more with a Marxist view of the world than with any kind of philosophical idealism because he thought it was the actual real world of events that mattered, what happened or did not happen. This led on to his conviction that, awkward and embarrassing though it might be, the Christian faith made real claims. At a time when many theologians and philosophers were trying to find a way round that particular stumbling block he continued to insist that the Christian faith was committed to certain propositions that, however difficult to justify, were in the end either true or false. This included belief that the tomb of Jesus had been found empty and he had been raised to a universal contemporaneity.

Just before the pastor and theologian Dietrich Bonhoeffer was hanged for his part in the attempt to assassinate Adolf Hitler he said: 'This is the end – for me the beginning of life.'[5] The first part of that statement is a straightforwardly factual assertion. His physical life was coming to an end, a statement proved true some time later by his lifeless body. The second part of the statement is all metaphor. There is a beginning, like a baby born into the world. But it won't be with a physical body or with anything we can see now. It won't be a beginning in time because it is in eternal life. It is the beginning of life but it won't be a life like the one we know. We cannot describe what is meant by life in the phrase 'for me the beginning of life'; nevertheless I believe it is possible to grasp that a serious claim is being made. The qualifications do indeed go on and on. 'Yes, it will be me but not me in the form you have known; yes it is a beginning but not like any beginning we have experienced in the material world; yes, it is life but not like the life we know now.' Despite all these qualifications, which continue so long as the question 'What do you mean?' is pressed, I believe it is possible to grasp the claim Bonhoeffer is making either to share his faith or reject it.

The Christian faith makes claims. These can be stated only in a series of images that continually need qualifying. Stanley Spencer served as a medical orderly in Macedonia in the First World War. When he was walking through the Vardar Hills he said he was aware of the dangers that lay ahead but at the same time, as he wrote, 'I suddenly had a feeling of the completeness and fitness and ultimate redemption of everything . . . I felt I was a walking altar of praise.'[6]

Altars do not of course walk, nor do they praise. But we can still understand what Spencer means by these metaphors. Similarly we could press the meaning of the words he uses – 'completeness and fitness and ultimate redemption' – and never get an entirely satisfactory answer, yet still grasp what Spencer is saying and claiming.

In one of his poems, R. S. Thomas has the lines:

> To yield to an unfelt pressure that, irresistible
> In itself, has the character of everything
> But coercion?[7]

These line are full of contradictions. If it is unfelt, in what way can it be a pressure? If it is irresistible, how can it be without any coercion? Yet of course it is with such contradictions and paradoxes alone that a person can convey the particular character of their religious experience of the interaction of their will with the divine leading.

The poet and painter David Jones thought that the nineteenth century experienced what he called 'The Break' and that his view was shared by his contemporaries in the 1930s.[8] By this he meant two things. First, the dominant cultural and religious ideology that had unified Europe for more than a thousand years no longer existed. All that was left were fragmentary individual visions. Second, the world was now dominated by technology, so that the arts seemed to be marginalized. They had no use in such a society and their previous role as signs no longer had any widespread public resonance. Their work was 'idiosyncratic and personal in expression and experimental in technique, intimate and private rather than public and corporate'.[9] 'The priest and the artist are already in the catacombs, but *separate* catacombs, for the technician divides to rule.'[10] There was no corporate tradition and one could not be looked for without a renewal of the whole culture. Writing after the Second World War he remarked that the situation at that time was even more pronounced and dire than it had seemed in the 1930s.

There is no 'symbolic order', to use a phrase of the art critic Peter Fuller. What Jones and his fellow artists and poets were conscious of is equally applicable to the more general use of religious language, with one further point. In so far as religious narratives and symbols did survive in the wider culture, they have for the most part lost their spiritual and emotional resonance. This is even more the case now than it was in the time of David Jones. In the early 1960s, the percentage of people who attended church was not all that much higher than it is now, but some knowledge of Christian stories and themes could be assumed in the wider culture. That started to disappear during that decade and now we have the third and fourth generation of people growing up for whom, in the case of the majority, Christianity is a foreign language and what goes on in church is strange if not alien. 'It's weird', as one teenager known to me remarked.

This situation is reinforced by the lack of religious literacy in our society. The art historian Sir Roy Strong refers to a conversation he had with a lecturer in English at one of our leading universities. She had presented them with George Herbert's poem 'Redemption' and asked them what it meant. They did not know. She then offered the word 'redeemed' to see if that jogged their memories of a pawnshop. Then one of the students said 'I've got it. It's about the class struggle.'[11]

Against this depressing background and the thin religious culture of our time it has really been only in the arts, especially in music, that something of the freshness, meaning and vitality of religious faith has been able to break through. But music by itself is not enough and the struggle with words has to continue.

The positive and negative ways

R. S. Thomas wrote a poem about absence which reads:

> It is this great absence
> that is like a presence, that compels
> me to address it without hope
> of a reply.[12]

From a literal point of view, an absence and a presence are opposite states and only a deranged person would address someone who isn't there, especially if they knew there was no hope of an answer. Yet, the poet suggests, it is only through such paradoxes, when ordinary description runs into the sand, that we can begin to understand what it is for God to be God.

W. H. Auden was no less serious a Christian than R. S. Thomas but he deliberately chose a different, more positive, playful approach to life. In 'Epistle to a Godson', he wonders what to offer his godson as nourishment for the journey of life and suggests:

> Nothing obscene or unpleasant: only
>
> the unscarred overfed enjoy Calvary
> as a verbal event. Nor satiric: no
>   scorn will ashame the Adversary.
>   Nor shoddily made: to give a stunning
>
> display of concinnity and elegance
> is the least we can do, and its dominant
>   mood should be that of a Carnival.
>   Let us hymn the small but journal wonders
>
> of Nature and of households, and then finish
> on a serio-comic note with legends
>   of ultimate eucatastrophe,
>   regeneration beyond the waters.[13]

In those few lines, there is a distinctive way of looking at the world and celebrating. There is also a serious claim being made. If some of those words were considered literally they would soon disintegrate into nonsense: What exactly is 'regeneration beyond the waters'? On the other hand, if the lines were all set out in ordinary prose it would be likely to come across as stale or banal. Their magical mood and outrageous look into the future all lie in the words, words being used to wonderful effect.

The poems of R. S. Thomas and W. H. Auden are good examples of the two main approaches to the use of words in the Christian tradition, the via positiva and the via negativa or Apophatic way. The via positiva, as exemplified by Auden, says that language can point the way but it continually needs to be qualified. Language has to be made and unmade, remade and unmade again ad infinitum. Famous words of Samuel Beckett apply with particular aptness and force to the use of religious language: 'Fail again. Fail better.'[14] The via negativa or Apophatic way, as exemplified by Thomas, recognizes that there is a point when words fail totally and we simply have to wait in silence.

There is a long and hugely sophisticated debate rooted in ancient Greek thought, reaching a height with St Thomas Aquinas and flourishing in our own times about the way words might be said to be used about God in the same sense that we use them in ordinary life (univocal) and the way their sense as applied to God is different (equivocal). In practice, this means that everything we say about God is as untrue as it is true, so every analogy, metaphor, image, symbol or picture immediately has to be set aside or denied by another one that, in its turn, has to be qualified again and again. Only in this way is it possible to suggest, point to or hint at a reality that is not an object in the world of objects or a thing in the world of things. Most thoughtful people, for example, have great difficulty with the idea of God being a person or an individual. But God is not a person or an individual in any ordinary sense of the words. A study of the hymns and devotional literature of the Church, as well as the Bible, quickly reveals that impersonal images are used just as frequently as personal ones. Most believers will address the divine in personal terms but know perfectly well that this needs to be qualified not only by impersonal images such as sun, light, air or water but also by ideas of divine indwelling.

The via negativa takes the truth about endless qualification being necessary to its logical conclusion. This is a wordless waiting. Instead of continuing to make and break every image, it goes beyond all images into what is variously called a cloud, or darkness. A classical exponent of this approach is John of the Cross, who was quoted almost verbatim in T. S. Eliot's *Four Quartets*. A passage in that poem takes the three words 'faith', 'hope' and 'love' and says that they have such limited, finite, human associations that we have to put them aside altogether and simply be still 'and wait without hope'. The words are not altogether useless, however, for 'the faith and the love and the hope are all in the waiting.'[15]

This was a theme independently and powerfully stated by Simone Weil, the French intellectual of Jewish background and Christian conviction, in the essays collected together under the title *Waiting on God*.[16] As already implied, it was also a major theme in the poems of R. S. Thomas, of which 'Kneeling' is one example:

> Moments of great calm,
> Kneeling before an altar
> Of wood in a stone church
> In summer, waiting for the God
> To speak: the air a staircase
> For silence: the sun's light
> Ringing me, as though I acted
> A great rôle. And the audiences
> Still. All that close throng
> Of spirits waiting, as I,
> For the message.
> Prompt me, God;
> But not yet. When I speak,
> Though it be you who speak
> Through me, something is lost.
> The meaning is in the waiting.[17]

Inevitably, being human we project on to God much of ourselves and imagine a God we most want or most fear. It is only by waiting on God in silence that we can become more open to God making himself known to us more as he is and less in terms of our hopes and fears. And even if we put together words that seem to us some divine touch upon us, even then as Thomas puts it, 'something is lost.'

A classical exponent of this way, the anonymous fourth-century author of *The Cloud of Unknowing* sums up the theme of his book in the words:

Now you put a question to me asking, 'How shall I think about God, and what is God?' And to this I can only answer you, 'I do not know.' With your question you have brought me into that same darkness and into that same cloud of unknowing into which I would wish you to come yourself . . . God may be well loved, but cannot be thought of. God may be reached and held close by means of love; but by means of thought never. And therefore, even though it is good occasionally to think of the kindness and the great worth of God in particular aspects, and even though it is a joy that is a proper part of contemplation, nevertheless in this work it should be cast down and covered with a cloud of forgetting. You are to step above it with great courage and with determination, and with a devout and pleasant stirring of love; and you are to try to pierce that darkness which is above you. You are to strike that thick cloud of unknowing with a sharp dart of longing love; and you are not to retreat, no matter what comes to pass.[18]

That passage, powerful as it is, does not perhaps convey the reality of the darkness, the sense of the absence of God, the sheer dereliction. Those who have walked this path, like John of the Cross, talk about 'the dark night of the soul'. In his book *The Wound of Knowledge*, an astonishingly mature work written when he was only 24, which I suspect future generations might well judge to be a classic of our time, Rowan Williams examined Christian spirituality from the New Testament to St John of the Cross. He argued on the basis of those foundational documents that a Christian spirituality is far removed from the kind of ersatz comfort that people today look for in spirituality. Rather it is an identification with Christ on the cross in his dereliction, and in him with all those who live in a hell of one kind or another. This is a real night, a real darkness that offers only the consolation that to be there is to be where Christ was and is.[19] This experience can also be described as one of the absence of God, as Simone Weil and others have known it. This is not simply an intellectual denial of his reality or an inability to feel any divine presence, but an overwhelming sense of the horror and bleakness of the world, a world totally stripped of any kind of enchantment.

The novelist Philip Pullman, in his recreation of the Gospel story, has Jesus reflecting in the Garden of Gethsemane on the verse of the psalm 'The fool has said in his heart that there is no God' but, try as hard as he can, he cannot see God in his creation. No sound comes from God; there is only a terrible emptiness and silence. Then Pullman's Jesus reflects on whether God might be present in that absence and continues:

> God, is there any difference between saying that and saying that you're not there at all? I can imagine some philosophical smartarse of a priest in years to come pulling the wool over his poor followers' eyes: 'God's great absence is, of course, the very sign of his presence' or some such drivel. The people will hear his words, and think how clever he is to say such things, and they'll try and believe it; and they'll go home puzzled and hungry, because it makes no sense at all. That priest is worse than the fool in the psalm, who at least is an honest man. When the fool prays to you and gets no answer, he decides that God's great absence means he's not bloody well there.[20]

This is a fair point robustly made that needs addressing. Simply put, what if any difference is there between an experience of the absence of God and his actual absence?

First, as Simone Weil put it, 'God can only be present in creation in the form of absence.'[21] This is not gobbledygook but an obvious point. God is not an object in the world of objects, a thing in the world of things. Therefore he cannot be located, identified, or pointed to within the created world. Christians and many others believe that God is the ground of all existence, the fount from whom moment by moment the universe flows and in whom it is held in being but who cannot be known except as that ground or fount.

Second, it is likely that when mystics, poets and many ordinary people experience the absence of God, that will not be all they claim to experience. They will often want to witness to moments of grace or illumination or insight; to some moment or time when they believe God has touched their lives.

Third, the Christian faith puts a high premium on faithfulness, on keeping going through every kind of difficulty, even when life seems bleak and God absent. In *Four Quartets*, Eliot acknowledges moments of illumination when, as sometimes when we hear music, we are taken out of ourselves, but insists that these are fleeting and what matters is the disciplined practice of the Christian life.[22]

Rowan Williams has recently explored the limits of language, the points at which normal discourse comes to a halt and how this more general phenomenon relates to the language of religion. What he says in relation to our capacity to choose will be discussed in Chapter 10, but what particularly interests Williams are the points at which language no longer seems adequate, breaks down and is reduced to silence.[23]

That theme of Rowan Williams is particularly relevant to the relation between the two ways of using language about God, the via positiva and the negative or Apophatic way. When we use a figure of speech to indicate a religious truth it has, as was said earlier, to be qualified time and again; made, broken and remade endlessly. So there comes a point where we are either reduced to silence or we are prepared to rest in a poetic paradox that makes no sense as ordinarily understood but which nevertheless does convey what the believer is trying to communicate. The religious poetry of Eliot and Thomas, as already shown, is steeped in such paradoxes.

Summary

In himself, God is unknown and unknowable by our limited, finite minds. However, as many philosophers now agree, words find their meaning in the context in which they are used. Religious believers find themselves part of a tradition whose words are rooted in specific practices. For example, a phrase such as 'I put my trust in God' is rooted in a particular attitude to the events of life supported by prayer, which is itself part of the liturgical life of a community informed by the words of Scripture. This outlook on life is expressed in particular forms of behaviour. At the heart of this is the conviction that the one addressed is trustworthy or faithful. So the words are rooted in a way of thinking, praying, speaking and acting that is shared with others. It is in that context that their meaning is known.

The assumption behind such traditions in the world's major monotheistic religions is that God has chosen to disclose enough of his purpose for us to live by. Nevertheless the severely limited capacity of religious language must never be forgotten. In Marilynne Robinson's novel *Lila*, the central character is a formerly destitute young woman who marries an aged pastor, John Ames. The faith of John Ames is fundamental to his being and he is a genuinely good man who prays much of the time and who does his best to communicate it to his flock. But he is acutely aware that there is a huge gap between what his faith means to him and the inadequacy of the words when they come out. This gap is focused in the way that when Lila first turned up in his church she listened with an intensity that unnerved him. She really wanted to hear something that spoke to her sadness and anger, but he knows he can never put into words anything that will really convey what he in fact believes.

> There was a seriousness about her that seemed almost like a kind of anger. As though she might say 'I came here from whatever unspeakable distance and from whatever unimaginable otherness just to oblige your prayers. Now say something with a little meaning in it.' My sermon was like ashes on my tongue.[24]

Religious language offers a perspective on life; its pleasures and pains, its delights and torments, its mundane routines and ecstatic moments, its beauties and horrors, and seeks to hold such experiences together in a total unified vision. This is not simply an intellectual stance, it is commitment to a way of life within a living tradition. Indeed without that commitment the stance has no reality. It takes on substance in a particular style of speech and conduct.

This does not mean that religious language is only about a perspective on existence rooted in a way of living. As has been argued, it makes serious claims, which in the end are either true or false. These are not ruled out of court because they cannot be verified or falsified in the same way as a scientific proposition can be. What matters is that something is communicated. When Bertrand Russell as a young man walked in Richmond Park agonizing about whether or not there was a God, his language was a tapestry of metaphor but what he was doing and saying was not meaningless. There was a claim that something was the case, a claim that he later came to disbelieve.[25] When, as happens now, a growing number of people tick the box 'No religion' on the census form, they may not have a very clear or informed view about what they reject but they can grasp enough of what is meant to know that it is not their view.

There is an ultimate mystery about existence. Nevertheless for the believer there is commitment to a particular way of seeing and living life as a member of a wider community that draws its wisdom from the past as well new insights from the present. This commitment implies claims about what is the case. Within the wider context of 'unknowing', this commitment and the claims it makes are beautifully summed up in one of the best-loved passages in the New Testament, 1 Corinthians 13, St Paul's great hymn of love. In the King James (Authorized) Version, he ends with the words:

> For now we see through a glass, darkly; but then face to face: now I know in part; but then shall I know even as also I am known. And now abideth faith, hope, charity, these three; but the greatest of these is charity.
>
> (1 Corinthians 13.12–13 AV)

The hope expressed in this passage is that although now we see through a glass darkly – which in modern versions is sometimes translated as seeing 'only puzzling reflections in a mirror' – then we shall see face to face. Now our knowledge is limited and partial but then we shall know as we are known. Other parts of the New Testament express this hope differently, in cosmic rather than personal terms and involving the whole of our life together, not just our life as individuals; but the point is that there is a future in which God's purpose of love will find its perfect consummation. This is a claim that will turn out to be true or false and is to be lived out now in faith, hope and love.

It is important to note that at this stage no argument has been put forward that these claims are true. They may be totally untrue. The purpose of this chapter has been a more limited one, simply to show how religious language works and what it might mean to inhabit a religious tradition.

4

Pursuing the truth

Science and religion

I have the greatest possible respect for serious scientists. This was reinforced during my time at King's College, London, and further strengthened when I chaired the House of Lords Select Committee on Stem Cell Research and again when I was involved with the Human Fertilisation and Embryology Authority (HFEA) and on the Nuffield Council on Bioethics. Once a year the HFEA had a meeting with its scientific advisors, whose task was to monitor relevant cutting-edge scientific research going on around the world. Our task was to judge what might relate to the area for which we had a responsibility so that we could begin to think about its legal and ethical implications. It is the careful, painstaking, patient work of such scientists over many years that have enabled many parents who would otherwise be childless to have children, and other parents who would otherwise pass on an inheritable disease to have children free of that disease. I became full of admiration for the intelligence and dedication of scientists working in that field. And that is just one field of scientific research.

It is a combination of such research, with its application in appropriate technology, that has given our society such confidence in the whole scientific enterprise as a way of getting at the truth. I do not have a sentimental view of scientists. They are subject to the same ambitions, vanities and weaknesses as the rest of us. There is always a scramble to get papers published in the best journals and from time to time we read of a scandal where someone has falsified the evidence behind their alleged results. Moreover scientific research now is nearly always tied up with commercial considerations of one kind or another. But all that having been said, the scientific method achieves results in which we can have confidence. When we board a plane we are expressing our confidence in the generations of fundamental research and experimental testing that have led to our doing this on the assumption that we will be safe. So when we talk about science being able to give us certainties, it is this practical kind of certainty we have in mind. Strictly speaking, scientific theories are always open to modification in the light of new evidence, but as our practice shows, we do in fact treat them as certainties. We live our lives on the basis that they are true.

In sharp contrast to this, religions, which have been going far longer than modern science, seem to offer nothing certain – only different competing views of the world, some of which seem totally incompatible with one another. I can understand therefore why some people are inclined to dismiss religious claims out of hand and put their trust in scientific method alone to unravel all the mysteries of the universe. Indeed when engaged in dialogue with Richard Dawkins I have heard him say as much. But however understandable, this claim will not stand up.

First, it has long been recognized that there are different kinds of question that call for different kinds of answers. If someone asks how I am writing this book, the answer will be a description of what I am doing: typing on my PC, for example. If someone asks why I am writing it, the kind of answer will be very different. It will be about what purpose I am trying to achieve, and this might be for a mixture of reasons. So it is that scientists, qua scientists, explore and map out how the world evolved or how our brain works when we are thinking. But those same scientists when they come out of the laboratory and go for an evening stroll, looking up at the sky perhaps and reflecting on the day, not just on the work done, but their relationships with others, might indeed wonder what it all adds up to. They may come to the conclusion that they have no idea or even that no answer is possible to such questions. But they will have questions on their mind that cannot simply be answered in the lab alone. One indication of this is that a survey of scientists in the United States some years ago showed that the percentage of religious believers among scientists was much the same as it was in the country as a whole, and this included some very distinguished ones.

In fact the so-called 'clash of science and religion' is one of the great myths of our time. One example of this is the debate on evolution, not least the dramatic story told about the encounter of Samuel Wilberforce and Thomas Huxley in 1851.[1] The wider truth about the Church and evolution is very different from the received account. At the same 1851 meeting of the Association for the Advancement of Science, the customary sermon was preached by Frederick Temple, later Archbishop of Canterbury, in which he said that God creates by secondary causes over a long period of time. Or as the novelist Charles Kingsley wrote in a letter to Charles Darwin, evolution is a great thing for Christianity because 'We knew of old that God was so wise that he could make all things; but, behold, he is so much wiser than even that, that he can make all things make themselves.'[2] Historians of science note that there was no undue delay among the Christian public in accepting the theory of evolution, and by the end of the century the intellectual battle was over.

Darwin himself never thought there was any incompatibility between his scientific findings and religious belief, and he himself never totally lost his faith in God. He did lose his earlier Christian conviction but this was partly because he had been working with a literalistic view of the Bible, partly because of the apparent cruelty in the evolutionary process and above all because of the death of his beloved daughter.

The creation of the myth about science and religion, especially as focused on stories like the encounter of Samuel Wilberforce and Thomas Huxley, seems akin to the development of myths connected with the cult surrounding particular saints in earlier centuries: we are suckers for a good story, especially one that reinforces what we want to believe. The reason I stress the mythological nature of the alleged incompatibility of religion and science is that it detracts from the real difficulties of faith, as indeed the history of Darwin himself shows. As mentioned, it was not evolution itself that undermined his faith but its apparently cruel character, together with his personal grief over his daughter. Indeed I used to tease Richard Dawkins by saying 'There are so many good arguments against the truth of religion why do you keep dragging science into it?' I believe that there are real, very serious objections to religious belief, and because they are real and serious it is important not to be distracted by the alleged clash with science.

Proofs and the phenomenon of faith

From the beginning of recorded history, philosophers and children alike have thought that there must be some cause of the universe being here. We know that in the world nothing happens by itself. If we see a balloon floating over the fence we look for a reason and perhaps find this in a children's birthday party happening next door. It is entirely natural, therefore, that we should apply the same kind of reasoning to the question of existence as a whole. Eventually the process of reasoning leads to the word 'God' and the child asks, as they do, 'Then who made God?' At that point we come to the end-stop in this process of reasoning. A theologian will step in at that point with a definition of God as uncreated and complete in himself, the uncaused cause of all things.

In one form or another, this process of reasoning has been at the heart of the five so-called proofs for the existence of God, from Aristotle to Aquinas and beyond. Although there remain a few serious defenders, today most philosophers find difficulty with them. First, because of the complexity of the concept of causality and what we might actually mean by saying that something is a cause. Second, what I have always taken to be the heart of Kant's criticism of such arguments, namely that they assume what we are trying to prove. Our ordinary human process of reasoning does indeed suggest that there must be a cause of the universe being here. But we do not know whether such reasoning, which works so well within the world, applies to its existence in the first place. It might be nice if it did, but to assume that it does is to assume there is a rational purpose akin to our own, or rather of which our rationality might be a pale reflection. It is that assumption we have to question. The implication of this is that we have to accept the limitations of human reason when it tries to reach beyond its own sphere of the finite and limited, into the totality of things. This conclusion works both ways. The essentially limited nature of human reason means that we can no more prove there is no God than we can prove there is. Human reason is indeed a very powerful tool but we simply do not know if its assumptions apply when we try to move beyond the limited and finite. The question of whether or not there is a self-sufficient, uncaused cause of all things must remain open.

Another process of reasoning, popular in the eighteenth century, suggested that the world is such a wonderful, complex phenomenon, there must be a highly intelligent designer behind it. The world is indeed awesome, not least in the way we ourselves exist as a result of billions of years of evolution. The problem here is that we have no standards of comparison. If I am walking along and see a row of cabbages, I rightly draw the conclusion that a gardener has been at work. This is because I have in my mind a clear picture of a vegetable patch on the one hand and a bit of scrubland on the other. I know into which category I put the row of cabbages. But we do not have two categories of universe, one designed and the other not designed. There is only one universe and we cannot tell whether or not it is the handiwork of an intelligent designer because we have nothing to compare it with. The current view of some scientists that we might be part of a multiverse does not affect this argument because every sphere of existence in a multiverse would still be finite and limited. We do not have a designed and an undesigned multiverse with which to make a comparison.

A fair amount has been written in recent years about the so-called anthropic principle, which focuses on the fact that the set of conditions that made it possible for human life to evolve in the first place was very limited, and one tiny change in any one of those determinants would mean we would not be here. So it looks as though to achieve that uniquely special set of circumstances that brought about human life (anthropos), there must have been a designer that had this in mind in the first place. It is indeed mind-boggling, totally awesome, that the universe is so finely tuned to produce us: but this is not the same as saying this amounts to a rationally compelling argument that there is a divine designer. First, whether or not there is a designer God, we are here anyway and we can describe the evolutionary process that has led to our being here without reference to God. Second, as before, we do not have a category of finely tuned universes designed to produce humanity to compare with another category that is not finely tuned.

Again we do not know and again the argument works both ways. The fact that we have come about through a long process of evolution does not of itself mean there is no God because to say this would need a standard of comparison, which we simply do not have. The question of whether there is an intelligent designer of the universe or not must remain an open one.

These arguments do not work as strict proofs. All we can say is that such chains of reasoning can help to open up the mind to the possibility that there might be a God who creates *ex nihilo*. Or as Rowan Williams has argued, they indicate the point at which the nexus of cause and effect no longer applies, we are reduced to silence 'and if there is anything to be said it will be in a different mode altogether'.[3]

There is one more traditional approach to this question, and that is to explore what any definition of God must logically entail. God is by definition that than which a greater cannot be thought. From this it has been argued that God must necessarily exist. It is an argument that has had some theological resonance for believers and a fascination for philosophers, even today. But there are several confusions here. For a believer, God does indeed necessarily exist in the sense that being God he is eternal and complete in himself and cannot be anything other than that. But that is different from saying that a process of reasoning can show that he does in fact necessarily exist as a matter of logic. Even more fundamentally, when we say God is that than which a greater cannot be conceived, that applies to qualities like goodness, wisdom, intelligence and so on but it does not apply to existence which, in the jargon, is not a predicate. So there is no way a purely disinterested, rational argument can convince the non-believer that there is a God by the sheer force of logic. The issue, from that point of view, remains open.

Although these so-called proofs continue to receive a certain amount of academic attention, this whole approach is fundamentally mis-conceived, for three reasons. First, even if someone was convinced by a chain of logic that there is a God, what would this amount to? It could simply lead to a person saying, 'So, yes, there is a God.' But that statement is very far from an expression of faith in God as understood by the monotheistic religions of the world. For them, God is one who by definition makes a total difference to our lives. This means we can only know God if we are aware of ourselves as a creature beholden for our existence to a creator; if we know ourselves to be moment by moment dependent for our existence on a power beyond ourselves, the root of our being and the ground of all being. That is, to emphasize the theme of the previous chapter, we give meaning to the word 'God' within the context of a particular way of seeing and living life, and a sense of ultimate dependence is at the heart of this.

This point brings out the second way attempts to prove the existence of God are misconceived. It is that the God we are being asked to believe in has to be given some characteristics, otherwise we don't know what it is we are being asked to assent to. Even if a person found the argument from causality persuasive, the God assented to would simply be the uncaused cause of things. We would not know if that uncaused cause was good or wise or, on the con-trary, indifferent or hostile to human well-being.

The third reason why that approach is unsatisfactory is that it seems so unreal and artificial. The phenomenology of faith – that is, any description of how people come to faith or for that matter lose it, from the inside – paints a very different picture of what is going on.

Everyone's spiritual journey is different but while rational reflec-tion plays an important part and should do so, as I will emphasize,

I would suggest that religious faith tends to make its way into people before they are fully aware of it, and it is as they become aware of it that they also become aware of the rational arguments for and against a belief that has already in some way got inside them. For some people, faith will have gone in with their mother's milk. For others, there has been an admired role model in the family, at school, in the local community or at church. For some people, their journey is a gradual, deepening one over many years. For others, there has been a key point, perhaps after a crisis caused by a divorce, bereavement or an illness in the family, when they are driven to discover within themselves deeper resources for living that they thought they did not need before. For others, particularly at university, they may have been presented with the challenge of Jesus Christ, which has drawn their imagination and taken hold of their lives. From a Christian point of view, this inner dimension of the growth into faith will involve some form of acknowledgement and response that makes a total difference to the way life is seen and lived. Dag Hammarskjöld was a brilliant Secretary General of the United Nations during some of the world's most dangerous years. When he died in a mysterious air crash in the Congo, some of his secret diaries were found. The entry for Whitsun 1961 reads: 'at some moment I did answer Yes to Someone – or Something – and from that hour I was certain that existence is meaningful and that, therefore, my life, in self-surrender, had a goal.'[4]

Reasoning

John Henry Newman, writing of his intellectual journey from the Church of England to become a Roman Catholic, wrote that 'The whole man moves; paper logic is but the record of it.'[5] This is true in that the whole man or woman does indeed move. We move as spiritual, emotional, moral, reasonable and volitional beings. But it is important to emphasize that rationality, or considerations of reasonableness, are an essential part of that movement and not just the record of it. We think our way into faith as well as feel our way into it. This means much more than exploring the traditional proofs. It means testing a growing faith against every aspect of experience in order to see whether it is possible to have a view of life consistent and coherent with all aspects of experience. A rational faith is not one that is the product of some detached logical process, it is one that has been thought through in relation to what we know of life in all its aspects, scientific, aesthetic, moral and personal. We are rational beings and rightly seek such a coherent and consistent view. The philosophical theologian Austin Farrer was one of the most brilliant men of his generation but in one sermon he reflected on the simple evangelical faith of his mother:

> You have known women like her, though few, perhaps, as good –
> a more unphilosophical mind it would be difficult to find . . . the
> centre of your Christian conviction, whatever you may think, will be
> where my mother's was – in your exploration of grace, in your walk-
> ing with God. But faith perishes if it is walled in, or confined. If it is
> anywhere, it must be everywhere, like God himself: if God is in your
> life, he is in all things, for he is God. You must be able to spread the
> area of your recognition for him, and the basis of your conviction
> about him, as widely as your thought will range.[6]

That, in my experience, gets it right. By whatever process it has come about, a person finds himself or herself if not with full faith, at least with some feeling for it, and having that faith, the mind seeks to relate it to the totality of experience. As far as rationality is concerned the key sentence is 'You must be able to spread the area of your recognition for him, and the basis of your conviction about him, as widely as your thought will range.'

Pascal imagines God saying 'Console yourself; you would not seek me if you had not found me.'[7] Faith is always a seeking faith; as St Bernard put it:

> God has no better gift to give to those who seek him than himself.
> But here is a paradox, that no one can seek the Lord who has not
> already found him. It is thy will, O God, to be found that thou may-
> est be sought, to be sought that thou mayest more truly be found.[8]

It is that seeking faith – and every faith is a seeking faith – that drives our minds to obtain greater understanding. *Credo ut intelligam* said St Anselm; I trust in order that I might understand better. This is not an attempt to evade the arguments against belief. On the contrary, they are powerful. It is that if we are not able to spread the area of our recognition of him and the basis of our conviction about him in any particular area, then our faith is likely to be eroded. In short, a rational view of the universe is one consistent and coherent not only within itself but with all we experience.[9]

As I go on to argue in this book, I take the arguments against the idea of a wise and loving power behind the universe with deadly seriousness and think they are almost compelling in their persuasiveness. But at this point it is necessary to point out that there can be no possibility of faith without a genuine openness to the possibility of its truth, an openness that teeters on the edge of finding it true and a willingness to trust the truth that is disclosed. There is an analogy here with human relationships. Making a relationship with someone depends on a growing degree of openness and trust. By contrast, a settled attitude of cynicism would preclude from the outset any possibility of a real relationship. Trust, in some sense, is a precondition. This is not to deny that we come to distrust some people and can feel badly let down. This happens all too often. Nevertheless trust opens up possibilities that a hardened scepticism closes down from the start. This openness is also part of what is meant by rationality. A rational person, believer and non-believer alike, will be genuinely open to the arguments of the other.

What is fundamental to those who find themselves on the road to faith is that they are drawn or attracted to that in which they are coming to believe. It is beginning to take hold. That is why there has been for so many Christians such a close relationship between God and beauty. In the same way that beauty draws us, so does the moral beauty of a good person and so, for a believer, does the Christian picture of God. 'For the God who said "Out of darkness light shall shine," has caused his light to shine in our hearts, the light which is knowledge of the glory of God in the face of Jesus Christ' (2 Corinthians 4.6). St Augustine had a strong aesthetic sense and loved the sights and sounds of North Africa, but he comes to see this beauty as but a weak reflection of the ineffable beauty of God, to whom he prays in the words:

> Late have I loved you, beauty so old and so new. Late have I loved you. And see, you were within and I was in the external world and sought you there, and in my unlovely state I plunged into those lovely created things you have made. You were with me, and I was not with you. The lovely things kept me far from you, though if they did not have their existence in you, they had no existence at all. You called and cried out loud and shattered my deafness. You were radiant and resplendent, you put to flight my blindness. You were fragrant and I drew in my breath and now pant after you. I tasted you, and I feel that hunger and thirst for you. You touched me, and I am set on fire to attain the peace which is yours.[10]

What happens is that there is an allure, an enchantment that draws us towards it; in the fullness of faith this simply takes hold. Usually this works first of all through created things, through the beauty of nature or music, for example, or through the spiritual quality of a saint or Christian believer. Sometimes it can work through books, as it did for C. S. Lewis, who describes how before he was a believer he began to find himself drawn to great writers in the past who happened to be Christians, such as George Herbert and John Donne. It is not that he ceased to admire people writing from a different perspective but, as he put it, deliberately changing a line from the twelfth-century French poem *The Song of Roland*, 'Christians are wrong, but all the rest are bores'[11] – which is probably a bit hard on the rest. In fact Lewis is another good example of someone with a powerful aesthetic sense that drew him through and beyond experiences of natural beauty to God.[12]

The anonymous author of the fourteenth-century mystical work *The Cloud of Unknowing* has a phrase T. S. Eliot used tellingly towards the end of 'Little Gidding' in *Four Quartets*: 'the drawing of this Love and the voice of this Calling'.[13] There is a drawing but also, as is made clear in the quotation from St Augustine quoted above, an awareness of being called in a way that invites a response.

None of this is to deny what is central to the teaching of Jesus, namely the need for repentance. This is not about beating oneself on the breast trying to feel bad about oneself. The Greek word *metanoia* contains the word for 'mind' and indicates the need to rethink; to rethink one's whole life in the light of truth's disclosure. So it is that C. S. Lewis in a famous passage says that there came a point when he knelt and admitted that God was God, 'The most dejected and reluctant convert in all England.'[14] But while this might have been true for Lewis at one particular point, it does not do justice to the other aspect of his faith, the fact that in ways known and unknown he had been drawn along the way to the source and standard of all beauty. For the only proper reason for kneeling and admitting that God is God is the recognition that he is good, all good, our true and everlasting good.

It has sometimes been suggested that Christianity is a faith you might simply decide to commit yourself to. Pascal, for example, with his famous wager, argues that there is everything to gain by belief in God and nothing to lose, therefore we might as well commit ourselves to it. Others have suggested that it is a kind of hypothesis that goes with a worthwhile way of life and this alone is enough for people to give themselves to it. This whole approach is to misunderstand the nature of faith. Christianity does involve a personal commitment but it has a fundamental structure of recognition and response. It is only because of the recognition of something that attracts us, and in the end of that which is supremely worth loving, that a commitment is made. It is true that people can be drawn by a particular way of life and want to be part of it, as the philosopher Roger Scruton has come to appreciate the Church of England as part of the culture to which he belongs and which he values, but on my understanding of his recent books it is a misreading to think of this simply as a naked decision. It is a response to that which attracts and calls in and through the institution he has come to appreciate.

It is true that a person can be drawn first one way and then another, a situation that Bishop Blougram explored in Robert Browning's poem about him. The bishop suggests that the world is like a chessboard with black and white squares. We see both, but to which should we give priority? We may settle down in unbelief, then:

> Just when we are safest, there's a sunset-touch,
> A fancy from a flower-bell, some one's death,
> A chorus-ending from Euripides, –
> And that's enough for fifty hopes and fears.[15]

At that point 'The grand Perhaps' comes to the fore again. The bishop then goes on to give various practical reasons why a life of faith diversified by doubt is to be chosen in preference to one of doubt diversified by faith. However, although radical doubts can coexist with faith, if the faith is to be sustained in face of them it needs more than the moving experiences described by Browning in his poem, however important a role they might play as part of faith. From a Christian point of view, it is the God who has revealed himself in Jesus who provides the ultimate reference point, a God of such humility that he emptied himself to make himself known to us in human terms, and the extent of whose love is seen in the battered figure on the cross. This is the heart of Christian faith, which makes it possible to go on even in the face of persistent questioning.

In the move towards or away from faith, the whole person is involved. Austin Farrer wrote:

> What is the supreme motive of a truth-seeking mind? Is it to explode shams or to acknowledge realities? After all the detection of shams, the clarification of argument, and the sifting of evidence – after all criticism, all analysis – a man must make up his mind what there is most worthy of love, and most binding on conduct in the world of real existence. It is this decision, or this discovery, that is the supreme exercise of a truth-seeking intelligence.[16]

That truth-seeking intelligence is part of the whole person and is therefore integrally linked to his or her aesthetic and moral sense. The great Victorian agnostics who turned away from the Christian faith did not do so because of the rise of biblical criticism or the theory of evolution but because what Christians called on them to believe struck them as morally inferior to their own ethical beliefs and standards.[17] The same is true today. Too often it is not the alleged unreasonableness of faith that turns people away but something about it that has put them off, which strikes them as morally or aesthetically unattractive.[18] That said, for a faith to gain and hold our assent it must be reasonable, and by that I mean it must be able to give as coherent and consistent a view of as many aspects of life as possible. It must be able to hold together all that we know about the world, including what modern science reveals, in a unified world view. In so far as it is not able to do that, it will be gradually eroded and in the end crumble.

It is from the standpoint of what is most worthy of love and binding on conduct that believers seek to respond to the other injunction of Farrer, that they must be able to spread the area of their recognition for God, and the basis of their conviction about him, as widely as their thought will range. Clearly creation itself and the fact of evolution is one key area where their thought must range.

One aspect of faith fundamental to a believer is the conviction of being a creature, of being moment by moment dependent on the ground of all being, of being held in existence by the fount and origin of all things. This is a fundamental datum with vast implications. As Austin Farrer wrote, 'Because we have God under the root of our being, we cannot help but acknowledge him as the root of all the world's being.'[19] The mind moves from what we know within ourselves about our own life to what therefore must be true of the universe as a whole. So, Farrer again:

> To make you or me God must make half a universe. A man's body and a man's mind form a focus in which a world is concentrated, and drawn to a point. It may be in that point that I know existence but it is an existence that involves the world.[20]

When scientists take us back some 13.8 billion years to the origin of the universe, we do not see God there, for how could we? But we know our own being is held in existence by that from whom all things come into being, and that truth applies at every point in the past and the future. When we look at the long process of evolution by means of random mutation and natural selection, we do not see God there, for how could we? But we know the leading of God in our own life, and our own life exists only because that leading has been present throughout the length and breadth of the evolutionary process.

I have argued that none of the so-called proofs for the existence of God do what they set out to do. They leave the issue open. This raises the questions of how it is that a believer comes to believe and the nature of faith. I have suggested that as often as not, faith becomes part of people before they are fully aware of it, and that if they persist in the faith this will be because it has an attractive power that holds them in the face of all questions and doubts. For a Christian, that compelling power is focused on the picture of God given us in Jesus crucified and risen. It is vital that our intelligence is involved at every point but our intelligence is integrally linked to our whole being, so the whole of us will be involved in thinking through issues of faith.

I further suggested that there is no fundamental conflict between belief in God and accepting the theory of evolution as a hypothesis of great explanatory power. As a scientific theory it can always be refined but there is no reason to doubt its fundamental truth. Believers who know God as the ground of their own being and who are conscious of being drawn into a divine purpose will as a reasonable extension of this see that same God as the ground of the universe as a whole, and evolution with a purpose behind it.[21]

The real difficulty with evolution lies elsewhere, not in the theory itself but in its character. The first difficulty is presented by the means through which evolution comes about, a combination of random genetic mutation and natural selection. At the least it seems a very chancy way of bringing us about, like spinning a roulette wheel to see where the ball lands and having to do it billions of times to get the answer that is wanted. For random genetic mutation is by definition random; it is simply a spore, which happens to be thrown off without rhyme or reason. Yet as the biochemist and theologian Arthur Peacocke pointed out, it is just this combination of randomness and inflexibility, and only this combination, that makes development possible. If there were no mutation, nothing new could develop. However, if that were all there is, no development could be captured for the future. It is natural selection – that is, the inflexible rule that only what can adapt to a particular environment survives – that enables a development to be captured and retained for the future. What does not adapt simply perishes for ever. So although this might seem an odd method for a divine creator to use, that is in fact the means whereby we have evolved, and we can at least see its rationale.

That said, there is a harsher side to this process well captured in Tennyson's phrase that nature is red in tooth and claw. Much of the natural world seems to be characterized by the struggle to eat and avoid being eaten. This is brought home to us in the many wonderful nature films that have been shown on television in recent years. However natural, in the sense of being part of the processes of nature, this can be very upsetting. Two points can however be made. First, it has become increasingly recognized in recent years that co-operation has also played a crucial role in evolution. Indeed Richard Dawkins rather regrets the title of his best-known book *The Selfish Gene* because it gave the impression that selfishness was all that was involved. It is indeed true that the individual gene operates in such a way as to maximize the chance of replication and survival. But individual genes are always part of larger, more complex organisms and they very much depend on co-operation. The second point is that while the higher vertebrates have nervous systems and feel pain akin to ours, simpler organisms do not and it is a mistake to see them in anthropomorphic terms. Nevertheless the suffering of animals not only challenges our way of life but rightly raises a major question about the compatibility of this with a loving creator. Because there is no finally satisfying answer to this question, the issue of animal suffering will for many form part of the wider protest that is taken up in Chapter 14, 'Refusing to be comforted'.

For the Christian believer, faith that there is a creator of all things visible and invisible will seem supremely reasonable. This is because it means there is a rational purpose behind the existence of the world and a meaningful goal for it. Furthermore it makes sense of the fact that we have rational minds that can map out the universe at both cosmic and subatomic levels, and that this is done through mathematical equations of great elegance. We can also see why it is that all forms of beauty should draw us and moral obligations impel us. Everything fits together in a coherent and consistent whole. The one major exception of course is the presence of so much evil and pointless suffering, the main focus of this book. But leaving this major obstacle aside for the moment, the believer finds that everything fits together in a satisfying whole. It makes sense. It seems reasonable. The problem is that there is no compelling logic that can show that the universe should make sense. It may all be without purpose or meaning. That is in essence why the arguments discussed earlier cannot work as proofs. And what this brings out, therefore, is that when the believer is thinking along the lines sketched out in the earlier part of this paragraph, she or he is doing so with a mind already opened up to this perspective. Pascal is not quite right when he writes that 'The heart has its reasons of which the mind knows nothing.' It is rather that heart and mind move together, and the believer's mind moves with a heart already touched in some way, even if only in the form of an initial sympathetic exploration. So while believers cannot prove there is a rational purpose behind life, they can try to show what it looks and feels like from the standpoint of someone who believes there is such a purpose; and from that perspective it does indeed fit together in a coherent whole for which good reasons can be given.

5

Truth in its beauty

The pull of truth

The quest for truth and therefore the key value of truthfulness is fundamental to every worthwhile human endeavour. In science, for example, when an experimenter has been exposed as falsifying results, as occasionally happens, there is a proper frisson of horror in the scientific community. For the bedrock of scientific knowledge is a commitment to what experiments and tests reveal. Similarly in the judicial process, it is the truth that is sought, and those who lie face particular opprobrium. However because, sadly, lying is so much part of the mentality of some people, the stakes are raised, so that it is 'lying on oath' that is the offence. Again, in the UK Parliament, because political propaganda is so much taken for granted, there is a special category of offence, 'lying to parliament', which in the case of a minister would necessitate resigning from office.

Now it might be argued that in all these instances what we have is just some kind of contract undertaken in a person's long-term self-interest. For example, truth being fundamental to scientific discovery, anyone who wanted to practise as a scientist might accept that it is in his or her own interest to accept the rules of the game, as it were. But the vast majority of scientists would I think say that this kind of account simply fails to do justice to their deepest conviction, which is the imperative of truth, the deep desire to discover and map out things as they really are, whether it is in cosmology or at the subatomic level or any one of the many areas in between.

What is true of a range of human activities is also applicable to human relationships. Trust is fundamental to relationships and trust is integrally linked to truth telling. We may come, through hard experience, to distrust certain people or institutions, but human life proceeds on the assumption that for most of the time people mean more or less what they say. Without this there could in fact be no human relationships and no emergence of the human person. For this reason, it is particularly damaging when an ideology that is based on a lie, and uses lying systematically, takes over a whole society. The writer and later President of Czechoslovakia, Václav Havel, was a person who offered a heroic witness to truth in such a society. He argued that if, for example, a shop showed an obviously false piece of Communist propaganda in its window, we should do our best to pull it down. Even in such small ways it was important to protest against the lie. Six of his essays on this theme were collected together under the title *Living in Truth*. Then in one of his plays he depicts a man under arrest in such a system who resolutely keeps silence. There are interesting parallels with the silence of Christ before his accusers. In a situation where everyone is trying to mis-interpret, distort and twist what is said in order to achieve their aim, perhaps to achieve a conviction, it may be that the only way there can be a witness to truth is through silence. The imperative that drove Havel in the political realm he thought equally applicable in the artistic. Writing of the truth of the artist's inner experience, he said: 'There is only one art, whose sole criterion is the power, the authenticity, the revelatory insight, the courage and suggestiveness with which it seeks its truth or perhaps the urgency and profundity of this truth.'[1]

This truth goes wider than words and applies in every artistic medium. It is about artistic integrity, a willingness to set aside what will be immediately popular or saleable or fashionable in order to pursue a particular personal vision. There is a wonderful example of this in the life of the painter Henri Matisse. His vision, obsession even, was colour, and he persevered with this through years of hard-ship and critical neglect, even derision. At one fairly early stage in his career he did begin to sell some of his pictures and one dealer offered to take as many academic still-life paintings as he could produce for 400 francs apiece. Matisse wrote:

> One day, I had just finished one of these [still-life] pictures. It was
> as good as the previous one and very much like it. I knew that on
> delivery I would get the money I sorely needed. There was a tempta-
> tion to deliver it, but I knew that if I yielded it would be my artistic
> death. Looking back I realise that it required courage to destroy the
> picture, particularly as the hands of the butcher and the baker were
> outstretched waiting for the money. But I did destroy it. I count my
> emancipation from that day.[2]

That kind of single-mindedness, that almost ruthless integrity, is
rare, but without some element of it no real art is produced. When
it is present, the way a whole generation sees or feels about things
can be changed, as happened with the early modernists not only in
art, but music, poetry and the novel.

This quest for truth has its counterpart in the spiritual life with the
imperative to know oneself without self-deception or illusion. One
of the themes that run through the sermons and lectures of Rowan
Williams is this warning against self-deceit. The same point was
repeatedly made by Reinhold Niebuhr in relation to the economic
sphere and power politics, for interest groups and nations can be
even more dangerously in the grip of illusion and self-deception,
cloaking naked self-interest with fine moral rhetoric.

So strong is this imperative for truth that Plato and those many
millions who have been influenced by him down the centuries gave
the abstract noun 'truth' actual ontological status. Things were not
just more or less truthful, there was an essential truth that really
existed, as there was an essential goodness and beauty, a universal
reality that every aspect of truth reflected. It was a bold and beautiful vision and has acted as an ally of Christian faith in many cultures.
However, that formulation cannot stand up to philosophical scrutiny
today and we are much more inclined to tease out the different ways
the word 'truth' is used, rather than try to give ontological status to
some abstract value.

Nevertheless what still remains to puzzle us is the pull of truth, its
drawing power, its allure, the hold it has on us to pursue it whether
it is to our advantage to do so or not. There is an imperiousness

about truth, a categorical imperative. It has been suggested that this pull of truth has a simple evolutionary explanation, namely that for the earliest human beings an accurate knowledge of their prey, predators and physical surroundings was vital for survival. But every aspect of our behaviour has an evolutionary justification. This does not, however, go very far in explaining its significance for us. The pull of truth, artistic, scientific, intellectual and personal, is such that people are often willing to sacrifice their short-term benefits for it, as in the case of Matisse, even sometimes their life. Truth is a fundamental theme and image in St John's Gospel, where Christ is described as the truth because in him God is revealed. Yet there are those whose pursuit of truth leads them away from this con-clusion. If this path is followed in all honesty and integrity (and given the human inclination to self-deception and illusion, that is a big qualification), it must of course be followed. Jesus is reported as saying that every sin can be forgiven except the sin against the Holy Spirit. I have always taken that one unforgivable sin to refer to deliberately following a path knowing it is untrue and wilfully calling good evil and evil good. It is not that God does not wish to forgive people who do this, it is that they make themselves into people incapable of receiving forgiveness because they have so distorted their sense of what is true and untrue. If people are honestly following what they understand to be true, the situation is very different. Simone Weil, reflecting on this and in particular on how the honest quest for truth can lead them away from faith, resolved the issue in her own mind with the words: 'Christ likes us to prefer truth to him because, before being Christ, he is truth. If one turns aside from him to go towards the truth, one will not go far before falling into his arms.'[3] This was obviously written very much out of her own experience, as we can see in the seriousness with which she took atheism.

John Masefield wrote a poem on truth that begins:

> Man with his burning soul
> Has but an hour of breath

> To build a ship of truth
> In which his soul may sail –
> Sail on the sea of death,
> For death takes toll
> Of beauty, courage, youth,
> Of all but truth.

It continues:

> Stripped of all purple robes,
> Stripped of all golden lies,
> I will not be afraid,
> Truth will preserve through death.[4]

It is a poem of hopeful agnosticism, not the full Christian vision. But it witnesses to this extraordinary quality present in humanity, the serious desire for truth, for total integrity. However often we deceive ourselves or suffer from illusions, and however much we reinforce those deceptions and illusions through our mutual collusions, we recognize that deeper than the purple robes and golden lies is a haunting imperative to recognize and follow truth. There is a paradox here in serious atheism, for the very integrity that might have led a person to believe that the universe is inhospitable to value itself witnesses to something profoundly beautiful in human beings.

The lure of beauty

It is clear from this that our quest for truth is integrally linked to certain moral qualities: a capacity to put aside the self-seeking ego, a certain humility, a willingness to resist short-term fashions in the service of a difficult long-term goal requiring patience and persistence. What is interesting about these moral qualities is that when they are present in a particular person they have a highly attractive quality. We might even dare to think of certain forms of goodness we may have encountered as having a beauty to them. Some qualities, we say, are admirable, and in admiring them, or more specially the person in whom they reside, we recognize an ideal we would like for ourselves and all human beings. It is no accident that the Greek word *kalos*, usually translated 'good', also means 'beautiful'. The truly good is beautiful; so it is that St Augustine, as quoted earlier, addresses God as 'beauty most ancient and withal so fresh'. Beauty is not a fashionable word in either philosophical or artistic circles and there is a certain hesitancy in our culture today about using it. But as has been written by one of the leading theologians of the twentieth century, 'We can be sure that whoever sneers at her name as if she were the ornament of a bourgeois past – whether he admits it or not – can no longer pray and soon will no longer be able to love.'[5]

It is not surprising that Christians down the ages have seen this lure of truth as the touch of God upon us, and the ontological reality of truth residing in God himself. But that is not my point here. The point is the way the imperative of truth, of integrity in all its forms, artistic, personal and political, haunts us. It is part of the grandeur of humanity that this is so, part of what makes up the beauty of life. Take the person who is a convinced atheist, who thinks there is no purpose to existence other than any we may wish to bestow on it, and that all human values are in defiance of a universe essentially indifferent to them. When such a person continues to assert the importance of living well, there is a profound beauty here. A Christian will see here a fact crying out for a wider theological interpretation, but even if that is rejected there is something here that is noble, grand and beautiful in itself for itself. The same can be said about the human quest for truth in the scientific, artistic or philosophical realms.

What is no less remarkable is the way the truth of the universe yields itself to formulations that are variously described as elegant and beautiful. A whole range of cosmologists and mathematical physicists have recently talked of the beauty of the equations with which they pursue truth at the outer edges of our understanding. This was also true of earlier scientists. It has been pointed out that James Clerk Maxwell sought to bring together light, electricity and magnetism, once classified as separate factors, in a unified theorem by seeking beauty in his equations. All this fits in with the concept of beauty in the Middle Ages when words like 'symmetry', 'balance' and 'harmony' were all repeated by theorists. They saw the source of all this in the divine wisdom who orders all things well, a wisdom that in the Scriptures is described as beautiful.[6]

In addition to the struggle to respond to the truth of things with artistic integrity, all genuine works of art are characterized by form. Art forms are always changing but without form of one kind or another there can be no art. It is form that distinguishes music and poetry from mere cacophony, novels and drama from aimless happenings. Form by itself is not enough to produce art. Form gives shape to the otherwise shapeless and it pleases us, but by itself it might just mean attractive decoration or wallpaper. In genuine art, the form is integrally linked to the struggle for truth and the integrity of the artist. When all three are present there will be true beauty, not mere prettiness or attractiveness but something powerful – a 'terrible beauty', to use the phrase of W. B. Yeats in his poem 'Easter, 1916'.[7]

Beauty in its many forms is what helps to make life worthwhile for so many human beings. The beauties to be found in landscape and nature more generally, in the arts – perhaps especially in music – and in the characters of the best people they know are what lift life out of a mundane struggle to survive. And as recent work in science shows, beauty is a fundamental constituent of the equations that reveal the universe to us. Beauty involves our conceptual, perceptual and affective capacities; our capacity to perceive, think and feel. But it does so without any particular purpose in mind, which is why the concept of play is central in many accounts of aesthetics. The conclusion of a recent three-volume history of aesthetics is summed up in the words:

> Our aesthetic experience is best understood, as Plato held, as a form of love. And like love for other persons, our love of beauty is not just cognitive, affective and perceptual but crucially too involves desire: to be with its object and to know it. It means too that, like love of persons, aesthetic experience is a way of connecting to the world that is pleasurable and painful, unconditional and yet uncertain, of the moment and yet indefinitely extended. Thus if play in freedom is

central to the capacity for taking the kind of interest in the world that we call aesthetic, it is the kind of freedom possessed by – and possessing – those who love.[8]

The triad of truth, beauty and goodness have usually been taken together as being of equal standing, with each fitting harmoniously, one with the others. This harmony was, however, fiercely disputed by Friedrich Nietzsche. Like Arthur Schopenhauer, Nietzsche was acutely aware of the horrors of existence but in contrast to Schopenhauer, who saw art as a refuge and escape, thought of art as a glorious act of defiance. Instead of simply resigning ourselves to life in all its horrors and looking for an alternative world in art, Nietzsche saw art as a way of taking hold of life, of magnificent human assertion, and especially was this true in tragedy. As he put it:

> Tragedy does *not* teach 'resignation – To represent terrible and question-able things is in itself an instinct for power and magnificence in an artist: he does not fear them – There is no such thing as pessimistic art – Art affirms ... For a philosopher to say, 'the good and the beautiful are one' is infamy: if he goes on to add, 'also the true,' one ought to thrash him. Truth is ugly.
> We possess *art* lest we *perish of the truth*.[9]

This bold claim needs a little unpacking. First, there is a clear con-tradiction. For Nietzsche says that 'Truth is ugly' yet he also claims that the metaphysical comfort tragedy leaves is because 'life is at the bottom of things, despite all the changes of appearances, indestruct-ibly powerful and pleasurable.'[10] That last sentence indicates that life for all its horrors is magnificent and is to be affirmed. If that is true, as Nietzsche claims, then it cannot at the same time be true that 'we perish of the truth'. For he believes we can face the truth, even its darkest side, and still find life pleasurable.

Tragedy deals with what is unresolved, with what cannot be con-soled, yet it creates that which people have termed beautiful. Nietzsche believed that this beauty cannot be at one with the good and that for philosophers to assert that they are is 'infamy'. This raises the old question, so often discussed, of the nature of tragedy. I take it first

63

to involve large forces mainly beyond our control. For the Greeks, this was fate or the gods; for us moderns it is often the determining factors of history, especially economic forces. To take just one example, Arthur Miller's play *A View from the Bridge*: here these larger forces are the poverty in Sicily and the consequent pressure on people to immigrate to New York, together with the policy of the government to control immigration. There are also powerful psychosexual forces at work in the unrecognized feelings of the longshoreman (docker) Eddie Carbone for his underage niece Catherine who lives with him and his wife. When the couple share their flat with two illegal immigrants from Sicily and one of them also falls in love with Catherine, the plot moves to what was seen from the first by a lawyer friend as an inevitable tragedy. There is a terrible betrayal of the illegals by Eddie to the police, which ends in his death. The lawyer, who acts like the chorus in a Greek tragedy, full of foreboding about what was to happen, comments at the end.

> Most of the time now we settle for half and I like it better. But the truth is holy, and even as I know how wrong he was, and his death useless, I tremble, for I confess that something perversely pure calls to me from his memory – not purely good but himself purely, for he allowed himself to be wholly known and for that I think I will love him more than all my sensible clients. And yet, it is better to settle for half, it must be! And so I mourn him – I admit it – with a certain . . . alarm.[11]

Then when watching tragedy on the stage there is what the literary critic F. R. Leavis called 'a sense of enhanced vitality'. This comes from the recognition that some positive value or values have been more sharply outlined and affirmed by death.

> The experience is constructive or positive, and involves recognising positive value as in some way defined and vindicated by death . . . It is as if we were challenged at the profoundest level with the question 'In what does the significance of life reside?'[12]

In *A View from the Bridge*, one value is the sacred bond of loyalty to fellow immigrants fleeing poverty. But there are also the more complex values embodied in Eddie Carbone himself, about which the lawyer is so understandably ambivalent.

The value of what is destroyed is somehow brought into sight by its very destruction. We see this very clearly in, for example, Shakespeare's *King Lear*. Cordelia, the one person who truly loved Lear, dies. What is done cannot be undone. Evil as expressed in the attitudes of the other sisters and the weakness of Lear himself have in one way triumphed. We feel a sense of pity and outrage precisely because we are so sharply aware of the values Cordelia embodies and the others deny. The tragedy brings them into sharper focus. Events have conspired to defeat the bearer of those values but that serves only to affirm their abiding significance and pose the question stated by Leavis to ourselves.

What this brings out is that, contrary to Nietzsche, beauty and goodness are indeed linked. This is seen in the artistic beauty of a tragedy, not only in its form as a work of art but in the way it heightens the goodness that seems to lose out in the course of events, but which in fact shines through more brightly. This is so, for example, in relation to the goodness of Cordelia in *King Lear*, which we might at the same time want to describe as beautiful.

What then of the link to truth? As already mentioned, the search for truth in any sphere cannot be divorced from moral qualities, first of all because it requires a transcending of the ego to focus on what is there. It involves a laying aside of all the vanities and personal interests that drive so much of our behaviour. It requires a deep seriousness together with a sustained attention to the other. This is the quality so powerfully written about by Simone Weil and taken up by Iris Murdoch. We can see a good example of what is involved in some words of the painter John Constable. He said that in art there are two things to be avoided. One is imitation, simply reproducing the styles of the past. The other is what he termed 'bravura', and what is interesting is how he defined this as 'going beyond the truth'. In other words, the artist has to avoid simply splurging his or her own personality on to the canvas to draw attention to it. Rather what is necessary is an act of self-transcendence in which the artist is solely focused on the object or idea before him or her, letting its truth take hold. So it is that Constable let the landscape reveal its truth to him. When occasionally he departed from this he knew what he was doing, for he said that sometimes he put in a little 'eye salve', a pretty detail that he knew would appeal. Similarly Anselm Kiefer, interviewed before his major 2014 exhibition in London, said that as an artist he always strove for the truth. He did not think it was attainable, but it had to be struggled for.

So at the core of this triad of values of truth, beauty and goodness is the good, for without an act of self-transcendent, serious attention to the object or subject being considered, the search for truth will be led astray. That search for truth has to take into account every aspect of life including what is grotesque and terrible. When that is done, for example in a work of art, that work, by the very fact that it is recognized as a work of art, will have a dimension of beauty; and what is possible in the creation of a work of art may be possible for the universe as a whole. Creation itself may turn out to be a work of art whose totality makes up that which is sheerly beautiful. The issue of tragedy and whether it is possible to go beyond it is considered further in Chapter 16.

The present chapter has celebrated the integrity with which many human beings are capable of pursuing truth in every sphere of life. A different but related aspect of this is the way people struggle on heroically in the most difficult circumstances of crippling illness or deprivation. This is not just integrity in pursuit of ideas or artistic expression but in living courageously. They need not go on but they do. Albert Camus suggested that the great problem in life is suicide:

> There is but one truly serious philosophical problem and that is suicide. Judging whether life is or is not worth living amounts to answering the fundamental question of philosophy. All the rest – whether or not the world has three dimensions, whether the mind has nine or twelve categories – comes afterwards. These are games; one must first answer.[13]

That answer, whether life is worth living or not, has for Camus to come before any other. Far too many people do commit suicide; yet the great majority of us do not. 'I would rather die', says a character in Graham Greene's novel *The Power and the Glory*,[14] to which he receives the reply: 'Of course. That goes without saying. But we have to go on living.' Why? Sometimes when we meet people who survive in the most terrible circumstances we think to ourselves that if we were in that situation we could not go on – yet so many people do. No doubt this is accounted for partly by the animal will to survive bequeathed to us by evolution and partly by fear of taking one's own life. But deeper than that seems to be an inchoate sense that something great is at stake in life, something that cannot simply be measured by a utilitarian calculus of pain and pleasure. Samuel Beckett and Samuel Johnson, so unlike in the way they are perceived, did in fact have a great affinity of spirit, which was why Beckett started, though he never finished, a play about Johnson. Both were utterly serious about life, both faced its horrors, and for both of them it was a matter of going on going on.[15] Behind this was a fear of the void, of what Johnson called 'vacuity', which had to be filled up at all costs. For Beckett, it was language, going on talking, that filled the void, making 'a stain upon the silence'; for Johnson it was company. But for both of them going on going on was a serious, indeed the ultimate, moral endeavour. So here again we have a strange paradoxical witness to the glory of the human enterprise. Whether or not life has a given, good purpose behind it, innumerable human beings believe in themselves and their own lives enough to continue, sometimes despite the most adverse circumstances. There is a challenging, haunting beauty about this. Many have felt with Keats that 'Beauty is truth, truth beauty', as he wrote in his poem 'Ode on a Grecian Urn'. For a believer, this may go further, as expressed in the hymn 'O worship the Lord in the beauty of holiness' with its lines:

> Truth in its beauty and love in its tenderness,
> these are the offerings to lay on his shrine.

In earlier chapters, it was argued that rational argument by itself can neither prove nor disprove the reality of God and that our reasoning powers operate as part of the whole person. For a person of faith, those reasoning powers will seek to relate his or her belief to every aspect of creation, however challenging this sometimes seems. What has been suggested in this chapter is that there are important aspects of human experience, very widely shared across cultures, that keep us open to the possibility of a good power behind the universe. One is the imperative to follow truth wherever it leads. Another is the pulling power of beauty in nature, the arts and in life itself. The third is the presence of some truly good or holy people whose example exposes the hollowness of our own lives and challenges us to emulate them. In such people too, there is a moral and spiritual beauty that beckons us. This triad of goodness, truth and beauty, going back to Plato and the Greeks, has walked hand in hand with the Christian faith down the ages, has helped to shape our cultural and moral heritage and continues to influence it in significant ways. Its pull and lure and challenge continues to haunt us with the possibility of a spiritual dimension to life behind, beyond and within the tangible world.

6

A living tradition

One of the guiding principles of this book is to try to be true to the actual experience of people of faith and not posit some ideal scenario. It seeks to reflect the situation of faith from the inside. With that in mind, I would suggest that by whatever route and for whatever reason, if a person finds himself or herself thinking about the possibility of religious belief it will be from within a faith community, formal or informal, which is itself the product of a tradition. We do not think alone. We are all part of a cultural tradition that has formed us and with which we are in inner dialogue. For those thinking about faith, this will be in a more sharply defined tradition. They may have been brought up in the faith and then find that they are radically questioning it. But at that point, and until they leave, they stand within the tradition. Or they may have heard the Christian message preached, or heard about it from a friend, been attracted by it and drawn in to some Christian congregation. They may be very tentative and exploratory in their participation but they are feeling their way forwards from within a community, not as an isolated individual.

One writer in the New Testament begins his letter by stating the good news as he understands it:

> our theme is the Word which gives life. This life was made visible; we have seen it and bear our testimony; we declare to you the eternal life which was with the Father and was made visible to us.

He immediately goes on to say:

> It is this which we have seen and heard that we declare to you also, in order that you may share with us in a common life, that life which we share with the Father and his Son Jesus Christ.
>
> (1 John 1.1–3)

A key concept in that last paragraph is the Greek word *koinonia*, translated above as 'common life' and in other translations as 'fellowship'. It is a word that in the original Greek appears twice in that sentence, first to refer to the shared life of the community into which the believer has been drawn, second to refer to the shared life the believer enjoys through that community with the Father and his Son Jesus Christ. It is a remarkable claim. The congregation of very ordinary people in which the believer now finds himself or herself as a member is at the same time a way into the life God has shared with us in Jesus. It is not just a group of people gathered to learn about a particular religion, or for mutual support or good works, it is a doorway into the very life of God.

I am deliberately not saying anything about particular Christian denominations. The *koinonia* to which I am referring is what the 1662 Book of Common Prayer affirms when it says 'We are very members incorporate in the mystical body of thy Son, which is the blessed company of all faithful people.' This is not to deny the importance of the debates between different churches about where ultimate authority lies and how disagreements are to be handled, but they will not be discussed here. Whether people are Roman Catholics, Conservative Evangelicals, members of Pentecostal churches, Orthodox or Anglicans, I believe they will see themselves in that phrase from the Book of Common Prayer and will have the humility to leave it to God to judge degrees of faithfulness in others.

That said, three principles have to be made clear. First, the *koinonia* in which the believer finds himself or herself is the expression of a living tradition that goes back to Jesus and his circle of close followers and has its consummation in that Christ-filled community of perfect mutual giving and receiving of love we call the Communion of Saints.

Second, the Bible is best understood as itself an expression of this living tradition. Before the Bible there was the preaching, then collections of stories and sayings and then the accounts of Jesus and letters that later became collected together to form what we call the New Testament. For many years, there were discussions about what should be included. At some point what is now included was excluded and what is now excluded was included. It was only in the fifth century that agreement was reached about the canon of the New Testament. It was the community of Christians at the time who reached that conclusion, so it could be said that the authority of the community is the decisive one. But it is not as simple as that because in forming the Canon they were above all trying to recognize and affirm what was apostolic and therefore authoritative for the community.

So the third principle is that the Scriptures are authoritative for the Christian community in every age and nothing can be laid down as essential to the Christian faith that cannot be firmly grounded in Scripture. The Bible is at once the product of the Christian community and the touchstone of its living, developing tradition.[1]

I recognize that this last statement is not uncontroversial and that the Catechism of the Roman Catholic Church, for example, will state the relationship between tradition and Scripture somewhat differently. But my hope is that any disagreement on this point will not detract from my main theme, which is that to become and grow as a Christian is to be fed and nourished by a living tradition persisting through space and time.

What is a living tradition and what does it mean to inhabit it? Despite the great emphasis in our society on present changing fashions, the ceaselessly moving now, almost every family knows something of tradition even if only in the form of stories about their grandparents. More widely, we can become aware of a cultural tradition, so someone who reads novels will have some sense of what it means to belong to a reading public that has persisted for 200 years or more. Someone in the West who appreciates art will have some sense of belonging to a tradition that goes back to the Renaissance and before that to the Romans and Greeks. Although a cultural tradition and a living one may overlap in many ways, the difference between them can be seen in the contrast between the ways an art historian might approach Byzantine art and the attitude of a member of the

71

Orthodox Church. For the latter, art, in the form of icons, whether as painted panels, mosaics or frescos, whether on a wall or free-standing, bring home the reality of the heavenly realm present with us now. Icons are painted – or to use the technical term, written – according to age-old techniques and in prayer. Although the approach of the Church in the West placed more emphasis on the educative and didactic element in art, the role of paintings and image in prayer was still important and remains so today, as we see in the legal cases concerned with people wearing the cross at work. But for the Orthodox it is fundamental, and this is because of their strong sense of belonging to a living tradition.

The late Donald Allchin described how on a visit to a monastery the abbot showed him the library and noted how different his attitude to the books was from that of the average Westerner. He wrote:

> We look at books chronologically and classify them in terms of influences and development. To the Abbot they all had a simultaneous existence and composed a simultaneous order. They were all books useful for the life of the spirit. Their authors were fathers and teachers who had become friends, to whom one spoke in church and at other times; it was of little importance whether they had lived six hundred, twelve hundred or fifty years ago.[2]

It was this understanding of tradition that T. S. Eliot regarded as of fundamental importance for a writer when he wrote that 'The historical sense involves a perception, not only of the pastness of the past, but of its presence.'[3] Similarly in the political realm, Edmund Burke argued that we need to understand society in an organic sense, as a living, developing body, one in which we see ourselves belonging to a community that is the product of the past and has an obligation to the future.[4]

For the Orthodox, the eternal dimension of the community is always present and is manifest in the way a church is decorated, with Christ Pantocrator in the dome surrounded by angels, the Virgin and Child in the apse and scenes from the life of Christ and the saints around the wall. As the eighth-century Patriarch Germanos put it: 'The Church is the earthly heaven in which the heavenly God lives and moves.' Although other Christian churches do not have this truth so powerfully displayed in iconographic terms, it is there in the liturgy shared by them all when in the Eucharist the congregation are bidden to lift up their hearts and pray 'Therefore with angels and archangels, and with all the company of heaven . . .'

This living tradition is very different from a dead traditionalism that seeks to preserve old ways of doing things for their own sake. First of all a living religious tradition is one in which the past is taken up into the present in a way that nourishes the soul now, or in more specifically Christian terms, enables us to share in the divine life God shares with us in Christ. Second, a living tradition enables us to see our present culture in both its newness and its ephemeral nature. Without a strong base in tradition it is very easy for people simply to be caught up in and taken along by the culture in which they are set. A tradition gives us a distance from contemporary culture. That distance enables us to see that culture more objectively, in both its continuity and discontinuity from the past. Not least it enables the person of faith to make a faithful response to it, discriminating between genuinely new truths that need to be assimilated by the tradition and passing fashions. This is never an easy task, and mistakes can be made by those who inhabit a tradition, both in the direction of adapting too quickly to the prevailing cultural norms or, more usually, reacting against them for too long before recognizing truths that have to be reckoned with. My own Anglican tradition came to terms with new historico-critical methods of looking at the Bible in the nineteenth century, artificial contraception in the first part of the twentieth, marriage after divorce in the second half, female bishops in the twenty-first century and is going through a period of turbulence over gay relationships. The point is, however, that a living tradition is one that is in principle able to respond and develop in each age, not despising in any way the wisdom of the past but responding to what is perceived to be the leading of the Spirit in the present.

A person can begin with a sense of belonging to a cultural tradition and find that this draws him or her into one that is more than this, which becomes for them a living one. As mentioned earlier, C. S. Lewis found that even as an atheist he was strongly drawn to works by Christian writers, as indeed was T. S. Eliot. Both writers moved from a position of admiration for Christian literature into one in which they found themselves inhabiting the living tradition of which it was a part. But as will be made clear in Chapter 17, in the case of Eliot this did not mean the closure of the sceptical part of his mind. Even in the case of Lewis, well known for his apparent doctrinal certainty, the sceptical side of him remained alive and came very much to the fore when his wife died. He could not have written the books he wrote towards the end of his life with their many helpful illuminations without having faced within himself the toughest questions.

The Jewish community offers an interesting example of how racial, cultural and religious traditions can coexist in one people with very blurred boundaries between them. For some Jews, being Jewish is a matter of solidarity with their own people, a people who have suffered so much, but involves nothing in the way of belief or practice. For others, some degree of observance matters very much (though the amount will vary hugely), but they will sit light to many funda- mental beliefs. This is in contrast to those for whom both the observance and the beliefs matter greatly. Again, for others what really matters is belonging to a community that provides a moral perspective and imperative, so while strongly identifying with Judaism they may still describe themselves as agnostic or atheistic. So Judaism is a living tradition but one whose meaning varies greatly depending on which branch of Judaism the person belongs to and his or her personal experience.

I would suggest that Christianity is a living tradition in the follow- ing sense. In the previous chapter, I argued that the Christian tradition did in the end depend on certain core beliefs, and those beliefs are fundamental to the argument of this book. That said, it has much to learn from Liberal and Reform Judaism in allowing latitude to individuals in how they relate to those beliefs at any one point in their life cycle. If there is an ultimate 'unknowingness' about

God, and what matters is commitment to a way of love rooted in trust and upheld by hope, this can coexist with a fair degree of scepticism at any one point, for the fact is that people's intellectual adherence to particular doctrines will vary greatly at different times in their life. There is a traditional phrase in the liturgy of the Church that well encapsulates how an individual might approach the matter: 'Regard not our sins but the faith of the Church.' It is the faith of the Church that matters, or more accurately, the presence of Christ in his Church and his unceasing prayer to the Father from within our human struggles. The individual with all his or her doubts and scepticism can be accommodated.

7

What do we know about Jesus and why does it matter?

The Jesus of history?

The world in which we live, at once so beautiful and so full of horrors, is one in which we look for meaning. I argued in earlier chapters that the quest for a given meaning to life with which we might align ourselves remains a valid question but there is no rational proof, or disproof, on whether there is a God. However, the imperative of truth of which we are conscious as human beings, and the lure of beauty, together with the way these qualities come together in certain lives of sheer goodness, continue to haunt us with the possibility that there may be an ultimate reality in which they have their source and standard. In the last chapter, I suggested that people of faith, or those feeling their way sympathetically towards faith, will find themselves within a living tradition. By this is meant a tapestry of words and music and liturgical action that hints at hidden depths and a wider meaning yet to be known; one that puts forward a disciplined way of life that both enhances our joys and enables us better to cope with life's tragedies. This will be a tradition whose past spiritual riches relate to the present, offering help to living now. This does not mean that people will at any one point believe all that the tradition claims but they will have begun to find elements within it helpful. If they did not find it a living one, in that sense, they would not be where we are now in terms of the argument of this book. What has been said so far, however, could apply to a number of religious traditions. Clearly, Sikhs, Muslims and Hindus, as well as Christians, find their tradition a living one or they would not identify themselves with it. So we have to face the fact that the words from the first letter of John quoted in

Chapter 6 make a quite specific and distinctive claim. For ease of reference, they are quoted again here:

> our theme is the Word which gives life. This life was made visible; we have seen it and bear our testimony; we declare to you the eternal life which was with the Father and was made visible to us. It is this which we have seen and heard that we declare to you also, in order that you may share with us in a common life, that life which we share with the Father and his Son Jesus Christ.
>
> (1 John 1.1–3)

This claims that to enter into the shared life of the community of Christians is at the same time to be taken into the life God has shared with us in Christ. It is to be drawn into the life of God himself as he has made himself known to us in his Son. Can this claim stand up to scrutiny? This is a question that has two crucial parts. First, what do we know for sure about Jesus, what he taught and who he thought he was? Second, how did the Christian community come to think he was a unique revelation of God, and was that conviction justified on the evidence presented in the New Testament?

It is important to note that no attempt is being made here to prove that Jesus was who the Church claims him to be, and in any case what would such proof consist of? The task is a more modest one, to show that for someone reflecting on this particular religious tradition it is reasonable to believe there is a proper continuity between the basis of that tradition in Jesus and the developed faith of the community.

So what do we know for sure about Jesus? I recognize that for some, who may have been sympathetic to the kind of argument presented in the preceding chapters, the very name is, sadly, a switch-off. It may be that they have had an unfortunate encounter with someone who tried to convert them in a clumsy manner, or they have found the whole Christian thing extremely unattractive. But while that is undoubtedly the case for far too many, it is not possible to continue with the argument presented in this book without considering what can truthfully be said about Jesus. An attempt will be made here to do this in as objective a manner as possible, one that might gain the assent of believer and non-believer alike.

The first challenge is to try to understand and describe Jesus in the context of his own time, on the basis of the best evidence available. And this means there is an immediate danger to be aware of, which is to project on to him some ideal from our own time. During the nineteenth century, arising out of the new biblical scholarship in Germany, there were a number of famous attempts to get behind the biblical accounts and reconstruct the story of Jesus in a new way. Then Albert Schweitzer in his book *The Quest of the Historical Jesus* did a survey of these attempts and came to the conclusion that the scholars had looked down the long well of history and simply seen their own faces at the bottom.

Although it could reasonably be argued that biblical scholars are more rigorous today in evaluating the evidence than their forebears – indeed paradoxically they tend to greater scepticism than their secular counterparts – they are not immune from this criticism of Schweitzer's. In the 1960s, for example, when support for liberation movements was running high, a book was published that argued that Jesus should be seen as a political revolutionary who aimed at the overthrow of the Roman Empire. At the same time, other works sought to put forward Jesus as a guru figure akin to those from India who were also fashionable at the time.

The reason why we tend to reconstruct the figure of Jesus in a way that fits in with our own culture is not just that we want someone who resonates with our own times but that we forget that 'The past is a foreign country: they do things differently there.'[1] And they certainly do things very differently in the world of the New Testament. Most obviously, casting out demons was, according to all four Gospels, clearly a central element in the ministry of Jesus and one of crucial importance to him. This is an activity we find it almost impossible to make proper sense of. It is true that in some areas in some countries of the world today this is part of the culture but it certainly isn't part of our own. If someone claims to be possessed by an evil spirit we try to get him or her to see a psychiatrist. It is true that both the Roman Catholic Church and the Church of England have a place for exorcism, with licensed exorcists, but this ministry is used very sparingly and carefully and fully alert to any possible psychiatric elements. We simply have to accept that the idea of evil spirits taking hold of people was part of the culture in which Jesus ministered in a way that it is not in ours.

Another even more testing example is the conviction shared by all the early strands of the New Testament, including apparently by Jesus himself (though this is more disputed), that the end of the world as we know it was to come very soon. Indeed this was the rock Schweitzer came up against and may have been one reason why he put aside both his musical career and his biblical scholarship to retrain as a doctor to work at Lambaréné in Central Africa.

Over the past 30 years or so, there has been a new quest for the historical Jesus, as well as an international Jesus seminar on the subject. This quest, while fully aware of the pitfalls later revealed in nineteenth-century attempts to recover the Jesus of history, works on the assumption that it is possible through the most rigorous scholarship to set out the main outlines of the life and teaching of Jesus in a way that can be respected as such by a very wide range of informed opinion among believers and non-believers alike.

The evidence that any quest has to work with is provided by the four Gospel accounts. The evidence outside those accounts is very limited indeed. Each Gospel is written with a different audience in mind, from a particular perspective and from within a particular cultural milieu. One of the priorities of New Testament scholarship in recent decades has been to tease out these different perspectives. So whereas for most of Christian history the assumption has been that the four different accounts of Jesus can all be reconciled and put together to form a unified, composite picture, no such assumption is made in modern scholarship. Indeed the opposite – it is taken for granted that the pictures presented are different and that not all differences can be harmonized. The exposition of the distinctive picture given by each of the four Gospel writers has been a richly rewarding one, but what we have are four different perspectives, not one.

Each of the four writers had earlier material to work on. For example, the writer of St Matthew's Gospel had the Gospel of Mark, material he shared with the writer of the Gospel of Luke, as well as access to a tradition the others did not use or know of. Luke had St Mark's Gospel, material shared with Matthew and access to material unique to him. The sources behind the fourth Gospel are more complex and less certain. But all the sources used by the writers will have been remembered and recorded for a particular purpose.

Behind the Gospels and the possible written sources on which they drew, scholars have detected material shaped or formed in a particular way to meet some question or issue in church life at the time. And behind all written sources, both those that have survived and those we surmise once existed, lies an oral tradition and the earliest preaching of the Christian Church. Why do we remember some things and not others? Why do we record some things and not others? The answer we give to that question for ourselves is the answer we give to the earliest Christian memories. Certain stories and sayings were remembered and written down either because they were particularly vivid and memorable or because they helped to address an issue the Church was facing at the time – or, more likely, both.

So in trying to reconstruct the life and teaching of Jesus, scholars have to dig into and through these various layers, trying so far as they can to distinguish what went before from later accretions or interpretations. It is a difficult and complex task in which there can never be final certainty. Nevertheless there is now some agreement on a basic outline of what Jesus did and said. There will always be differences of emphasis and there is no finality, but what is put forward here has strong scholarly support. It is stated as succinctly as possible, with the minimum of supporting biblical references and without glossing over the difficulties.

The starting point for this picture is that Jesus must be seen as a Jew shaped by the Judaism of the first century. This highlights another problem. All the Gospels were written after the fledgling Christian community had broken away from the Synagogue, and the sources we have reflect that split, with the hostility that ensued. With all the above in mind, the outline runs as follows.

At about the age of 30, Jesus appeared on the public stage in the Galilee region proclaiming that the long-expected reign of God in human affairs had arrived. He called people to change their whole stance on life and put their trust in the good news he was bringing. Though reluctant to satisfy people's desire for miracles, especially those who wanted signs to prove that what he was saying was true, he was driven by compassion to heal many of the people who pleaded with him for a cure. Similarly he cast out evil spirits from those who were afflicted in this way. He saw these healings of body, mind and spirit as signs that the rule of God was indeed breaking the stranglehold that evil had on the world.

Proclaiming that the rule of God 'is upon you', his teaching has a great sense of urgency to it. Many of the stories he told are designed to bring home to people the seriousness of the present situation and the urgency of making a response to it now. This response involved changing their whole outlook on life and living from henceforth under the rule of God, or within his divine milieu. Jesus' radical and memorable ethical teaching is designed to set out what this implied, both in terms of character and behaviour. It is not legislation for how society is to operate in the long term but an imperative for personal change now in the light of what God really wants of us. In bringing this message home to people, Jesus acted as a freelance rabbi, sometimes teaching in the synagogue and often discussing disputed questions with the main body of religious teachers at the time, the Pharisees, some of whom he felt close to and others whose teaching he strongly contradicted.

Jesus did not act alone. He gathered around him a small band of intimate followers, and the fact that there were twelve of these is an indication that he saw himself as bringing into being a renewed Israel or people of God. He confined his mission to the people of Israel but particularly went out of his way to reach out to and eat with those whose way of life had put themselves on the margins of Jewish life. His unforgettable teaching on this theme is designed to show that his ministry of searching out those on the edge and including them in the people of God reflected the pattern of God's eternal approach to humanity as a whole.

Jesus knew he had to take his message from Galilee to Jerusalem, the centre and focus of Jewish life, and he knew also that this would bring increasing opposition, rejection and probable death. He accepted this and came to see it as a price that had to be paid for bringing into being God's new order of things.

Jesus knew himself called to announce this new age and to gather round himself the makings of a renewed people of God. Beyond this what he said about himself is enigmatic. The title he used of himself, 'Son of Man', can just mean 'human being'. He associated this Son of Man with having to suffer, but as he used the term it also carried associations from a passage in the book of Daniel, in which the Son of Man is ultimately triumphant.

Jesus did go up to Jerusalem and he taught in the temple precincts. In particular, there was a clash with the temple authorities, on whom most of Jerusalem was financially dependent at the time. He foresaw that in God's new age the old temple of stone would give way to a new spiritual temple, the indwelling of God in his renewed people.

He was then arrested, tried, crucified and buried.

From then on it is no longer possible to achieve any kind of consensus. This is because the Christian community came into being as a result of the conviction that God had raised Jesus from the dead and that he would come again soon in glory. At that point the divine kingdom he had inaugurated on earth would find its fulfilment and consummation.

That last paragraph brings out why it is so difficult to get behind the New Testament documents to find out 'what actually happened', for every page in the New Testament is written up from the standpoint of faith in the resurrection of Jesus and his living spiritual presence in the Church. So there is a sense that we can fully enter into it only with what Pope Benedict XVI called a 'hermeneutic of faith'. A believing Christian reads the New Testament as part of the same community of faith from which it came, with the same fundamental assumptions. This is not to deny the importance of serious, objective scholarship, which can be engaged in by believer and non-believer alike, and what this might produce in the way of an agreed portrait of Jesus. As already indicated, it is possible to affirm significant common ground. But on the resurrection and its implications for reading the New Testament as a living document, there will inevitably be a parting of the ways. And that is why, although scholars work to find sources and antecedents of the Gospel accounts, the believer will quite properly take the Gospels in their entirety, with their different perspectives, as mediating to them the living Christ. They come from a community of faith and speak to that same community of faith now.

A. N. Wilson, who has both written a book and made a television programme about the historical Jesus, now believes that it is impossible to reconstruct the historical life of Jesus. He thinks that every line in the New Testament is written from faith to faith and we cannot peel away these successive layers of interpretation to find out what Jesus really said or did.[2] As the previous two paragraphs here make clear, Wilson is absolutely right in affirming that the New Testament is written by people with faith in Christ to the community that shared that faith, but his total scepticism about reconstructing the figure of Jesus is not justified. While it is always open to dispute and modification, the outline presented here has strong scholarly support.

Jesus raised from the dead?

What we know for certain is that many of the first Christians claimed that the risen Christ appeared to them. St Paul wrote to the church at Corinth reminding them of what he had first preached to them:

> First and foremost, I handed on to you the tradition I had received: that Christ died for our sins, in accordance with the scriptures; that he was buried; that he was raised to life on the third day, in accordance with the scriptures; and that he appeared to Cephas, and afterwards to the Twelve. Then he appeared to over five hundred of our brothers

at once, most of whom are still alive, though some have died. Then
he appeared to James, and afterwards to all the apostles. Last of all he
appeared to me too.

(1 Corinthians 15.3–8)

The significance of this passage was not only that it was written early,
about the year 51, but that the words Paul uses at the beginning are
the words for receiving and handing on a tradition. So even before
he first went to Corinth there was a tradition about the death and
resurrection of Christ that was being handed on.

In addition to the claim that the risen Christ had appeared to a
good many of his followers after his death there are also the accounts
that the tomb of Christ was found empty early on the Sunday morning, the third day after Christ's crucifixion on the Friday. A majority
view among scholars in recent years has been that the appearance
stories are the earliest and most reliable, and that the story of the
empty tomb is later and less to be relied on. Other distinguished New
Testament scholars, however, have taken a contrary point of view,
arguing that the story of finding the tomb empty can also be taken
as an early witness to the resurrection – this is a view I share.[3]

Together with the internal evidence of the New Testament, two
other facts are relevant. First, the opponents of the first Christian
preaching never produced a body to undermine the claims that
Christ had been raised from the dead. Second, no monument was
built over the grave of Jesus at the time. These points are not decisive but they are factors to be taken into account. They mean that
even if the Christian claim is untrue, there is no obvious alternative
explanation of the Christian account.

It is important to note that the resurrection of Jesus is not about
the resuscitation of a dead body. It is about the transfiguration of
his human body into the stuff of eternity, into what Paul called a
spiritual body. For the author of St John's Gospel, with its very different perspective from that of the first three, or Synoptic Gospels,
the going up of Jesus to Jerusalem was at the same time his going
up to be glorified; and that glorification consisted of the crucifixion,

resurrection and going to the Father as part of one movement. In the light of this, it could be argued that the resurrection appearances of the risen Christ were from the eternal realm, objective in character, but in their actual content reflecting the situation of the person to whom he appeared.[4]

When all this has been said, however, there is still the general argument of the philosopher David Hume about miracles, that on the basis of human experience it is much more likely that the disciples were mistaken in their belief that Christ had been raised from the dead, than that what they claimed was true. That is correct. However it is not just human experience in general that has to be taken into account in evaluating the life of Jesus. It has to be seen against the background of the people of Israel as a whole and their conviction that God would indeed act at some point to right all that is wrong and establish his rule in human affairs. Furthermore we have to note the proclamation by Jesus of that rule and his conviction that his mission to proclaim it would be vindicated in some way.

Here we are presented with a stark choice. There is no escaping the fact that Jesus announced that the rule of God was at hand and believed it was breaking into the world in his words and deeds. Then it all seemed to end in total failure. He was killed, his closest followers fled and the life of the world continued on its wicked way. Nothing had changed. God had not established his justice on earth. Jesus was a misguided failure, just one among many.

Or, God had raised him from the dead; the rule of God had indeed been established: not in the world as a whole yet but in Jesus himself as a pledge and foretaste of its universal sway, and in those who one by one were being drawn into his undying life. That is what the first Christians believed and proclaimed. In the resurrection, God had shown his hand and Jesus had been vindicated both in his message and in his person. Now, in the Christian community, his presence can be known. St John's Gospel records Judas, not Iscariot, asking 'Lord, how has it come about that you mean to disclose yourself to us and not to the world?', to which Jesus replies 'Anyone who loves me will heed what I say; then my Father will love him, and we will come to him and make our dwelling with him' (John 14.22). In the same teaching, the so-called 'last discourse' (John chapters 13—17), the writer makes it clear that to love Jesus is to obey him, and this means loving one another. When we do this he dwells in us and we dwell in him.

The Jesus of history and the Christ of faith

Some of the earliest Christian preaching was that God had vindicated Jesus in both his message and his person and that he was now at the right hand of glory. But as the passage from 1 John quoted earlier makes clear, that message quickly came to be formulated in a fuller form. In Jesus, the life of God is made manifest; the very heart of God has been made accessible in a human life and we can share that life. And this brings to the fore the second part of the question indicated earlier. How did the Church come to make its enormous claims about Jesus and can they be rooted in what Jesus actually taught or implied about himself? The challenge presented by this question can be highlighted by noting the contrast between the central theme of the first three Gospels and that of the fourth.

In the fourth Gospel, the message of Jesus is Jesus himself. He is the way, the truth and the life; the light of the world and the bread of life, to mention just a few of the metaphors used. But in the first three Gospels, as stated earlier, his message is the rule of God. He appears to have been reluctant even to claim the title of Messiah, so associated was it with misleading ideas. He preferred the neutral term Son of Man, which he filled out with both a vocation to suffering and a conviction of final victory. So in what way, if any, can the claims in the fourth Gospel find a historical basis in the others? In what way can the proclamation of Paul about Christ be justified by appeal to the Jesus of history? There are five features that need to be taken into account which, stated very briefly, are as follows.

First, there is the strikingly intimate relationship Jesus had with the one he addressed as 'Father', *abba* in the original Aramaic, which was preserved in the text. Second, there is the authority with which he claimed to act in the name of God, forgiving sins for example. Third, there is the authority with which he taught. In the Sermon on the Mount, he sets up a series of contrasts between what the Torah said and what he himself was teaching: 'You have heard that our fore-fathers were told ... But what I tell you is this' (Matthew 5.21–48). The Gospels record that the people were amazed that in contrast to other religious teachers of the time he taught with authority. Fourth, integrally linked to these other aspects was the authority he assumed to announce and bring in the divine rule; a divine rule breaking into this world through what he said and did. When he was accused of casting out demons because he was in league with Beelzebub he pointed out that if this really were the case then Satan would be divided against himself. Furthermore it would pose a question about other exorcists at the time who were thought to be doing the work of God. In short, 'if it is by the finger of God that I drive out demons, then be sure the kingdom of God has already come upon you' (Luke 11.20). Fifth and finally, as mentioned earlier, there was the central thrust of his ministry, reaching out to those outside the mainstream which, as he made clear in his parables, was to be taken as a sign of the way God reaches out to include all of us.

C. S. Lewis is often quoted as saying that Jesus was either God or mad. This is not, I think, a helpful way of putting the matter because Jesus did not go around teaching that he was God. Rather he lived his life on intimate terms with God, as a son to a father, seeking to be fully responsive and obedient to the Father's good purpose. Indeed the fourth Gospel, which has Jesus making the most explicit claims for himself, at the same time has him making it clear that the Son is totally given over to the Father and that he seeks only to do his will and reveal his glory. That said, the truth in Lewis's statement is that Jesus clearly spoke and acted as though he had the authority of God, and we are presented with a choice of either recognizing that authority for what Jesus claimed it to be or saying that he was under an illusion.

If Jesus was fully human, as the Church has always claimed him to be, then his self-understanding must always have taken a human

form. This would have included the limitations of the culture of
the time but more than that it would have had an exploratory,
developing aspect to it. Jesus had a normal Jewish childhood and
education. He grew and learnt through the ordinary experiences
of life as a young man and in the course of his ministry. There is
no reason to think that he fully knew who he was even at the end.
In short, he trusted fully in God for his own identity as much as
for his mission. He gave himself fully over to his vocation to live
as an intimate son of his father and to act with divine authority in
bringing in the kingdom, even through death. The rest was handed
over. Some words of Dietrich Bonhoeffer capture the spirit of this
well. When Bonhoeffer was in prison for his part in the attempt to
assassinate Hitler he wrote a poem called 'Who am I?', contrasting
the way he seemed to others, confident and serene, and how he felt
inside himself, confused and afraid. He ends:

> Who am I? They mock me, these lonely questions of mine.
> Whoever I am, thou knowest, O God, I am thine.[5]

In a similar way, Jesus puts the question of who he is into the hands
of the one he trusted to the uttermost.

So once again a great deal hangs on what we make of the claim that
Jesus was raised from the dead. If he was indeed raised from the dead,
then it was not just his message and mission that was confirmed
but the authority with which he taught and acted, an authority he
claimed to be that of God. The resurrection, in the words of the
German theologian Wolfhart Pannenberg, is a 'retroactive validation'
of Jesus in his person as well as his message. To put it in terms that
later came to be used, the loving relationship the historical Jesus
had with the one he called Father is shown by the resurrection to
be at the same time an eternal relationship of the divine Son to the
Father. So we can say that the ultimate unknowingness of Jesus
about himself and the humility with which he lived a fully human
life in relation to the Father are the very preconditions for his being
in reality the divine Son. To think of Jesus as a God walking about
on earth or going about teaching people he was God, apart from

being untrue would in fact undermine the Christian claim about him; for the Christian claim is that he is truly human as well as fully divine. That divinity is revealed in and through his humanity, not apart from it. The utter dependence and responsive love Jesus showed are part of the creaturely humanity in which the divine is revealed. At the same time the resurrection reveals that these characteristics are also part of the life of the eternal Godhead.

A contemporary picture?

One further issue remains to be considered in this chapter. Although, as shown, it is possible to construct the main outlines of the mission and teaching of Jesus as it is to be understood in the context of his own culture, is it possible to paint a picture of him for our own times? A picture that has imaginative and spiritual force? And does it matter whether we can or not?

The difficulty of this emerges when we consider what can be constructed about some other historical figures, Samuel Johnson for example. We know a great deal about Johnson from different sources. There is the famous picture of him given by James Boswell when Johnson was at the height of his powers. There is the more intimate side of Johnson revealed by Hester Thrale, who found him at once fascinating and a burden. There are various accounts of him by other contemporaries. There is what Johnson himself wrote in his many essays, sermons, his dictionary and critical works, in which he has no hesitation in expressing his strong views on a whole range of subjects. We are able to view Johnson in his home town of Lichfield and at the centre of a convivial circle in London as well as on his travels in the Hebrides. Then there are his diaries and prayers. From these we know Johnson from the inside; how he felt about himself and how he felt in his relation to God. Using this range of material we feel it is possible in some sense really to know Johnson, both in how he came across to a range of other people in his public persona, and from his most intimate thoughts. The result is that in recent years we have had a number of superb biographies.

Reconstructing the life of Jesus in a way that makes it possible for us to know him in that sense is much more difficult, indeed impossible. First, of course, it is much easier to enter into the culture of early modernity shared by Johnson than it is into first-century Palestine. Second, the materials about Jesus are less extensive and more fragmentary. More important, whereas with Johnson we have a great deal of what he himself wrote, Jesus wrote nothing, and what he said comes to us through the memories of others. Above all, however, whereas we have the intimate diaries and prayers of Johnson, which give us access to his most private feelings, we do not have similar documents for Jesus.

We can also note that while we have a number of visual portraits of Johnson, we do not have one of Jesus. The early story that he was painted by Luke is obviously a legend and the early Church saw no contradiction in representing him sometimes like a young Roman youth in the style of Apollo and at other times as a bearded god-like figure in the style of Jupiter. Not surprisingly, when people have tried to understand Jesus in terms that resonated in their own culture, there have been very different pictures, from Dostoyevsky's Prince Myshkin in *The Idiot*, based on the idea of a Russian *staretz*, or holy man, to Pier Paolo Pasolini's Marxist Jesus in his 1964 film *The Gospel According to St. Matthew*.

As mentioned above, we can enter into the inner life of Samuel Johnson through his private diaries and prayers; we have nothing equivalent for Jesus. Or do we? What about the fourth Gospel, which does indeed contain intimate disclosures to his close friends and long prayers? The fourth Gospel remains an enigma. It is now recognized that there is much more history embedded in it than was once thought; nevertheless, that said, we cannot escape the fact that the whole world of thought in St John's Gospel is very different from, say, that of St Mark. Nor are they easily compatible. Most obviously, as already indicated, the main message of Jesus in Mark is the rule of God whereas in John, Jesus teaches about himself as the life and light of the world, the one through whom the Father is to be seen. The traditional view is that the fourth Gospel was written by one of the close friends of Jesus, John the beloved disciple, who was therefore in a position to pass on this more intimate side of Jesus. This is an attractive view but the differences both of message and thought-world are very great. The other view is that what we have in this Gospel is a profound reflection on the total Christian experience, not just the historical Jesus but Jesus risen, ascended and glorified and dwelling in the Church through the Holy Spirit and guiding it into all truth. The fourth Gospel is the profoundest of the Gospels but it is best seen in terms of Robert Browning's poem on it, 'A Death in the Desert', with its lines 'What first were guessed as points, I now knew stars.'[6] In other words, it draws out the implications of what is present in the Synoptic Gospels in the light of the total Christian experience. It is quite possible that the Gospel was based on an eyewitness account by John the beloved disciple, whoever he was, but it comes to us as reflected on by a circle of people in Ephesus whose ruling theme is mystical love.

The other great theologian in the New Testament, in addition to the author of the fourth Gospel, is Paul. Although he shows awareness of the main ethical teaching of Jesus and can distinguish this from his own views, he did not seem to have any interest in the historical Jesus as such. His message was the living Christ whom he had encountered on the road to Damascus and the new creation this Christ has brought into being.[7]

The implication of these considerations is that there can be no definitive picture of Jesus for our time or for any time. Novelists, playwrights, painters, musicians, film-makers will enter into the Gospels with a greater or lesser degree of serious spiritual intent and will use their creative imaginations to make something they believe will resonate with our time and culture. This is the main conclusion of the book by A. N. Wilson referred to earlier. After a period of hostility to the Bible he rediscovered its authority. A turning point was seeing the interpretation of the book of Job in etchings by William Blake. This reinforced for him the essential role of the imagination in reading the Bible, what Blake referred to as 'the divine arts of imagination'.[8]

So we come back to the living tradition embodied in the Christian community. Week by week and day by day this community is nourished by regular, systematic reading of the Scriptures and perhaps also by some post-canonical writings. It is through these words that the mind of Christ is formed in his people and the Spirit comes to dwell in their hearts. This tradition finds its definitive focus in the sacramental sharing of bread and wine. The living Christ is in the totality of the tradition, past and present, but definitively in the canonical Scriptures. It is good that artists of all kinds should use their spiritual imaginations to bring to life the Jesus of history in terms that resonate with our culture or one of the many subcultures of which it is formed. But more important from the point of view of Christian faith is the daily formation not just by what Jesus is remembered as saying or doing but by the stars which once were seen as points. Those stars are the total impact of Christ on the first Christians, but spreading out from there over the whole of Christian history. It is no accident that the Church observes a special calendar in which are celebrated not just the main festivals associated with Jesus but the commemoration of the martyrs and saints of every age. For as Gerard Manley Hopkins put it:

> Christ plays in ten thousand places,
> Lovely in limbs, and lovely in eyes not his
> To the Father through the features of men's faces.[9]

Summary

It is possible to achieve a degree of scholarly consensus on the broad outlines of the life and teaching of Jesus within the context of his own time. This makes it clear that while he has to be understood within the Judaism that shaped him, he cannot be understood simply as another great moral teacher. Rather he confronted the people of his time with the challenge and choice of responding to the imminent reign of God in human affairs that was breaking the power of evil in the world through his words and actions.

Whether Jesus is regarded as mistaken in acting with the authority of God depends on the view taken of the preaching of his first followers that God raised him from death to an eternal life within the Godhead. If this is believed, then both his mission and his person are affirmed as having an eternal significance. The whole New Testament is written up from this perspective: that God had indeed raised Jesus from the dead and that he lives for evermore, especially in his body on earth, the Christian community. From within this faith perspective, it is possible to see how the life of the historical Jesus, who lived in perfect filial response to the one he called Father, is a working out in time of an eternal relationship. The union of the Father and the Son within God is grounded in Jesus, the Word made flesh. The Christ of faith was not invented later by Paul or John. It was not an add-on. It was inherent in what Jesus said and did. It was, however, the conviction of the first disciples that he had been raised from the dead to a universal contemporaneity that enables its truth to be seen.

I recognize that this argument is a circular one. If people find the tradition a living one, even in a questioning, tentative way, they will be open to reading the New Testament from the same perspective as those who first wrote it. The argument that there is a proper continuity between the historical Jesus and the faith of the Church is unlikely, however, to convince those totally outside the tradition, because a similar kind of argument can be made, for example, about the relationship between the Qur'an and Islam today, or about that between the Hebrew Scriptures and the Talmud and contemporary Judaism. In both cases, it will be argued by adherents of the faith that their tradition is firmly rooted in its foundation documents. So the question of how we are to understand the relationship between different religious traditions and how we are to evaluate their truth arises. This will be considered in the next chapter. The purpose of the argument in this chapter has been a more limited one: to show how the passage from 1 John quoted earlier – that to become part of the *koinonia* or shared life of the Christian community is also to be taken into the *koinonia* or shared life of the Father and the

Son – arose naturally out of the experience of the first Christians, an experience rooted in the historical Jesus, and why it is an authentic way of summing up their faith.

I recognize that for a good number of readers this chapter will be a difficult one; not, I hope, because it is difficult to understand but because of the large claim that the Christian Church makes. It brings us up short for two reasons. First, because of what has been called 'the scandal of particularity', the claim that God has acted uniquely and definitively at one particular time and place in history. Second, because it is clear from the account given above that so much hangs on what a person believes about the claim that God raised Jesus from the dead and through his Spirit lives in the Christian community today. These are formidable difficulties, in no way to be underestimated. But as will be clear in the final chapters of this book, my own understanding of how we can best live with both the beauty and the horror of life does depend crucially on our understanding of Jesus.

8

One religion among many

It was acknowledged in the last chapter that though a plausible argument can be made that the developed faith of the Church bears an integral relationship to the historic Jesus, a similar argument might be made for other religious traditions. For them too, it might be shown that there is a coherent relationship between their founding figure or foundation documents and later developments. In all such cases, the argument will be made from inside the tradition in some sense, even if it is only one of broad sympathy with it. The crucial question remains as to how one can come to discriminate between one tradition and others in such a way as to make a rational choice between them. Or it may prove impossible to do so.

A popular answer is that we don't have to choose between different religions because they are all basically saying the same thing. This simply isn't true. They are saying different and in some respects mutually contradictory things. The Abrahamic faiths may be united in believing that there is one God, maker of heaven and earth and of all things visible and invisible. Yet as was discussed in Chapter 2, Buddhism regards such questions as to whether or not there is a creator as unprofitable, a distraction from the real issue, which is the problem of suffering and how to respond to it. Within the Abrahamic faiths claims are made about Jesus, which again are not compatible one with another. At best Jews will regard Jesus as an inspired but misguided prophet. Islam does regard him as a true prophet, second only to Muhammad. But that is very different from what is said in the Nicene Creed that he is 'of one substance' or 'of one being' with the Father, a statement of Christian orthodoxy accepted by all mainstream Christian denominations.

Another popular argument is to say that though the religions seem to be saying very different things, the essence of each one is the same. When asked what this essence is, people have different answers, but there is a more fundamental difficulty with this whole approach. To argue that the core of each religion is the same is to assume a bird's-eye view floating above them all. There is no such view. We are all bedded down in our own culture and language. This does not mean that no rational discussion between religions is possible. It is. But it does mean we cannot take up a neutral stand in order to pick and choose between them. To say there is an essence of every religion that they all have in common assumes we are in a position to survey them all from above in order to decide what that essence is and recognize it in each of them. But there is no point from which we can take up that lofty neutral stand. It does not exist. So two extreme points of view need to be set to one side. One says that all religions are really saying the same thing. They are not. The other says that because we all inhabit our own linguistic and cultural world no rational choices between different world views is possible. The fact that people from within different traditions can discuss with one another and understand one another assumes, rightly, that rational choices can be made.

The starting point, however, has to be from within one's own religious or cultural tradition, whatever that happens to be. From that point, it is possible to enter into rich and fruitful relationships with people of other faiths. The principles on which such a relationship is possible and fruitful are important. In my experience, there are three that are fundamental.

The first is to let the dialogue partners speak for themselves and define themselves in their own terms. We all tend to have stereotyped views, even caricatures, of religions other than our own, spectacles through which we see them. So it is fundamental that they themselves should say what they believe and describe what their religion means to them. Our role is first to attend and listen.

The second is to affirm as much common ground as possible. However incompatible two religions might seem at the outset, it is always possible to find some common ground, if not in terms of beliefs, at least within a set of values that are shared.

The third is to share what is distinctive about each faith. When a relationship of respect and trust has been built up and some common ground has been established, it is not just possible to share differences but essential if the dialogue is to be authentic. Some people have a false view of interfaith dialogue, thinking it is about leaving one's own most cherished beliefs behind in order to find a lowest common denominator. The opposite is true. In order for the dialogue to be real and not just polite noises, it is essential to bring into the relationship what is sharply different as well as what converges. In my experience, when the participants have got to know one another, this is quite possible to do.

I have been part of two serious interfaith groups. First, for many years I was a member of the Manor House Group in London, which consisted of Jewish rabbis and Christian ministers. We used to meet twice a year for a day's discussion on a particular theme, and in addition go away for a weekend together. In this way, relationships were built up and there was huge mutual enrichment. In such groups, participants not only gain respect for the religion of the other but also find their own understanding enlarged of the other religion as well as their own. One feature that emerged in the Manor House Group was the often amusing non-theological differences.[1]

The other group was the Oxford Abraham Group, which I convened when I was Bishop of Oxford, consisting, as its title suggests, of Jewish, Christian and Muslim theologians. Our method was to take a subject, with a short paper delivered by a participant from each of the three religions. This led into a discussion on where there might be common ground, where differences remained and how these differences might be approached in the future. So we took the major figures of the religions, Moses, Jesus and Muhammad, as well as traditional and contemporary subjects of concern to the three faiths.[2]

While groups that include all faiths have their place, in my experience it is this in-depth discussion with two or three faiths that is likely to be most real, enriching and helpful.

For such groups to progress, it is probably essential for each of the participants to make theological space for the others from within their own religious perspective. Obviously if someone comes into such a group believing that all religious approaches other than his or her own are totally false, it is difficult to engage much further.

From a Christian point of view, this theological space is provided first of all by a view of God as a God of loving kindness. It would be totally contradictory to think of a loving God confining all life-giving knowledge of himself to one chosen tradition. The New Testament is clear that some knowledge of God is available simply by reflecting on the world. As Paul put it:

> For all that can be known of God lies plain before their eyes; indeed God himself has disclosed it to them. Ever since the world began his invisible attributes, that is to say his everlasting power and deity, have been visible to the eye of reason, in the things he has made.
>
> (Romans 1.19–20)

It is true that he goes on to say that people have not honoured God as they should but that does not take away the fundamental point that in principle God can be known by everyone. The same principle applies to our behaviour. Although Paul agreed that the Jewish people had the privilege of a special disclosure of what God wants of his people in the Torah, he says of non-Jews: 'although they have no law, they are their own law; they show that what the law requires is inscribed on their hearts, and to this their conscience gives supporting witness' (Romans 2.14–15).

It was this understanding that Paul put into practice when he preached to the Athenian intellectuals as reported in Acts 17. Speaking about the human quest for God, he even appealed to their own poets, as he said:

> They were to seek God in the hope that, groping after him, they might find him; though indeed he is not far from each one of us, for in him we live and move, in him we exist; as some of your own poets have said, 'We are also his offspring.'
>
> (Acts 17.27–29)

In St John's Gospel, the defining image in the prologue is the *logos*, or word. This was a key concept in both Greek philosophy and, in a very different way, Jewish religious thought. In using this term, the writer is wanting to affirm as much common ground as possible in both traditions. Famously, St Augustine in his religious pilgrimage said that he had come across the whole of the prologue in the philosophies he studied in his pre-Christian days except the claim that 'the Word became flesh' (John 1.14). In other words, although the Christian faith makes a claim about the uniqueness of Christ, his appearing is not in a vacuum. He comes, and can be encountered today, in relation to the symbols and philosophical ideas of different societies. It was this approach that was taken by the group of Christian thinkers known as the Christian Apologists in the second century. They affirmed the philosophical outlook of the intellectuals of the time, showing how it found its natural fulfilment in the Christian faith. This was also the approach taken by the Jesuits to Confucianism in China in the seventeenth century and followed by many Christians of all denominations in other cultures since then, including Hindu-dominated India.

In the twentieth century, this approach received more formal affirmation with talk about 'the hidden Christ' in other religions, or of Christ as the one in whom the insights of other faiths find their proper focus and fulfilment. However, there is a difficulty with this approach since it runs contrary to the principle laid out above that in interfaith dialogue participants must define themselves in their own terms. So while a Christian might indeed look to see Christ in people of other faiths, and give thanks for this, it is more appropriate to keep this for prayer rather than bring it into theological discussion with them.

The other way a Christian will leave theological space for other religious traditions is through an awareness that because each one of us is bedded down in our own culture and language, our own outlook at any one point will be severely limited, and the true God will by definition be beyond anything my partial mind can grasp now. What I believe now, and indeed what everyone else believes now, will in the end be corrected, enlarged and enriched by the final disclosure of truth, and on the way to this our dialogue with people of other faiths can begin to bring this about. Hence genuine dialogue is always an enlarging and enriching experience of God, not only through a better understanding of others and their faiths but in the deeper understanding of our own.

Some Christians stress the exclusive nature of their faith by pointing to verses in John's Gospel that seem to suggest we can know God only in and through Christ. But as argued above, this did not stop the author of the fourth Gospel, Paul and Christians in every age from also seeing something of the truth of God in other religions and philosophies. Furthermore there are some very challenging sayings of Jesus, such as the parable in Matthew 25, which suggests that the final criterion of judgement is not what we have believed but how we have responded to the needs of others. An orthodox Christian will believe that when all is revealed there will be at the heart of truth a God who is for us, and that the definitive expression of this is Jesus crucified and risen. But just because he is for us, and not against us, he will surely welcome all those who have responded truthfully to the light within them and responded to the needs of those around them. Meanwhile the Christian will bear in mind the words of Jesus, 'Not everyone who says to me "Lord, Lord" will enter the kingdom of Heaven, but only those who do the will of my heavenly Father' (Matthew 7.21).

A distinction is sometimes made between general and special revelation. There is a general revelation in the sense that some knowledge of God can be gleaned by everyone simply by reflecting on creation and their own inner life. As Immanuel Kant put it: 'Two things fill the mind with ever increasing wonder and awe, the more often and the more intensely the mind of thought is drawn to them: the starry sky above me and the moral law within me.'[3] But in addition to this it is claimed that God has chosen to disclose himself in a special way. We might think of a parent who acts lovingly to all her children, and then one day risks her life by jumping into a rough sea to rescue just one of them. This action does not contradict what the children know of her already, her love for each of them; rather it definitively reveals the extent of that love. Furthermore the other children know she would have done the same for them in similar circumstances. What this simple analogy also brings out is that from a Christian perspective our knowledge of God is integrally linked to our rescue or redemption. As will be discussed later, Christians claim that we know God in a special, intimate way because he came among us to save us from ourselves, from our own self-destruction, and to unite us to himself for now and all eternity.

Christians believe that God's special disclosure of himself began with the formation of the people of Israel, to whom he revealed what he wanted of them. This was a community shaped and built up by fundamental moral qualities: 'He has told you, O mortal, what is good; and what does the LORD require of you but to do justice, and to love kindness, and to walk humbly with your God?' (Micah 6.8 NRSV). That vocation of the Jewish community continues.[4] But from a Christian perspective the vocation of the people of Israel to live in response to God like a faithful son to a trustworthy father comes to a definitive focus in Jesus. Then, through him, the call to live such a life comes to all people. This vocation is one of responsiveness and trust but also, as the previous chapter argued, it means coming to share, through Christ, in the divine life itself.

This claim means that Christians have to face up to 'the scandal of particularity', mentioned at the end of Chapter 7. There is a scandal because rather than seeing the divine equally revealed everywhere, Christians proclaim a particular person at a particular time and place to be the definitive disclosure of God in human terms. This inevitably raises difficult questions about those not brought into contact with this disclosure. Are they to be left out?

It would seem, however, that revelation in any profound and intimate sense must have a particular focus as well as a general disclosure. There is a particularity about the example quoted earlier of a mother saving one of her children from drowning. Furthermore it is fundamental to Christian conviction that the sharp focus in Jesus was designed to move out from there to include the whole of humanity.

God has chosen to work his purpose from within the flux of history. That implies particularity, but it is a particularity that has as its goal a universal embrace.

There is another difficulty however. If there is a particular revelation at a particular time and place in history, it will be bound up with that time and place for ever. As history moves on, it will be left ever further behind. This is an acute problem for many today because the culture of our own time seems so distant and different from the culture of first-century Judaism in which Jesus lived. Again, however, Christians have to face up to this. If revelation is particular it will in some sense be linked to the past. But this is where what was said earlier about belonging to a living tradition comes to the fore. It is part of Christian conviction that the Holy Spirit dwells in the Christian community and is leading it into all truth. That conviction is strongly present in the New Testament, especially in St John's Gospel. So Christians are not simply looking back to a figure of the past, they are part of a community in which the Holy Spirit takes the things of Jesus and brings them alive in every age in relation to the insights and challenges of that age.

A living tradition will inevitably be characterized by turbulence as it seeks to relate insights gathered from the past to the changes of the present. Some will see more clearly than others how those insights apply in a fresh context; others will believe that such applications are a false rather than a true development. Only time will tell if they are right or not. This turbulence is not comfortable; but it is a sign that the tradition is indeed a living, developing one, not ossified. It comes to a focus in the present in a community organically related to both the past and the future. At its heart is the one who, in words quoted earlier, said: 'I am the first and the last, and I am the living One; I was dead and now I am alive for evermore' (Revelation 1.17–18).

This living one is known through the pages of the Bible, whose dynamic has shaped not just the life of the Church down the ages but whole cultures in their political, cultural and artistic development. That impulse continues to inspire and impel today, not just in personal life but in many forms of artistic endeavour, especially music. In terms of the argument of this book, the Bible and its unfolding dynamic is the foundation witness to the living one who enhances our celebration of life while at the same time enabling us to avoid despair when faced with its horrors.

9

Why did it all begin?

A life of our own

A character in one of Evelyn Waugh's novels, now teaching in a ghastly independent school, had once been a clergyman but had lost his faith. He explains how his great doubt came upon him. 'Once granted the first step, I can see that everything else follows – Tower of Babel, Babylonian captivity, Incarnation, Church, bishops, incense, everything – but what I couldn't see, and what I cannot see now, is *why* did it all begin?'[1] He asked his bishop and his mother, and getting no satisfactory answer he resigned his living and became a schoolmaster instead. Some, even religious people, will agree that this is a question we are not in a position to answer. So the rest of what I write in this chapter, though it is rooted in the New Testament, is best understood as the surmise of one very limited human mind.

What we know for certain is that we have a life of our own and that we have to stand on our own feet and take responsibility for our lives. This fundamental autonomy belongs to every aspect of the created order, for to be created means just that, to have a life of one's own whether as an electron, a gnat, a cat or a person. As was argued in Chapter 4, God does not just make the world, he makes the world make itself. We may or may not be aware of the God dimension but we are all aware of the world making itself. This is the fundamental assumption behind all our actions and the whole scientific enterprise. We are shaping both our own lives and the future.

When, according to the book of Genesis, God says 'Let there be', he does just that: he lets things be to go their own way. From the standpoint of faith, however, he does not then abandon the world, for he remains the ground of all being, holding things in existence.

The miracle continues, that things exist in all their isness and particularity. They might not exist, but they do. The fact that they do is because moment by moment they are held in existence by the fount from whom all being flows. At the heart of all monotheistic religion, therefore, is this awareness of the fundamental dependence of all that exists on a greater reality and another dimension; a sense that I am a creature alongside other creatures. I am dependent on the air I breathe, the millions of interactions in my body, on the stability of natural processes in my environment but beyond, in and through all this, I am dependent on that from whom all things exist.

Although God is present as the ground of all being, there is a profound sense in which God, in giving us a life of our own, has put us outside himself. We possess independence, the capacity to make choices, the freedom to make something of ourselves and the world. This is an obvious but fundamental point that can be affirmed as common ground by both Christians and secular humanists.

For the monotheist, however, this responsibility for our own lives goes along with a consciousness of our creaturely status, and an acknowledgement of the creative source of all things who is utterly other, transcending anything we can conceive. Yet, particularly on the Indian subcontinent and in the mystical tradition of all religions, there is an emphasis on God being 'in' all things. At one extreme this merges into pantheism, in which God becomes almost identical to all things, but if this were really the case it is difficult to see that the word 'God' can retain any meaning. But short of that there are a number of ways it is possible and appropriate to think of God in all things. He is first of all in all things as the ground of being, as already discussed. He is in all things, in the sense that he is not distant from the creative process but at its very heart. He is closer to us than our own breathing, as St Augustine put it. More than that, he is clearly in a truly good person in a way that he is not in a malevolent one. Jesus said that where two or three are gathered together in his name, there he is in their midst. Not least – one of the major themes of the fourth Gospel as well as the letters of

John – is that where there is love in the Christian community, there God is dwelling within them.

The Christian conviction is that God does indeed give us a life of our own and responsibility for leading it, but that he wills to come to dwell in us, and through the sharing of his life with us in Christ brings this about. In the 1662 Book of Common Prayer service of Holy Communion, there is the Prayer of Humble Access in which people pray that through receiving the body and blood of Christ, they 'may evermore dwell in him, and he in us'. This mutual in-dwelling is a major theme of John's Gospel. It is not only that through Christ, God comes to dwell in us but that we come to dwell in him. We are taken into the very life of the Godhead. This idea of an indwelling God finds powerful emphasis in some of the later letters in the New Testament. The bridge thrown across the abyss between the uncreated source of all things and creation is the person of Jesus Christ. But through Christ, God works first to fill the Church, and then all things, with his presence. It is this theme that is spelt out so profoundly in the letters to the Colossians and Ephesians. First, 'For it is in Christ that the complete being of the Godhead dwells embodied' (Colossians 2.9 NEB). Second, the God who fills Christ Jesus wills to fill those who are his. The great prayer in Ephesians ends up 'that you may be filled with all the fullness of God' (Ephesians 3.19 NRSV). Third, the purpose of God does not end there. It is to fill all things with his presence. For the Church is 'his body, the fullness of him who fills all in all' (Ephesians 1.23 NRSV). In these verses, there is set out the most extraordinary vocation and destiny for human beings. We are to be filled with all the fullness of God. But this vocation and destiny is not for us alone but for the whole created order. For God is the one who is to fill all in all.

This mutual indwelling of God and humanity in Christ is also approached in the New Testament in another way. When Mary Magdalene meets the risen Christ on the first Easter morning, he says to her: 'go to my brothers, and tell them that I am ascending to my Father and your Father, to my God and your God' (John 20.17). This again is a remarkable passage. He calls his disciples brothers and he says that his Father is their Father and his God is their God. In short, he is taking them into the same relationship with God that he himself eternally enjoys.

One of the most memorable scenes in the New Testament is the baptism of Jesus by John the Baptist. In that scene, the Father is present, as the one who says to Jesus, 'You are my beloved Son; in you I take delight' (Mark 1.11). The Holy Spirit is also present, symbolized by a dove. That is the threefold relationship in which Jesus lived out his whole ministry. He lived as beloved Son to his Father and was enabled to do so because he was filled by the Holy Spirit.

St Matthew's Gospel ends with the risen Christ saying to his disciples:

> Go therefore to all nations and make them my disciples; baptize them in the name of the Father and the Son and the Holy Spirit, and teach them to observe all that I have commanded them. I will be with you always, to the end of time.
>
> (Matthew 28.19–20)

Since then, that is just what the Church has done, baptizing people in the name of the Holy Trinity. This is not just a formula. It is the very life of the Godhead into which people are taken by their faith and baptism. Through Christ believers share the relationship with God that he eternally enjoys. We too are his daughters and sons, called to live out that filial relationship to the Father through the Holy Spirit who dwells within us.

In Genesis 18, there is a story of how God appeared to Abraham in the guise of three angels. This story, called the Hospitality of Abraham, because he offered them food and drink, was from an early stage in Christian history seen as a foreshadowing of God's disclosure of himself as Holy Trinity. In the early fifteenth century, it was the subject of one of the most beautiful and moving of all icons, by the Russian Andrei Rublev. It shows three angels, depicted with harmonious elegance and beauty, sitting around a table. The perspective is such that the viewer looking at the icon is drawn into the scene, to take his or her place at the table. On the table is a chalice and a lamb. The viewer is being invited into the very life of the Godhead. Moreover this invitation comes especially through the invitation to share in the eucharistic feast, the foretaste of the heavenly banquet, made possible by the sacrificial death of Christ.

The doctrine of God as Holy Trinity is usually presented as a great puzzle and stumbling block. But mind is a social reality. Babies get talked into talking by others and then begin to do that talking within themselves that we call thinking. Mind is essentially interpersonal. So with all the proper stress on the limitations of language in talking about God at all and the way all metaphors have to be qualified, as stressed in Chapter 3, it makes sense to think of our interpersonal minds as pale reflections of that which exists in fuller, perfect form in God. At the same time, we know that we are a unity. There is in God a deeper personal communion than can be found in any two persons and a greater unity than can be found in any one person.[2]

The doctrine of God as Holy Trinity is not just a formula to be said at the beginning of services or when Christians make the sign of the cross, it is the very life of God into which we are taken and the lifeblood of God flowing in our spiritual veins. All this gives substance to 1 John 1.1–3, discussed in an earlier chapter, that in coming to share the life of the Christian community we come also to share the life of God himself.

All human beings, by virtue of their humanity, are made in the image of God; that is, we can think, choose, love and pray. But our vocation is not just to live as that image but to grow into the divine likeness. St Paul wrote: 'we all see as in a mirror the glory of the Lord, and we are being transformed into his likeness with ever-increasing glory' (2 Corinthians 3.18).

'God is love; he who dwells in love is dwelling in God, and God in him' (1 John 4.16). God is love in the sense that his whole being is orientated towards the good of the other. He is wholly given up to bringing about the well-being and eternal happiness of others. It is his very essence; it is what he is. The writer of the epistle affirms that when we love one another it is this divine love dwelling in us, and we who are dwelling in God – *Ubi caritas est, Deus ibi est.* To love God and others is to share in the divine nature. The writer of the second letter of Peter says that divine power has been bestowed on us, 'that . . . you may become partakers of the divine nature' (2 Peter 1.4 ESV). This is the basis of a central theme of Orthodox Christianity, that of theosis, or our deification in and through Christ. It is there in the early church fathers such as Irenaeus, who said that as God came to share our life in the Incarnation so we are destined to share the divine life and become what he is. It is there in Athanasius, who said that 'The Word became flesh that we, partakers of His Spirit, might be deified.' It is there in Cyril of Alexandria, who asserted that 'He became man that we might become divine.'[3]

This chapter began with the loss of faith by a clergyman who couldn't answer the question why it all began; why on earth God had created the universe in the first place. A Christian answer is that God is love, and it is the nature of love to create. Why do parents have children? Of course from an evolutionary point of view, we are driven to do this by a genetic imperative. But these days having children is a conscious choice. Most parents would reject the idea that they have children just to support them in their old age, though that was indeed a consideration of telling force in earlier societies. The reason has something to do with the mystery of love, that it is of the essence of love to create and give itself over to what is other. And some people, who for whatever reason do not have children, express this creative side of love by giving themselves over to others in a different way. I think of a married couple, both doctors, who did not have children of their own and who spent nearly all their lives running a rural hospital in South Africa.

It is of the very essence of God to create, so he brings into being a universe. First of all for its own sake, and as far as humanity is concerned, for our sake, that we may enjoy a life of our own. But second, so that freely we may come to share his nature by growing into his likeness. This comes about as we are drawn into the divine life and as that life comes to dwell in us. God is love and his purpose is that we should grow in our capacity to love, and in this way both reflect and be transfigured by his glory.

God's work of art

One of the features that has distinguished *Homo sapiens* from other creatures is our desire to make works of art. Even in the Ice Age in Europe, some 30,000 years ago, striking works were being produced.

Today art in its many forms – novels and poetry, music, painting and conceptual art, drama, dance – is a hugely important part of people's lives. Much of this is for straightforward enjoyment and entertainment, and nothing wrong with that. Nevertheless there is a seriousness about the arts and what they mean, both in the life of a culture and in individual lives, which indicates that they are more than just escapism. Indeed as mentioned earlier, for a good number of thoughtful people the arts, particularly music, probably play something of the role that religion did in the lives of their nineteenth-century forebears. Stanley Spencer went beyond the artists already quoted not only in seeing beauty in unexpected places and ways and wanting to be truthful to what he saw but in linking this with the capacity to love. As he wrote:

> Love is the essential power in the creation of art and love is not a talent. Love reveals and more accurately describes the nature and meaning of things than any mere lecture on technique can do. And it establishes once and for all time the final and perfect *identity* of every created thing.[4]

Perhaps we should think of creation itself – and in particular us human beings within it – as a work of art. What links our human creativity and the amazing wrestling of the divine with our human recalcitrance is Ephesians 2.10: 'We are God's *poiema*, his work of art'. If we recognize artistic integrity, that fierce and uncompromising persistence in expressing a particular way of seeing and feeling about the world, how can the integrity of divine love, wrestling to realize his vision for us, be less?

'We are God's work of art' – and as the rest of the sentence goes on: 'created in Christ Jesus for the good works which God has already designated to make up our way of life' (Ephesians 2.10 NJB). When artists are asked why they do what they do, they are more than likely to reply that this is just something they have to do, this is their very being or essence, who they are. They cannot imagine not doing it. Similarly it is the very essence of God to create. When parents are asked why they have children, what are they to reply? Is there not something in the nature of love to create an other or others?

Some theologians, like the aestheticians quoted earlier, have used the image of play. This image serves a useful purpose in indicating that the creation of the universe, like play, exists for itself, as an end in itself and not a means to another end. However, the image of play perhaps implies something too easy, whereas God pours himself into creation. He gives himself to it, not just in the cross but in the process of creation itself. As far as we human beings are concerned, we have been created in the image of God but are called to grow into his likeness. Indeed our supreme vocation and destiny, if we will have it, is to be filled with all the fullness of God. In the same way, as Stanley Spencer said, it is love that establishes the identify of anything; the love of God does this for us not just by observing us with a gaze of love but by drawing out the potential we have within us to grow into his likeness. This is at once deadly serious and yet also in some sense play. W. H. Auden was fond of the aphorism of Nietzsche: 'Maturity – to recover the seriousness one had as a child at play'.[5]

St Paul twice uses an unfortunate image of human beings as clay in the hands of God the great potter, who is free to do with his pots what he wants. But we are not just clay, we are thinking, talking, feeling clay, able to suffer and argue back. God the great artist has set himself the hugely ambitious task of creating a work of art not just out of inanimate matter like clay but always in relation to creatures who are free to rebel, who have to be persuaded and who, according to the traditional Christian story, have to be won over and wooed back to their creator. From this perspective it is not just our world that is beautiful but human beings. As we pursue truth and are drawn into the beauty of an unfolding purpose we become supreme works of art that reflect the glory of the creator.

10

The mystery of good and evil

Free to choose?

Over the years, the philosopher John Gray has been the most consistent critic of the view probably held by most liberal thinkers and politicians today. This progressive view assumes that the terrible things happening in the world today can be stopped and that with the right political, economic and social policies in place the ills of the world can be remedied. In particular, Gray has been critical of those who use the word 'evil' about a person like Saddam Hussein, without realizing that we are all blighted and that what we see in him is, to a greater or lesser extent, a persistent feature of all human behaviour. As he writes:

> If their feverish rhetoric means anything, it is that evil can be vanquished. In believing this, those who govern us at the present time reject a central insight of western religion, which is found also in Greek tragic drama and the work of the Roman historians: destructive human conflict is rooted in flaws within human beings themselves. In this old-fashioned understanding, evil is a propensity to destructive and self-destructive behaviour that is humanly universal. The restraints of morality exist to curb this innate human frailty; but morality is a fragile artifice that regularly breaks down. Dealing with evil requires an acceptance that it never goes away.[1]

This is indeed 'a central insight of Western religion', classically expressed from Augustine to Reinhold Niebuhr. For reasons that need not concern us here, Gray looks for the explanation of this neither in religion nor in Freud; rather 'it may be some version of evolutionary psychology that can best illuminate the human proclivity to hatred and destruction'.[2]

Evolutionary psychology is indeed a good place to begin, and the starting point is some awareness of our own motivation, as well as the observation of how other people behave, especially children. The obvious point is that we are born with a drive to satisfy our wants. Without this we simply would not survive. The babe strives to find his mother's breast, and later to get what he wants, often in a series of clashes with parents who will be trying to get their child to take into account what other people want as well. Therefore fundamental to our behaviour throughout life is a struggle to do all that is necessary to stay alive and flourish, which in practice at a mundane level usually means a drive to avoid pain and gain pleasure. Yet however difficult to manage, this in itself cannot be regarded as a flaw of creation, for without it we would not be here. Without the drive to stay alive and therefore the drive to satisfy our basic material wants, we would not survive.

It is also important to note, however, that this is not the only drive evolution has left us. There is the instinct of parents to look after and protect their young, which can very often be imitated at an early stage when, for example, a tiny child starts looking after her dolls in the same way her mother looks after her.

To be socialized, to grow into a mature adult, means taking other people and their needs into account as well as one's own. This is usually possible to some extent but becomes very difficult if there is a shortage of resources and a struggle ensues for what little there is. It is also not helped by the predominant economic philosophy in the world today, one of rampant, highly competitive capitalism, which works to harden the drive to pursue one's own interests even at the expense of other people. This drive to stay alive is further reinforced when we are part of a group that is pursuing its own interests, whether a neighbourhood, a tribe or a country. For whereas as individuals we have some capacity, inspired by a religious or ethical view, to transcend our own interests, and sometimes to put them aside in favour of other people, such altruism is hardly possible for a group. This was the argument of Reinhold Niebuhr's classic book *Moral Man and Immoral Society*,[3] which he later wished he had called 'Immoral Man and Even More Immoral Society'. We see the dilemma in its sharpest form with the paradox of patriotism, which transmutes the individual's capacity to transcend self-interest into an absolute loyalty to the state, which of its nature pursues its own interests. What is true of the state can also be true of a tribal, ethnic or religious grouping. And this can have a terrifying dimension when it is fed by fear based on misconceptions and propaganda. Hence the terrible blight of anti-Semitism and what happened in places like Srebrenica and Rwanda, and what is happening today with Sunni and Shia suicide bombers. What seems to happen with genocide and mass killing is that the human face of the other is simply blotted out. So we have the terrible phenomenon of groups of people of different ethnicity or religion who might have lived side by side in tolerable peace for generations suddenly finding themselves caught up in a frenzy of killing.

Sometimes it is a system of economic exploitation built up over the centuries that blinds us to the human face of the other, as happened with the institution of slavery and more recently in Apartheid South Africa. The caste system in India works in a similar fashion in the way people treat the Dalits, the former untouchables. More widely, the rampant capitalism that dominates the world today leads to some people in every country being exploited as though they were less than human. There are good people every- where protesting and working to combat these evils by revealing the human face behind the suffering, but the fact is that there are powerful forces at work that often blind us to the human cost.

Does what has been described so far need any further, meta- physical explanation for the terrible things we human beings do to one another? Given our basic drive to survive, our need to belong to organized groups and our timidity in standing out against them, together with sufficiently hard social or economic conditions, it takes only a little wicked or misguided rhetoric to set mischief afloat. The kind of breakdown of civilized living that happens, and could occur in an even more terrifying way, is described in Cormac McCarthy's novel *The Road*.[4] In this book, a father and son are trying to stay alive in a post-apocalyptic landscape. What the cause of this is we never quite know. It could be a series of nuclear explosions or a climate-change catastrophe. But the result is that there is virtually nothing left to eat or drink, and the people who survive are divided up into small marauding bands who will kill anyone who stands in their way. What is so disconcerting is the fact that it did not seem to dawn on so many who read and 'enjoyed' this book that something like this really could happen. We human beings are fully capable of bringing such a situation about and behaving in it as the book describes, of a war of all against all.

What makes the book possible and readable is that the father, through whose eyes we see this desperate world, has still kept his human sympathy and moral sense. At the end there is a tiny glimmer of hope when he and his son encounter someone else who similarly seems to have kept alive his human sensibility and sympathy. And this brings out the most fundamental of all points. However much our psychology has been shaped by the evolutionary imperative to live and survive, we are not totally at the mercy of its drives. We have a consciousness that will occasionally glimmer with an awareness that something other than the pursuit of self-interest or survival at all costs is being asked of us. I believe we have, within limits (which might be very much narrower than we imagine), some genuine options in our lives and that these options have a moral dimension. This docs not mean there is a 'will' existing independently of who I am or that choices are somehow free of constraints, internal and external. What it does mean is, as Rowan Williams has put it: 'I talk to myself, I imagine courses of action and test whether they will fit into the narrative of myself that I am constructing; I look at these images and work out my attitude towards them.'[5]

I am persuaded of this capacity to make genuine choices for four reasons. First, my own experience: I know I can choose to do one thing rather than another. In the words of Samuel Mountjoy, the central character of William Golding's novel *Free Fall*, we know the capacity to choose as we know 'the taste of potatoes'.[6] Now there are those who argue that this personal experience of freedom is quite compatible with a totally deterministic view and that they simply represent two different ways of talking about the same phenomenon. Although this 'compatibilist' theory has its supporters, I take an 'incompatibilist' position, which regards a fully determinist view as incompatible with a belief that the will is in some respects genuinely free. So, second, I believe our choices can, within tight limits, be freely chosen because a totally deterministic position is self-undermining. If everything is fully determined then so is the statement that this is the case and it can therefore have no claim to be true. For a statement to be judged true, we must be able to recognize it as such, and it is not possible to do this if everything we say is simply the result of physiological or psychological factors over which we have no control. Third, if the results of all our reflection and agonizing over what we should do were simply the expression of the strongest neurological drives going into the brain, what evolutionary function would the brain serve? The brain has evolved for some purpose, and that purpose is to enable us to reflect on the future, consider the consequences of our actions and try to act in such a way as will best serve our interests. There is also the moral dimension whereby we come to consider the interests of others as well as ourselves, but the point now is that the brain has evolved for a purpose, and part of that purpose is to give us scope to reflect and choose.

The fourth reason is the one put forward by Rowan Williams in his analysis of language mentioned in Chapter 3. A basic presupposition of his book is that we are embodied intelligences who use language to negotiate and make our way in the world. Understanding 'may best be understood as a matter of knowing what to do or say next'.[7] A question then arises about the relation between language and the world we inhabit. Williams rejects all attempts to see this purely in terms of physical stimuli or cause and effect. Rather there is a prior matrix of language that holds together the material world, other people and ourselves. We do not know the world apart from the language in which it is saturated. Indeed the world comes to be in and through our language. Like a smile or frown, it cannot be reduced to what is material but can only come to us in the form of the material. This process of knowing takes place in time as a continual process, always unfinished business. So language in some sense tracks what is before us, as it makes itself known. Paradox, metaphor, silence, the breakdown of normal discourse, seem to indicate that 'there is a "sense" before we *make* sense.'[8] This is an exploration into truth, for, to use a phrase of George Steiner's, 'We are a mammal who can bear false witness.'[9]

As was made clear at the beginning of this chapter, the drive to stay alive, the struggle to survive – that is, to pursue one's own interests – cannot in itself be considered an evil, for it is a fundamental feature of the whole evolutionary process of which we are a part, and we would not be here without it. One of the features that distinguishes us from non-human creatures, however, is not only that we can become aware of the other and that other's interests, but we can reflect and decide how far those interests should be taken into account in modifying our own. To grow up from a young child to an adult is to grow into a recognition that these choices form a very fundamental part of living and constitute a major challenge. Recognition of a moral claim on us, a claim that calls for a response, varies of course with the circumstances in which we find ourselves and the extent of our moral growth at the time. But growth and the call to grow are the key concepts. From a Christian point of view, this has a particular dimension, in that we are made in the image of God, and this means that, in however an opaque, faltering fashion, we have the capacity to think, choose, pray and love as part of our humanity. Through this we are called to grow into the divine likeness. That growing likeness is also a growing capacity to reflect the divine glory.

From this point of view, the deliberate rejection of a moral claim we are becoming aware of, this turning away from the call to grow as a human being, is not just wrong, it is 'sin', for it is a turning away from God's call. If it continues it becomes that hardening of the heart that the Bible continually castigates. This means that sin is really about refusing to move on. It is getting stuck at a particular stage of development, leading to retarded moral and spiritual growth.

While it is true that whole nations, tribal groups or religious traditions can get caught up in a kind of mad hysteria, so that people find themselves swept into forms of behaviour they would previously have found totally reprehensible; nevertheless there will be some people who are culpable beyond the majority. It is for this reason that we have an International Criminal Court in which people can be found guilty of genocide, crimes against humanity or war crimes. Even in Nazi Germany when an unspeakable evil took hold of the whole culture, there were those who knew there was another way and who did their best to protect or shelter Jews, very often at the cost of their own lives. They were a tiny minority but that minority witnessed to the fact that what was happening was not inevitable, was not totally determined.[10]

In the Church of England's *Common Worship* Eucharist, worshippers confess what they have done wrong to God and their neighbour:

> in thought, word and deed,
> through negligence, through weakness,
> through our own deliberate fault.[11]

For some generations now, we have been encouraged to think well of ourselves and to develop a sense of our own worth. One result of this, however, is that we often find it difficult to identify with the prayers of penitence set out by the churches. But from a Christian point of view prayer is made not just as an individual but as part of the whole of humanity in Christ. Attending a Eucharist in Sweden, I recall how the Confession of the Church of Sweden captures this sense well when it includes the phrase:

> Through my sin I am guilty of more than I understand,
> And share in the world's alienation from you.

In confessing sin, we stand with the whole of torn and divided humanity in its alienation from God and put our trust in the same God who in Christ made himself one with that humanity.

That negligence, weakness and deliberate wrongdoing, when set in the context of extreme social, economic and political situations, seems enough to account for the terrible things we do to one another without bringing in any further religious dimension. So on the principle of 'Occam's razor', that we should not multiply explanations beyond what is absolutely necessary, what truth, if any, remains in the old Christian account of evil? What does it add? What does it account for that is not already explainable in non-religious terms?

Milton's myth

The Christian myth on the origin of evil, as given classic form by John Milton, has two parts. First, the idea of the devil as a fallen angel who tempts and seduces humanity, and second the story of our earliest ancestors being led astray, thereby tainting all subsequent human beings with 'original sin'; that is, an inescapable tendency towards doing wrong.

Angels are a beautiful idea, and there is no reason in principle why there should not be many other forms of creation that are invisible to us. But the concept of a personified evil, Satan, is another matter. In his classic study *Evil and the God of Love*,[12] John Hick rejected the concept of the devil, especially the idea of Satan as a fallen angel, on the grounds that angels, according to the story, were created perfect in a perfect environment. He argued that because our actions arise out of us and express our being, they could not therefore have sinned. The idea of fallen angels is self-contradictory, he argued. Yet is this the case? Perhaps there really is a mystery about evil, so that for sheer devilment people, or angels, are capable of going against the good, rather as small boys feel tempted to smash glass windows or pull the legs off live insects. And if this is so then even if they were created without a flaw in a sublime environment, would not this still be the case? Conscious of their freedom they might wilfully, for no rational reason, for sheer devilment, want to destroy the good.[13]

But there is another difficulty with the whole story. Life for creatures like ourselves, the product of an evolution in which the fittest
survive, is difficult enough anyway. We exist as embodied selves,
fragile, vulnerable and with Hamlet's 'the heartache and the thousand
natural shocks that flesh is heir to'. What kind of God is it who in
addition to this would have us tempted, tested and tormented beyond
what we can bear, using a force outside ourselves, and who has
deliberately given that force a free run in order to do just this? The
idea is morally intolerable. It seems better to think of angels as
a vivid way of talking about the grace of God as it touches, guides
and inspires us. As for temptation, it is the essence of a temptation
that there is something about it that draws or lures us. We do not
need to personify evil in order to account for this.

The second part of the myth, which is about a fall from grace in
the Garden of Eden, needs to be separated into its different elements.
First, it is obvious that something has gone badly wrong with human
life and that this antedates recorded human history. There has been
what John Henry Newman called a great 'aboriginal catastrophe',
for we are all born into a world that is seriously out of kilter, and
every human advance carries with it the possibility of some new
evil, of which the invention of atomic and later nuclear power is
only the most obvious example. Every community that has been
founded, whether on religious or secular grounds, to get away from
the old corrupt order and create a new form of life where there is
genuine care between human beings, finds itself coming unstuck
on the rock of the human ego. It is not usually long before a quarrel
and a split occur, with endless sundering after that.[14] A classic
example is the fact that there are now more than 500 versions
of Protestantism in the United States. Exactly the same fissiparous
tendency is present in all utopian and socialist movements. When
did this great aboriginal catastrophe occur? The short answer is that
we do not know, but there is a very imaginative account of what
might have happened in William Golding's novel *The Inheritors*.[15]
This pictures two tribal groups, one on the threshold of consciousness and one just over it. The first group do not have language but

they think in images, and what one individual pictures they all picture. They live and move as a unity. The other group does have language. They also have fire, alcohol and constant warring. In the transition, something has gone badly wrong.

According to the Genesis account, what went wrong had at its root something to do with our relationship to God. It involved a refusal to live as a finite, limited creature and involved a bid to put ourselves at the centre of the universe instead of our creator. This may not have been so much a deliberate rejection of God as an unwillingness to accept our creaturely status with all the vicissitudes of history. Thinking of ourselves in A. E. Housman's words, as 'a stranger, lonely and afraid in a world I never made',[16] we are subject to anxiety. We try to relieve that anxiety by investing some limited goal with absolute status. So, for example, someone comes to find the whole meaning of his existence in nationalism. He gives what is conditioned and finite an unconditional loyalty. In religious terms, he treats as God what is less than God. Religion itself is not immune to this process; indeed its very nature lends itself to it. As Reinhold Niebuhr put it:

> Religion is not, as is generally supposed, an inherently virtuous quest for God. It is merely the final battleground between God and man's self-esteem. In that battle, even the most pious practices may be instruments of human pride. The same man may in one moment regard Christ as his judge and in the next moment seek to prove that the figure, the standards and the righteousness of Christ bear a greater similarity to his own righteousness than to that of his enemy.[17]

This fundamental flaw has terrible social consequences. As Niebuhr said:

> The religious dimension of sin is man's rebellion against God, his effort to usurp the place of God. The moral and social dimension of sin is injustice. The ego which falsely makes itself the centre of existence in its pride and will-to-power inevitably subordinates other life to its will and thus does injustice to other life.[18]

It is this that throws light on John Gray's criticism of much liberal thought with its tendency to focus on one particular evil that must be got rid of at all costs, after which the world would be safe. That attitude is yet another example of giving an absolute status to what is less than absolute, of finding security by ignoring the partial, flawed nature of all human achievement.

The Nazi regime with its wicked anti-Semitism provides the most extreme and horrifying example of this expression of evil, and does so in two ways. First, by making loyalty to the state, in the form of the Führer, a principle that was to override all others; and, second, with its policy of a 'final solution' to the presence of Jews on its territory. The very phrase 'final solution' is telling, indicating an absolutizing of one feature, the end of which, the Nazis thought, would be the solution to their problems. The Communist regime in the Soviet Union provided another example, again through the way loyalty to the party and the state overrode all other considerations; and, second, through a willingness to pay the price of millions of deaths through the purges and the collectivization of farming in order to achieve a socialist goal. What this example brings out is that the goal can in itself be an altruistic one, not just a perverted one; but even this, if made into an unconditional imperative, can become demonic. Indeed one of the most perceptive post-Second World War German theologians, Helmut Thielicke, argued that just this had happened in both Nazi Germany and the Soviet Union. Both states had ceased to be the state described in Romans 13, which can legitimately seek our qualified loyalty, and had become the state described in Revelation 13, which in seeking an unconditional loyalty had usurped the place of God and thereby become demonic.[19]

The fall of Satan is a myth but it is one that illuminates our condition. Satan fell because his pride led him:

> To set himself in glory above his peers,
> He trusted to have equalled the Most High,
> If he opposed; and with ambitious aim
> Against the throne and monarchy of God,
> Raised impious war in Heav'n . . .[20]

It is often said that Milton projected something of himself into his picture of Satan. C. S. Lewis said this is 'true in a sense, but not in a sense peculiar to Milton. The Satan in Milton enables him to draw the character well, just as the Satan in us enables us to receive it.'[21]

It is for this reason that the horrors we inflict on one another cannot be accounted for only in terms of evolutionary psychology accentuated and reinforced by conditions of deprivation and stirred up by fear. There is something beyond that which has its roots in our reluctance to accept our vulnerable, creaturely status. This gives rise to a fundamental anxiety that can lead us to give absolute status to that which is less than absolute and which as a result becomes demonic.

At the heart of this is a wilful, irrational choice against the good. This choice arises out of us but is nevertheless freely chosen. Why we do this is indeed a mystery. There remains an ultimate mystery about iniquity.

The obverse of this truth, that the evil we do to one another cannot be fully explained in empirical terms, is that our capacity for genuine self-transcendence, for setting aside our own interests, even our own life for the sake of others, is also beyond what can be accounted for by our normal modes of explanation. We are capable both of greater evil and greater good than we care to think. Indeed as has often been pointed out, it is not just the presence of evil that poses a major question but the fact of good. There is much sheer goodness in the world and this has to be taken into account just much as the terrible wickedness. Both the mystery of evil and the mystery of good are rooted in our awareness of ourselves as self-determining agents daily conscious of courses of action with a moral dimension. We are born with a healthy desire to survive but we are called to grow beyond this into moral and spiritual maturity; in Christian terms, into the likeness of God.

A thread running through this chapter is that the capacity to do evil is rooted in human choice. It does not exist in its own right. The world we know and any other sphere of angels there may be is God's good creation and evil is not to be located in matter. Neither is there an equal and opposing agency to God. There is a famous phrase of St Augustine, *Mali enim natura est; sed amissio boni mali nomen accepit* (*De civitate Dei* 11.9), which has shaped nearly all Christian thinking on this subject. It is rendered by Rowan Williams as 'Evil is not some kind of object . . . but we give the name of "evil" to that process in which good is lost.'[22] Sometimes evil seems so powerful that it is experienced as a malign force. But this is not because it exists in its own right but because the fundamental energy of the universe in which we share, created good, is being misused and twisted by our choices.

Two other points need briefly to be made. If there is 'original sin' there is also 'original blessing', to use the title of a book by Matthew Fox. The world has been created good, life is a blessing and we have the capacity to recognize and respond to what is worthwhile. Second, not only can the doctrine of 'original sin' save us from an illusionary, destructive utopianism, keeping us realistic in what we can achieve in the political sphere, it can save us from undue pessimism about ourselves. The drive to pursue our own interests is part of our nature and without it we would not be here. The fact that we are so reluctant to temper this by taking into account the interests of others is the result of being born into and shaped by an environment that is already deeply flawed in this way. We still have to assume responsibility for our actions, but the fact that it is a struggle to grow beyond self-centred egoism is not wholly down to us.

11

Overcoming evil

The inner struggle

Evil is to be taken with the utmost seriousness. It affects every aspect of human life, personal and political, and every institution, including religion. In taking evil seriously, the first mistake to avoid is a binary view of the world in which evil is projected as 'the other'. Good and evil are tangled together at every point. They run through every heart. In particular, we have to face the fact that people rarely choose deliberately to do evil; they first of all convince themselves that they are doing good. Before they deceive others they deceive themselves. Religions, including Christianity, are particularly prone to this delusion. Some of the greatest evils have been perpetrated by those who deceived themselves, and those who colluded with them, into thinking they were doing good or serving God.

The world is tainted by evil and this means that any attempt to overcome it involves both profound self-knowledge and hard inner struggle. Both are to be seen in the story of Jesus being tempted in the wilderness. All three of the Synoptic Gospels record that after his baptism by John in the River Jordan in which he heard the words, 'You are my beloved Son; in you I delight', he spent time in the desert. Here he faced three temptations, each beginning with the challenge: 'If you are the Son of God . . .' He experienced the temptation to use his divine power to satisfy material needs, which he rejected on the grounds that 'Man is not to live on bread alone'. He also rejected the idea of establishing a human kingdom on earth by means he knew were wrong. Finally, according to Luke's order, he rejected the idea of winning people's allegiance by performing miraculous stunts (Luke 4.1–13). Luke, in placing this temptation third, is making a deliberate point because later in that Gospel the same temptation is taken up when Jesus is on the cross. There again he is challenged and mocked by the onlookers, the soldiers and one of the criminals to use his claimed status as Son of God to save himself by a stunning display of power.

The inner struggle of Jesus to realize his vocation in a way that was faithful to his calling was of a fierceness and intensity we cannot imagine. A tiny glimpse of it is given in the story of his prayer in the Garden of Gethsemane just before he was arrested. Twice he told his disciples to pray that they might be spared the great test or time of trial. He then first prayed that the cup of suffering might be taken from him, before submitting himself to the divine will whatever it turned out to be. According to Luke, although an angel brought him strength, 'in anguish of spirit he prayed the more urgently; and his sweat was like drops of blood falling to the ground' (Luke 22.44).

Sister Clare, who became the Reverend Mother of an Anglican religious order in Oxford known as the Sisters of the Love of God, whose vocation is contemplative prayer, used to describe how she came to join the community. It was in Cardiff during the Second World War, at the height of the Blitz when the docks were being bombed. She was working as a nurse amid the explosions and fire when she realized that the real battle was not up in the air between the Allied and Nazi planes, nor was it even on the ground where she was doing what she could for the injured. It was a spiritual battle that had to be fought and the heart of the struggle was prayer. What we know of the ministry of Jesus is that his sense of a spiritual battle was no less than this. It was one that involved great inner ordeals. When in the fourth century a number of Christians left the newly Christianized Roman Empire to go into the deserts of Egypt, they did so not primarily to flee the compromises of a newly fashionable Christianity or to get away from the world. It was because the desert was the front line in the struggle against evil. There, faced with nothing but the desert and the inner life, they discovered that the ordeal was indeed fiery. This inner struggle that Jesus underwent in order to remain true to himself and his Father's good purpose for him, was in order to ensure that the rule of God that he came to proclaim was indeed the rule of God and not just some distorted human projection.

Jesus saw society as being in the grip of evil, and the purpose of his ministry was to liberate it. He made it clear that the healings he performed, both of body and mind, were signs that the rule of God was even now releasing people from this bondage, and he intended the ministry of those he commissioned and sent out to be part of this process. In a dramatic image, he told his disciples when they returned from one mission: 'I saw Satan fall, like lightning, from heaven' (Luke 10.18).

After Jesus had been raised from the dead and made his presence known to his followers, they became convinced that what Jesus had proclaimed had indeed come to pass. In some decisive sense, his life, death and resurrection had broken the power of evil, overcome death and reconciled humanity to God. There have, however, been a number of different ways of expressing this, both in the New Testament itself and in the developed theology of the Church. There has never been an official doctrine of how Christ has been efficacious for our salvation; rather there have been a number of ideas, each of which has built on a particular image.

A rather surprising person, D. H. Lawrence, begins a poem: 'All that matters is to be at one with the living God.'[1] That succinctly states a central Christian conviction, which is why attempts to understand the purpose of Christ's mission have been called theories of the atonement (at-one-ment). They have used particular images to explore how as a result of Christ's death and resurrection humanity can now be said to be at one with God rather than estranged from him. It is important to remember that these are images or pictures with all the limitations that this implies, as argued in Chapter 3 of this book. A mistake has too often been made of pushing a particular image further than it was originally designed to go. For example, a popular early view held that Christ's death had ransomed us, and this image appears in some words of Jesus himself. It is a powerful image, conveying the idea both of being freed from captivity and the price that has to be paid for this. But things started to go wrong when people tried to work out in more detail to whom the ransom had been paid and what was the mechanism of the release. Other images, such as God's honour being offended or God's justice demanding a penalty, have also been stretched more than they were designed for. It is important to ask about each image whether it is in keeping with the picture of God given us in the teaching and example of Jesus himself. Some images, when pushed beyond their proper limit, should be rejected on these grounds. Behind all these images, is it possible to put in simple terms what Christ did for us? Austin Farrer wrote this:

> Everything that God does has an abyss of mystery in it, because it has God in it. But in the saving act of the incarnation God came all lengths to meet us, and dealt humanly with human creatures. If ever he made his way plain, it was there. The variety of parables express the love that went into the redemption, or the blessings that flow from it. They are not needed to state the thing that was done.
>
> What, then, did God do for his people's redemption? He came among them, bringing his kingdom, and he let events take their human course. He set the divine life in human neighbourhood. Men discovered it in struggling with it and were captured by it in crucifying it. What could be simpler? And what more divine?[2]

We notice, of course, that even in this simple statement a series of images is being used, some with powerful poetic effect, such as men 'were captured by it in crucifying it'. But given this it does express very well both the central thrust of the teaching and mission of Jesus and how this has in fact had an impact on Christians in their personal life.

What would the redemption of the world look like? It would quite simply be a world in which we were perfectly at one with God and one another. The old word 'atonement' gets it right. It would be a world at one with the root of its being, in tune with the divine music in our hearts and in harmony with one another. What are the barriers to this living union? If we take seriously the teaching and ministry of Jesus it is difficult to think that they come from the side of God. What characterizes the ministry of Jesus is that he went out of his way to include those whom others excluded. He mixed with them and had meals with them. And he taught that this pattern of his ministry was the pattern of God himself in his relation with us. He is like the shepherd who hunts the hills for the one lost sheep; the woman who scrabbles on the floor for the one lost coin. In another memorable parable, the Father stands outside his house scanning the horizon waiting for his wastrel son to return; when he does he embraces him warmly and gives a great party to celebrate his homecoming. God searches us out wherever we are; and it was clearly highly symbolic for the early Church that this should have gone to the lengths of being crucified between two criminals, to one of whom he said 'Today you will be with me in paradise.'

The barriers are not put up on God's side. That leaves us. Is there something about us, something within us, that erects them?

The barriers come down

When individuals realize the truth of the divine love for us, not just intellectually but when they take it into themselves and let it take hold, it breaks down all barriers. It melts the icy heart and dispels all feelings of self-pity or resentment. It is well expressed in the words of a hymn by Samuel Crossman (*c.*1624–83) to a haunting tune by John Ireland:

> My song is love unknown,
> My Saviour's love to me,
> Love to the loveless shown,
> That they might lovely be.
> O who am I,
> That for my sake
> My Lord should take
> Frail flesh and die?
>
> He came from His blest throne,
> Salvation to bestow;

But men made strange, and none
The longed-for Christ would know:
But O, my Friend,
My Friend indeed,
Who at my need
His life did spend.[3]

It is not sentimental or pietistic to appeal to the words of a hymn. The fact is that it is in such words that we see best how Christ continues to steal into people's lives, sometimes the most unlikely, and change them. The words of that hymn are particularly fine, both in the idea of men 'made strange' with its resonance of estrangement, and in the image of love for the loveless that they might lovely be, with its linking of goodness and beauty.

In Leo Tolstoy's novel *War and Peace*, a fashionable young army officer is given money by his father and told that it is all he can afford at the moment. The young officer, Nikolai Rostov, goes off and contrary to all his intentions and against his better judgement finds himself gambling. He is so trapped by his obsession that his losses spiral out of control into a huge sum that has to be paid next day. He goes to see his tough, gruff, fine old father and tries to put on a casual air.

'It can't be helped. It happens to everyone!' said the son in a free and easy tone, while in his heart he was feeling himself a worthless scoundrel whose whole life could not atone for his crime. He longed to kiss his father's hands, kneel and beg his forgiveness, while in a careless and even rude voice he was telling him that it happened to everyone!

The old count dropped his eyes when he heard these words from his son, and began to fidget about as though in search of something. 'Yes, yes,' he murmured. 'It will be difficult, I fear, difficult to raise . . . happens to everybody! Yes, yes, it might happen to anyone . . .' And with a furtive glance at his son's face the count went out of the room. Nikolai had been prepared for opposition, but had not at all expected this. 'Papa! Pa-pa!' he called after him, sobbing. 'Forgive me!' And clutching at his father's hand he pressed it to his lips and burst into tears.[4]

He had expected opposition but had met instead with understanding, kindness and self-sacrifice. It was this that pierced his heart, broke down his insouciance and brought about a deeper union with his father the other side of tears and sorrow. The barriers are not on God's side but ours. For God goes all the way to meet us and break them down. Our normal habit is to respond to any criticism in a defensive, self-justifying manner. But sometimes when others in their love for us make themselves vulnerable, this leads us to lower our guard.

The obverse of this divine seeking out, so that like the prodigal son in the parable far away from home we come to our senses, is the way the love thus shown raises a radical question mark over all our accepted notions of morality and propriety. Indeed once the truth of the Christian faith begins to dawn, the image that more than any other expresses its effect is that of a simple question mark. It leads us to question ourselves, not least about those areas of our lives on which we most pride ourselves, and it leads us to question the fundamental values that drive the society of which we are a part. This question mark is raised not just over our personal lives but over the political and economic systems of which we are a part and in which so many live in dire poverty or oppression. We come with our questions to God, perfectly proper questions about why there is so much suffering in life, but in the light of Christ, without ceasing to ask those questions, we find ourselves questioned in turn, in every aspect of our lives, personal, social and political.

If what God did is simply to come among us bringing his kingdom, setting the divine life in human neighbourhood – what about sin? People sometimes suggest that the kind of view suggested above does not take sin seriously enough. When we see or hear the news or read the newspapers, we are again and again appalled at what we human beings do to one another. People being killed, often in half-forgotten wars, more than four million killed in the Congo in recent years for example, not unrelated to the scramble for Congo's rich mineral resources; young gay men being hanged in Iran or women being stoned; the greed and reckless folly of some in the banking and financial sector that brought the world's economy to its knees, with people being thrown out of their jobs. The beheading of innocent civilians by Daesh and the endless bombings of one another by Shias and Sunnis. These things rightly make us angry. They fill us with a sense of moral outrage. And if that is how we feel, can a morally good God feel less? God is not a weak, anaemic God. He cares about us, he is deeply affected by us – and one aspect of this must be that he too is outraged at the cruelties we inflict on one another. This is what the Bible means by that terrifying phrase, 'the wrath of God'. If it is right to use human language about God at all, and we want to say God cares about us, then to care is to be affected, and then includes anger. Yet still he does not give up on us.

A young man is in prison for a series of crimes to feed a drug habit. In the course of these crimes, he has badly hurt people. But his mother regularly visits him in prison. She still loves him, has not given up on him. She is still angry and deeply grieving that he should have turned out like this, but she still loves him and wants to be with him. So with God and us. He still loves us and wants to be with us – he comes all lengths to meet us. But in meeting God's deep compassion and pity, we also meet his outrage – at those who sell drugs, for example, and ruin people's lives. What changes the relationship? What brings about at-one-ment between the mother and her son? She does not have to change her attitude. She loves him now and will continue to do so. It is he who has to change. The addict son has to realize the full extent of the hurt he has caused her and others. So he expresses his deep remorse and sorrow, and mother and son embrace in tears of sadness and joy. What has happened to her anger? It is somehow dissolved in the mutual tears and joy of mother and son. It is not as though everything is forgotten, but it is no longer on her mind and she certainly does not bring it up in conversation. So with God and us.

Descent into the world's darkness

Sin is a difficult subject for anyone to talk about in our time, for society seems unwilling to use that kind of language. Yet the reality of sin remains, as we know when we castigate domestic violence, trafficking, female genital mutilation, sexual abuse, gross misconduct, antisocial behaviour and greed in the financial sector. It is likely that when we contemplate our own shortcomings the language of the Book of Common Prayer, for example, will seem very over the top when it makes us say about them that 'Their burden is intolerable.' So it is important to remember that in his incarnation Christ identifies with humanity as a whole, and that he lived and died and rose again, 'for the sin of the whole world', as the Prayer of Consecration in the Book of Common Prayer puts it. In prayer, whether with others or on their own, Christians are alongside humanity as a whole. We stand with all people, with whatever horrors they are responsible for, because that is where Christ stood and continues to stand. That said, we can never distance ourselves, our own lives and motives and secret thoughts from those perpetrators of terrible things. Reinhold Niebuhr got it right when in the prayers he wrote during the Second World War he has sentences like:

> We pray for wicked and cruel men, whose arrogance reveals to us what the sin of our own hearts is like when it has conceived and brought forth its final fruit.
> We pray for ourselves who live in peace and quietness, that we may not regard our fortune as proof of our virtue or rest content to have our ease at the price of other men's sorrow and tribulation.[5]

God's love remains steadfast. It is we who have to change. What brings about change is an awareness of the lengths to which God has gone, at what cost, to remain with us in the prison of our pride and self-preoccupation. It is that love that enables us to face what we as human beings do to one another and God. Facing that can be painful. It is this kind of painful self-knowledge that is powerfully stated in a poem by Thomas Hardy:

> A cry from the green-grained sticks of the fire
>   Made me gaze where it seemed to be:
> 'Twas my own voice talking therefrom to me
> On how I had walked when my sun was higher –
>   My heart in its arrogancy.

'You held not to whatsoever was true,'
  Said my own voice talking to me:
'Whatsoever was just you were slack to see;
Kept not things lovely and pure in view,'
  Said my own voice talking to me.

'You slighted her that endureth all,'
  Said my own voice talking to me;
'Vaunteth not, trusteth hopefully;
That suffereth long and is kind withal,'
  Said my own voice talking to me.

'You taught not that which you set about,'
  Said my own voice talking to me;
'That the greatest of things is Charity. . . .'
  – And the sticks burnt low, and the fire went out,
  And my voice ceased talking to me.[6]

Sometimes we have to face such painful self-knowledge in this life. If not here, then in that purging self-knowledge that was termed purgatory: for looking into infinite compassion of divine love brings us at the same time face to face with ourselves.

Jesus came among humanity proclaiming the kingdom of God. He knew he had to take his message to the heart of the political and religious establishment in Jerusalem and he knew what the consequences would be. He knew it would result in opposition and death. But he offered his life to his Father and his friends. So at the Last Supper, he took the bread, broke it and thinking of the cross next day, said: 'This is my body which is given for you.' That broken body was the price of our redemption. It was not demanded of God but it is the cost to God of coming all the way to meet us at the point where we push him furthest away.

Simone Weil once wrote: 'All the criminal violence of the Roman Empire ran up against Christ and in him became pure suffering . . . The false god changes suffering into violence. The true God changes violence into suffering.'[7] That suffering was not just the terrible physical pain, one of the worst tortures devised by us cruel human beings, but the spiritual anguish of entering into the darkness of our alienation from God. On the cross Jesus cries out 'My God, my God why have you forsaken me?' In the seventeenth century in Spain, painters started to depict Jesus alone on the cross against a black background – alone and desolate rather than surrounded by crowds. It is perhaps this that Paul is trying to indicate when in a startling image he says that Christ was made sin for us, or in a more modern translation, 'Christ was innocent of sin, and yet for our sake God made him one with human sinfulness, so that in him we might be made one with the righteousness of God' (2 Corinthians 5.21). Jesus became one with human sinfulness. He enters into the literal hell of our estrangement from God. Indeed in Christian thought and art it is at this point that Jesus descends into hell to conquer death and release humanity from its grip. He enters hell on behalf of humanity, and because he is still the eternal Son at one with his Father, lifts that hell to God.

A line in a hymn by the Puritan writer Richard Baxter says that there is no darkness that we have to go through that Christ has not been through before. Yet there are many kinds of suffering that Christ did not experience – Alzheimer's, to take just one example. In Samuel Beckett's play *Waiting for Godot*, Estragon compares himself to Christ. Vladimir responds to this by saying: 'But where he lived, it was warm, it was dry!' Estragon retorts, 'Yes. And they crucified quick',[8] with its implication that his crucifixion is longer than Christ's. But while it is true that there are many kinds of suffering that Jesus did not experience, some of which seem just one long crucifixion, the most fundamental darkness is our alienation from God and it is this he entered and overcame. This is wonderfully symbolized in the Orthodox Icon of the Anastasis, in which Jesus descends into hell, breaks the power of the evil one and releases captive humanity.[9]

This image is also used by William Langland in *Piers Plowman*. He recounts the scene in hell in a way that recalls the apocryphal *Gospel of Nicodemus* and says he has heard secret words it is not granted to a human being to utter. 'My mercy it is that will judge mankind as they stand before me in Heaven. For surely I would be an unnatural kind of king if I did nothing to help my own kindred?'[10] The theme is also there in Julian of Norwich, who writes of Christ descending into hell and 'And when he was there, then he raised up the great host out of the deep abyss, which had been truly knit to him in high heaven.'[11] The mystery plays were another context in which this idea found powerful expression. I saw a great production at the National Theatre in London in which hell was depicted as a vast rubbish truck with its metal claws drawing everything in and grinding it up. In modern times, it has been central to the theology of Hans Urs von Balthasar, often regarded as the outstanding Catholic theologian of the twentieth century. For him, the phrase in the creed 'He descended into hell' is fundamental to the meaning of redemption and atonement, for it means that Christ has entered into and taken on himself the deepest darkness of humanity as a whole.

Visually and liturgically it is the Christian East that most powerfully conveys the sense of the whole of creation being altered by the Anastasis: of some fundamental shift in the foundation of things; of a descent to utter darkness that, through the resurrection, has united even the most estranged of creatures with God now and for ever. Matins on Holy Saturday in the Orthodox Church puts it this way:

> To earth hast Thou come down, O master, to save Adam: and not finding him on earth, Thou hast descended into Hades, seeking him there.
>
> Uplifted on the Cross, Thou hast uplifted with Thyself all living men; and then descending beneath the earth, Thou raisest all that lie buried there.
>
> The whole creation was altered by Thy Passion; for all things suffered with Thee, knowing, O Word, that Thou holdest all in unity.[12]

Christ not only enters our darkness, he is with us there holding us to God. Psalm 139 says:

if I go down to hell, thou art there also . . .

If I say, Peradventure the darkness shall cover me: then shall my
night be turned to day.

Yea, the darkness is no darkness with thee, but the night is as clear
as the day . . .

(vv. 7, 10–11 BCP)

In Jesus, God and humanity, heaven and earth, are joined never to
be unjoined. God holds frail, sinful humanity to himself through
all the vicissitudes of life and the unknown journey of death. He
laid down only two conditions for that relationship to be kept
open from our side. First, the necessity of *metanoia*, rethinking
and reordering our lives in the light of Jesus' message about God's
kingly rule; and second, our willingness to reach out to others as
God has reached out to us. 'Forgive us our sins as we forgive those
who sin against us' we pray daily. This is not a question of wiping
the slate clean. It is holding others in the same kind of relationship
in which God holds us.

There is a final point it is very easy to overlook. It is that if God
thought it necessary for our eternal salvation to enter the flux of
human history and change it from within, that necessity has not
changed. His work continues in and through human beings. First,
ceaselessly and secretly in the hearts of all people. But if that were
enough, the eternal Word would not have become flesh. Second,
God continues his redemptive purpose in a special way through his
body on earth, the communion of Christian believers. Whatever
the faults and failings of the Christian community, and they are
manifest and many, it has a special vocation and destiny to embody
now the life that God embodied in Jesus.

I recognize that what has been suggested in this chapter is basically unacceptable to most liberal-minded, progressive people in
Western Europe today. There is also an obvious riposte to what
I have said. The Church as a whole and individual Christians too
often come across as unredeemed, no better than other people
and sometimes worse. If Jesus brought about this great change in
humanity, why has it not made more difference not only to the

world but to his followers? Christians must have the humility to accept this charge. It is not one we can answer for ourselves. Only God knows the truth. When Randolph Churchill and Evelyn Waugh were serving together in Yugoslavia during the Second World War, they had a series of bitter quarrels. Eventually Churchill could stand it no more and shouted out: 'I thought you were meant to be a Christian and a Catholic?' To which Waugh replied: 'And think how much worse I would be if I wasn't.'[13] Christians do not claim to be better than other people. All they affirm is that they know themselves, in weakness and failure, to be held in Christ's grace.

12

Hope in the face of death

What happened to life after death?

For nineteen hundred years the great imperative for Christians was so to live this life that after death they might achieve a better one. Life was seen as a great moral obstacle course or training ground on the way to reaching heaven and avoiding hell. Mediaeval churches were dominated by great dooms, or depictions of the last judgement, in which these possible futures were set before the worshipper in stark visual terms. Although in the sixteenth century belief in purgatory was rejected by the Protestant reformers and emphasis placed on the sheer grace of God in Christ, the gaze of the believer was still directed towards the great goal of human life beyond death. All through the nineteenth century the many hymns that were written were still imbued with that vision. That focus on life after death radically shifted during the last 40 years of the twentieth century. Future historians examining Christianity in Britain in that century will note the dramatic change of perspective that came about, not least as reflected in the hymns written during that period on themes of social action, justice and human brotherhood. For those caught up in the rapidly expanding Pentecostal or Charismatic movements, the new music, in the form of refrains and choruses, was expressive of an intense religious experience rather than social action; but again, the emphasis was on the present, not the future.

While it can be argued that what happened at that time was a healthy corrective to an undue emphasis on the afterlife, which had dominated the Church for too long, what is really surprising is the way belief in life after death has for many Christians almost dropped out of active consideration altogether. I do not remember ever hearing a sermon directly on the subject of heaven and hell; indeed while always bringing the theme of Christian hope into funeral addresses, I do not think I have ever given over an ordinary Sunday sermon exclusively to the subject. A poll done a few years ago revealed that the percentage of churchgoers who believe in life after death was not much higher than in the population as a whole. Recent research is interesting in showing an increase in belief in ghosts, tarot cards and astrology among the population as a whole compared to 1950, bearing out G. K. Chesterton's dictum that when people stop believing in God they don't believe in nothing, they believe in anything.[1] However, whatever people as a whole believe or do not believe, the issue to be considered now is the hope of heaven within Christian belief.

Put starkly and simply, I believe that hope in the face of death is an essential element of Christian belief, a fundamental part of the structure of faith. Without this hope it is difficult to see how other elements can stand. It is not an aspect of faith that a Christian can sit light to or in any way regard as optional. This is not to argue that we should be thinking about it all the time or that we ought to get back to the pre-1960 orientation with its focus on heaven. On the contrary, the present emphasis on trying to let God work through us personally and politically to change the world for the better is a healthy one. But that emphasis is part of a whole view of life in which the hope of heaven is integral.

It is easy to understand why belief in an afterlife has been removed from its central place in Christian thought. First, we are all now so aware of the power of wishful thinking in our lives. It was above all Sigmund Freud, that great master of suspicion, who made us so wary of this. The result is that we find it difficult to believe that there really could be any such reality as a glorious heaven. Iris Murdoch summed this approach up in a lapidary phrase, 'Almost anything that consoles us is fake.'[2] Yet if we reflect on that sentence it immediately becomes clear that it is an assertion, an assumption. It is no more obviously true than the sentence 'what consoles must be true.' We would be right to approach the latter statement in a sceptical mood. It is also right to be sceptical about an approach that states almost as a matter of definition that anything that consoles is unreal. Most fair-minded people would admit that there can be both false and true consolation. Consolation cannot be ruled out a priori.

There is a deeply moving passage at the end of Chekhov's play *Uncle Vanya* in which Sonia tries to comfort her uncle. She acknowledges that his life has been one of tears and patient suffering and then she paints a picture of the very different life ahead for both of them:

> We shall rejoice and look back at all these troubles of ours with tender feelings, with a smile – and we shall have rest. I believe it, Uncle, I believe it fervently, passionately. We shall have rest! . . . We shall see all earthly evil, all our sufferings swept away by the grace which will fill the whole world, and our life will become peaceful, gentle, and sweet as a caress.

Vanya cries. Sonia wipes away his tears and she cries too. 'You've had no joy in your life, but wait, Uncle Vanya, wait. We shall rest. . . . We shall rest!'[3] It is a passage that lends itself to the charge of wishful thinking. Sonia's vision of heaven is set up in deliberate contrast to the unrelieved suffering of this life. But it cannot simply be dismissed on these grounds, for if the Christian hope of heaven is real it must inevitably be pictured in terms that contrast with much of this life. What kind of heaven we hope for depends on a range of other factors, above all the kind of God that is believed in.

The second reason is also due to another great master of suspicion, Karl Marx. Marx had some sympathy with religion, as we can judge from the quotation given in Chapter 2 about religion being the 'heart of a heartless world, and the soul of soulless conditions'. That paragraph continues:

> The abolition of religion as the illusory happiness of the people is the demand for their real happiness. To call on them to give up their illusions about their condition is to call on them to give up a condition that requires illusions. The criticism of religion is, therefore, in embryo, the criticism of that vale of tears of which religion is the halo.[4]

That criticism has been echoed in different ways by non-Marxists – by liberal progressives, for example, who believe we should concentrate all our energies on improving life now rather than on an afterlife, as well as in the popular jibe that someone can be so heavenly minded that they are of no earthly use. It is obvious that there is a great deal of truth in both the Marxist and the popular form of this criticism and it needs to be heeded. But the question that is at issue is whether action now to change the world and a belief in heaven are in principle incompatible. In fact justice now and justice as finally established in God's eternal kingdom are not in opposition, rather they need and support one another, as Austin Farrer stated so clearly: 'Heaven alone gives final meaning to any earthly hopes; and to take it the other way round, we have no way to grasp at heavenly hope than by pursuing hopeful tasks here below.'[5]

Most of us have been to funerals and heard the magnificent passage from the King James Version of the fifteenth chapter of St Paul's first letter to the Corinthians, one of the masterpieces of English prose. I never fail to be moved by Paul's final sentence. After the eloquent series of contrasts between our mortal and our immortal state, he ends up on a severely practical note: 'Therefore, my beloved brethren, be ye stedfast, unmoveable, always abounding in the work of the Lord, forasmuch as ye know that your labour is not in vain in the Lord' (1 Corinthians 15.58 AV).

The words 'in vain' could also be translated 'futile' or 'useless'. And I suppose all human beings will at least once in their lives have been overcome with a feeling that everything they do is in fact useless, a total waste, and indeed that life itself is getting nowhere, achieving nothing. It is the theme of the famous passage in Scripture from Ecclesiastes:

> Vanity of vanities, says the Teacher,
> vanity of vanities! All is vanity.
> What do people gain from all the toil
> at which they toil under the sun?
> (Ecclesiastes 1.2–3 NRSV)

Or as the translation in the Revised English Bible puts it: 'Futility, utter futility . . . everything is futile'.

It was this feeling that overcame Wilfred Owen in the trenches of the First World War. One wonderful poem written after seeing the body of a young soldier is called 'Futility'. Another called 'Last Words' reads:

> 'O Jesus Christ!' one fellow sighed.
> And kneeled, and bowed, tho' not in prayer, and died.
> And the Bullets sang 'In Vain',
> Machine Guns chuckled 'In Vain',
> Big Guns guffawed 'In Vain'.[6]

That refrain 'In Vain', runs through the next two verses. In contrast to that, Paul affirms: 'you know that in the Lord your labour is not in vain' (1 Corinthians 15.58 NRSV). This hope does not undermine our human efforts to implement God's justice on earth. It underpins, supports and strengthens those efforts.

The third reason why belief in an afterlife has been eroded, even among people of Christian faith, is because of all we now know about the interdependence of mind and body, the brain and human consciousness. Modern brain science is based on the premise that alterations in the brain can fundamentally affect mood and behaviour. It is easy to assume, therefore, that when the brain dies that is the end of us for ever. In fact, however, the Hebrew view of the human person, in which a Christian understanding is rooted, is that we are psychosomatic unities, an integrated whole of body, mind and spirit.

Why we should hope

Genesis 2 asserts that 'The LORD God formed a human being from the dust of the ground and breathed into his nostrils the breath of life, so that he became a living creature' (v. 7). Then, at the end of life, as the Church emphasizes and again in the Ash Wednesday service, 'Dust you are and to dust you shall return.' It is true that in the centuries immediately before Jesus belief in the idea of an immortal soul that survived the death of the body entered Judaism

143

and has remained a part of Christian thinking. But language about the soul should now be seen as pointing not to some invisible entity dwelling in the body but to the spiritual vocation and destiny of the whole person. We are not just material bodies, nor are we just thinking bodies. We are bodies with a potential orientation towards God, that can love and pray. Christian hope is rooted in a trust that the person we truly are, who is fully known to God alone, will be recreated or reformed in a form appropriate to an eternal mode of existence, whatever that turns out to be. We die but the person we truly are is lodged in the heart of God and God has willed for us an eternal life. This is what is meant by the credal statement about belief in the resurrection of the body. It is not about being resuscitated from our grave as in a painting by Stanley Spencer, but about a new form of existence altogether. As so often, Gerard Manley Hopkins gets it right:

> Enough! the Resurrection,
> A heart's-clarion! Away grief's gasping, | joyless days, dejection.
> Across my foundering deck shone
> A beacon, an eternal beam. | Flesh fade, and mortal trash
> Fall to the residuary worm; | world's wildfire, leave but ash:
> In a flash, at a trumpet crash,
> I am all at once what Christ is, | since he was what I am, and
> This Jack, joke, poor potsherd, | patch, matchwood, immortal diamond,
> Is immortal diamond.[7]

From one point of view, we are indeed nothing but a joke or a broken piece of pottery. But we are also immortal diamond, a jewel in the mind of God, and the resurrection reveals that truth. In Chapter 2, Ronald Dworkin was quoted to the effect that if we try to make something worthwhile of our lives, 'We make our lives tiny diamonds in the cosmic sands.' From the standpoint of Hopkins, those diamonds are immortal.

We cannot imagine the form those immortal diamonds will take. St Paul quotes Scripture in referring to '"things beyond our seeing, things beyond our hearing, things beyond our imagining, all prepared by God for those who love him"' (1 Corinthians 2.9). Beyond our imagining indeed, but that does not stop us using our God-given imagination as best we can. John Donne wrote:

> All mankind is of one author, and is one volume; when one man dies, one chapter is not torn out of the book but translated into a better language; and every chapter must be so translated; God employs several translators; some pieces are translated by age, some by sickness, some by war, some by justice; but God's hand is in every translation; and his hand shall bind up all our scattered leaves again, for that library where every book shall lie open to one another.[8]

That is one wonderful image. We are translated into a better language. Another image might be that each one of us is like a musical notation. In this life, we are played in flesh and blood but in another it will be in another instrument altogether. However we imagine it, the reality will be very different from what we can envisage now.

The Christian hope is fundamental to Christian faith for three reasons. First, the conviction that runs all through the Bible is that God is a just God, and however much life as we know it now seems to contradict this truth, he will finally act to right all that is wrong and establish true justice. It is this hope that is renewed time and again in the Hebrew Scriptures, focusing in the end on a messianic age. The first Christians entered into this hope and believed that it had been inaugurated in the life, death and resurrection of Jesus. But they saw this as a first stage, a pledge of his coming again in glory to bring about that final stage when 'God will be all in all.'

Marxism has often been seen as a Jewish heresy, with an earthly utopia brought about by human struggle taking the place of the messianic age brought about by God. But even a perfect Communist society, in which everyone gave according to their ability and received according to their need, would not meet the need for true justice; for the lives of countless dead, cut short in their prime, perhaps after a short, miserable and exploited existence, would still cry out to the heavens. As *Libertatis Conscientia*, the instruction on liberation theology issued by the Sacred Congregation for the Doctrine of the Faith in the Vatican, put it in 1986:

> For true justice must include everyone; it must bring the answer to the immense load of suffering born by all the generations; in fact without the resurrection of the dead and the Lord's judgement, there is no justice in the full sense of the term. The promise of the resurrection is freely made to meet the desire for true justice dwelling in the human heart.[9]

It is easy to misinterpret the point that is being made here. It is not being argued that because of the manifest injustice of this life there must be another one to compensate for it. This might indeed be open to the charge of wishful thinking. The point concerns the integrity of the Christian faith. For the conviction that God will in the end establish true justice is fundamental to both Christian and traditional Jewish faith, and without this it is difficult to see how such faith could survive in any recognizable form. Take away that element and the faith as a whole would collapse. So it is a fundamental element in the structure of the Christian faith in the sense that it cannot survive without a belief that there is a wise and loving power behind the universe. Nevertheless it is of course quite possible to argue that the whole structure is a fantasy.

The second reason why hope in the face of death is fundamental was classically put by St Paul when he wrote: 'I am convinced that there is nothing in death or life . . . nothing in all creation that can separate us from the love of God in Christ Jesus our Lord' (Romans 8.38–39). The Christian believer is conscious of a relationship with the living God who has made himself accessible to us in Jesus, and finds it impossible to believe that this would end with death. The Christ who holds us now holds us close to himself through and beyond death.

The third reason for hope is the resurrection of Jesus Christ from the dead, which the New Testament sees as a pledge and first fruit of our recreation. It would be very odd to believe in the resurrection of Jesus but not have hope for ourselves. And without belief in the

146

resurrection the Christian faith collapses. These three reasons are not reasons that will necessarily persuade a non-believer, but the point is to show that hope in the face of death is integral to the Christian faith, not an optional extra.

Some people have suggested that the conventional idea of heaven, in so far as it makes sense at all, has no appeal for them. They claim they would find it boring, a theme George Bernard Shaw had fun with in his play *Man and Superman*. But the dominant image of the kingdom in the teaching of Jesus is of a great feast or banquet – a party to which we are invited and to which we want to go. For many of us, our most relaxed and enjoyable moments are over meals with friends or family. Heaven is above all social. A prominent image in the Bible is of a transformed city, a new Jerusalem, for it is life with one another. St Augustine writes to a much respected widow, Italica, in 408 to assure her that those we love now will be better known then.

> For you ought not to consider yourself desolate while you have Christ dwelling in your heart by faith; nor ought you to sorrow as those heathens who have no hope, seeing that in regard to those friends, who are not lost but only called earlier than ourselves to the country whither we shall follow them, we have hope, resting on a most sure promise, that from this life we shall pass into that other life, in which they shall be to us more beloved as they shall be better known, and in which our pleasure of loving them shall not be alloyed by any fear of separation.[10]

It is a Communion of Saints, a communion of people filled with and transparent to the divine, bonded to one another by a mutually indwelling love. Within that there is the full expression of our creativity, as for example is nicely brought out in Rudyard Kipling's view of heaven in which everyone is an artist. It is also a state in which we are taken out of ourselves, as we sometimes are in this life by music, and in this way experience something of what is meant by a timeless moment. It will be a state in which all we know of earthly beauty is but a pale reflection of the reality then. C. S. Lewis has a fine passage in which he writes:

We do not want merely to *see* beauty, though, God knows, even that is bounty enough. We want something else which can hardly be put into words – to be united with the beauty we see, to pass into it, to receive it into ourselves, to bathe in it, to become part of it . . . that is why the poets tell us such lovely falsehoods . . . if we believe that God will one day *give* us the Morning Star and cause us to *put on* the splendour of the sun, then we may surmise that both the ancient myths and the modern poetry, so false as history, may be very near the truth as prophecy. At present we are on the outside of the world, the outside of the door. We discern the freshness and purity of the morning, but they do not make us fresh and pure. We cannot mingle with the splendours we see. Some day, God willing, we shall get *in*. When human souls have become as perfect in voluntary obedience as the inanimate creation is in its lifeless obedience, then they will put on its glory, or rather that greater glory of which nature is only the first sketch.[11]

Our vocation and destiny, if we will have it, is an unimaginable glory. It should be stressed that this heavenly glory is not to be seen as a reward for good conduct now. It is where the road of faith leads. It is not a medal pinned on the chest or a prize on speech day. It is the life of love coming into its own, all frustrations and limitations finally overcome.

The other hell

The Christian faith, however, not only holds out the hope of heaven, it also warns of the danger of hell. If Christians in the past dwelt too much on the horrors of this, the danger now is just the opposite, that people do not give it a thought. This is not just because of sentimentality. It is the result of genuine moral advance – we have become incapable of thinking of a God of loving kindness sentencing people to eternal torment, and this is a change in our whole understanding of God that has been reshaped by Jesus, both by his parables and by his life laid down for us.[12] These imply that God does not banish us, for he never gives up on us. But that is very different from saying that hell is unreal. Hell is very real. It is very real even now. A character in Samuel Beckett's play *Waiting for Godot* refers to 'the other hell'. Hell is very real, because we can create our own hell both now and in the hereafter and, sadly, we do. Furthermore given free will, hell is always a logical possibility. We are always free to spurn the love from which our being flows. We are always free to turn our back on the love that enfolds us and lock ourselves up in self-preoccupation, self-pity and resentment.

Universalism is the name given to the view that in the end every single human being will be 'saved'; that is, drawn into an eternal loving relationship with God. But while universalism can be the expression of Christian hope it cannot be a certainty, for free will implies that we can always choose to reject divine love. On the other hand, that love never lets us go. Julian of Norwich teetered on the edge of universalism but never fully affirmed it.[13] When T. S. Eliot was converted to the Christian faith he came to know and admire the American scholar Paul Elmer More but was deeply shocked that More did not believe in the reality of hell. 'Is your God Santa Claus?' he asked.[14] What we can say, without fear of logical contradiction, is that the love and mercy of God is infinite. One of William Golding's finest novels, *Pincher Martin*, is ostensibly about a shipwrecked sailor trying to climb up a rock to save himself from drowning. The book describes a desperate struggle to stay alive. As so often with Golding there is a brilliant twist at the end, which it would be unfair to reveal to those who still have the pleasure of reading the novel. It is sufficient to say that the book is about a different kind of struggle, one that has to do with the self and self-knowledge. Towards the end we read:

> The lightning crept in. The centre was unaware of anything but the claws and the threat. It focused its awareness on the crumbled serrations and the blazing red. The lightning came forward. Some of the lines pointed to the centre, waiting for the moment when they could pierce it. Others lay against the claws, playing over them, prying for a weakness, wearing them away in a compassion that was timeless and without mercy.[15]

It is a vivid image of the self as a pair of lobster claws being worn away by 'a compassion that was timeless and without mercy'.

The reality and pain of redemption was brilliantly brought out in one of the great neglected novels of the twentieth century, *Johanna at Daybreak*, by R. C. Hutchinson. The plot concerns a Dutch woman suffering from amnesia. Gradually, to her horror, her memory returns. What she has blocked out is that she betrayed her Jewish husband to the Nazis and abandoned her children, as a result of which one of them had become crippled. Eventually, after facing utter blackness, including the serious temptation to commit suicide, she makes her way to where her children are now living, where she is welcomed.

> Side by side – our hands still touching – we went into the house, to be greeted by the fumes from a pan of milk which someone had let boil over and by the pervasive bickering of children. Enveloped by that orchestra of inveterate sounds and smells, I realised I was back on the painful course I could never finally escape from – itself my one escape from the despotism of the past; the only course which could lead towards an ultimate tranquillity: the harsh, acceptable, exalting road.[16]

There is no sentimentality about this novel. She did something terrible as a result of which her husband is dead and one of her children is maimed. Facing this is harsh and painful. It is hell. Nevertheless the reality is that she was being welcomed back into the family.

This growth in painful self-knowledge is what is indicated by purgatory. It is a theme that runs all through T. S. Eliot's poem 'Little Gidding' in which, among other things, he sets out the gifts reserved for old age. This painful self-knowledge is a fire but that fire is the fire of God's love, at once holding us close and purifying us. For our only hope, or else despair, is 'To be redeemed from fire by fire.'[17]

Blessing God for our being

The Christian faith looks to a final state of affairs, a consummation of the whole creative process, in which the meaning of the whole can be seen and in the light of which all that went before is looked at anew. This final state of affairs can be described in the most abstract terms, as when Paul talks about 'God being all in all'. But if we want more emotional purchase on this we need to explore, in however speculative a fashion, what it might mean in practice. According to the Westminster Shorter Catechism, approved by the Church of Scotland in 1648, 'Man's chief end is to glorify God and to enjoy him for ever.' While this is true as far as it goes, it completely ignores the social dimension so strong in the Bible, the fact that we have a relationship not only with God but with one another. The Church has always affirmed the Communion of Saints, a communion of persons bonded and bound to one another in love. This, we could say, is the final stage of the evolutionary process. First matter, then life, then life becoming self-conscious with the formation of mind, then, in Christ, the emergence of God-filled life. This God-filled life is to be shared with all those willing to be 'in Christ', to bring about that Communion of Saints, that communion of persons indwelt and suffused with the love of God that is built up in this life but transcends space and time.

If we take the teaching of Jesus seriously it is clear that our final salvation depends not only on our relationship to God but even more on our relationships with one another. He taught that if we are bringing a gift to the altar and we remember that someone has a grievance against us, we are first to go and make peace with that person and only then come and offer the gift. Again, nothing is clearer or more insistent in his teaching than that we are to forgive one another as a precondition of our forgiveness by God. Daily, Christians pray 'Forgive us our sins as we forgive those who sin against us.' So that final state of affairs will be one in which human beings are reconciled with one another, not just with God. And it is just this that was the subject of an important challenge by Ivan Karamazov in Dostoyevsky's great novel. Ivan tells some horrific stories of cruelty to children and says 'It is not God I don't believe in, Alyosha; it's just that I return him my ticket.'[18] He then goes on to argue that no future harmony could justify a world in which such things happen:

I do not want a mother to embrace the torturer who had her child torn to pieces by his dogs! She has no right to forgive him! If she likes she can forgive him for herself, she can forgive the torturer for the immeasurable suffering he has inflicted on her as a mother; but she has no right to forgive him for the sufferings of her tortured child. She has no right to forgive the torturer for that, even if her child were to forgive him! And if that is so, if they have no right to forgive him, what becomes of the harmony? Is there in the whole world a being who could or would have the right to forgive? I don't want harmony. I don't want it, out of the love I bear to mankind. I want to remain with my suffering unavenged. I'd rather remain with my suffering unavenged and my indignation unappeased, *even if I were wrong*.[19]

This powerful moral protest has had a particular relevance in the light of the Holocaust and debates between Christians and Jews on the nature of forgiveness.[20] Christians have sometimes spoken too easily about forgiveness, and they need to hear the moral case against forgiving. Nevertheless there are some very powerful examples, by both Christians and Jews, of forgiveness being offered, even when the harm done was terrible indeed. What we can say is that without forgiveness – that is, a willingness, despite the hurt, to maintain a relationship with someone – there can be no ultimate harmony. And if the victim is willing to do that it would seem perverse of others, on behalf of the victim, to refuse to do so, which is the position of Ivan in the passage quoted. This is a point taken up again in Chapter 14, in a further look at Ivan Karamazov's challenge.

What would a triumphant outcome of the whole creative process look like? From the standpoint of human beings, would it not be a state of affairs in which every person was able to bless God for their existence; in which they were able to say, whatever they had been through, they are glad to exist? Existentialists used to talk about being thrown into existence. Certainly we did not ask to be here. We just find ourselves alive. From a Christian point of view, and perhaps even more from a Jewish one, life itself has always been regarded as a good gift. Yet, sadly, every year many people commit

suicide. For whatever combination of reasons, they do not find it
a gift that they want. In that final state of affairs, after whatever
processes of illumination or growth are necessary on the way, will
they be able after all to bless God for their being?

In his poem about his five senses, W. H. Auden wrote:

> I could (which you cannot)
> Find reasons fast enough
> To face the sky and roar
> In anger and despair
> At what is going on,
> Demanding that it name
> Whoever is to blame:
> The sky would only wait
> Till all my breath was gone
> And then reiterate
> As if I wasn't there
> That singular command
> I do not understand.
> *Bless what there is for being*,
> Which has to be obeyed, for
> What else am I made for,
> Agreeing or disagreeing?[21]

In that poem, Auden focuses simply on existence. But if we set this
in the wider context of the divine purpose then we can not only
'Bless what there is for being' but, in the words of the Book of
Common Prayer, bless God 'for the means of grace and the hope of
glory'. The means of grace are there to help us to grow in love, and
the hope of glory is the hope of a final state when we will have
grown in that love to the point of being filled and suffused by it.
At that point, after whatever mixture of beauty and horror had
gone before, all beings would bless God for their existence. Is such
a state of affairs possible? That seems to me the key consideration.
It is certainly a huge hope.

Meanwhile, are we able to bless what there is for being, especially
our own being? Our own life may have many blessings to it, but

153

those who are sensitive will still be racked by the suffering of so many others and wonder whether life is worth it. One such person was Charles Williams. Williams, a close friend of J. R. R. Tolkien and C. S. Lewis, had, according to all who knew him, a great capacity for enjoyment and delight in life. Yet according to the poet Ann Ridler, who knew him well, 'he would not have hesitated to decline the gift of life if he had been offered it', though she went on to add that 'he kept a private fantasy that we might, at some moment, sitting on a ledge somewhere out of Time, have been given the choice and said *Yes.*' Williams did not suffer from clinical depression nor did he have a death wish. It was simply that he was closely involved in the distress of the world. All seemed to him to be built on pain.[22]

This ambivalence about life was brilliantly stated in what Williams wrote about the book of Ecclesiastes, in which all is seen as vanity, all is futility. He sums up its message thus:

> For man's nature is such that he must prefer to live in hope of death than not live or hope at all. The single joy of existence is to know that existence will stop; by so much, and by so much only, existence is better than non-existence. And then it does stop, and there is an end.[23]

Prophets and mystics have their say, 'But Ecclesiastes spoke of what he knew, and of what many millions of others have known after him.'[24]

Charles Williams was a passionate believer in God, especially the incarnation of that God in Jesus. He was also, according to W. H. Auden, T. S. Eliot and those who knew him, the most genuinely good person they had ever met. So what are we to make of this attitude to life? Perhaps we have to say that something like this will be, for a person of faith who is sensitive to the anguish of the world, not just a passing mood but a strand in that faith.

13

Why suffering?

Rejecting the traditional answers

The three previous chapters have been concerned one way and another with evil. The effect of evil, whatever its source or cause, and whether or not it is finally overcome in a life after death, is to inflict suffering. The present chapter focuses on that suffering. Human beings in every period have known suffering. But there are at least two ways in which the question it raises about the possibility of a wise and loving power behind life is more acute today. First, previous generations took a much less sanguine view of what life offered. For the great St Augustine, who was deeply involved in the troubles and travail of this world, a key text was 'He who endures to the end shall be saved.' As the great nineteenth-century wit Canon Sydney Smith put it in his letter of advice on how to cope with low spirits, or as we should say, depression, 'Don't expect too much of human life, a sorry business at best.'[1] In the Fitzwilliam Museum in Cambridge, there is a painting by Salvator Rosa (1615–73) that contains the words 'Conception is sinful, birth a punishment, life hard labour, death inevitable.' It is true that for one of Samuel Beckett's characters, life is 'a punishment for having been born',[2] but most people today hope for something better than that. The much higher living standards for many of us in the West have made this possible, and the huge advances in medicine, not least in painkillers, means that we have far less excruciating pain to bear than our forebears. Second, however, because of 24-hour news coverage, which every minute of the day brings us news of a terrible tragedy or atrocity somewhere in the world, the fact of people suffering is never far away from us. Human affliction is with us all the time.

John Diamond was a much-liked and admired British journalist and broadcaster. Towards the end of his life he had a terrible cancer that left him unable to eat or speak. Yet he wrote: 'Still, bizarrely, I am happy.' He said that against all his professional and personal instincts he found himself 'an obsessive counter of blessings, a glass-half-full optimist rather than a half-empty cynic, a cheery spotter of silver linings cladding the greyest of skies.' Above all he valued a wife he loved and who, bizarrely, as he put it, loved him.[3] A year later, still somehow alive, he was asked to write an article for *The Observer*. The editor wrote to him: 'Just tell me, John, what the hell is the *point* of it all?' John Diamond said he did not feel the need for, nor could he discover any comfort in, religious faith. In the end, he described all the small ordinary details of his day, from reading the papers to watching television, and concluded: 'And that's all it's about.' It was 'about passing time', living for its own sake. 'Why am I happy? Because I am alive . . . this is the point of it all. You aren't happy? Yes you are: this, here, now, is what happiness is. Enjoy it.'[4]

This approach to life when afflicted with a terrible illness remains inspiring. And I suspect that the God who gives us life is far better pleased with someone who celebrates it, as John Diamond did, even though he had no religious faith, than with someone who has a carefully worked-out philosophy of what it is all about but lives without any zest or relish for the passing moments themselves.

That said, there are some for whom John Diamond's answer, admirable in itself, is not enough. The fact is that we are rational beings and as such we quite properly look for wider, more embracing levels of explanation. We do many things for their own sake but those things may still have a further purpose without detracting from the pleasure of the activity in itself. Indeed that purpose might enhance the pleasure. Some love cricket, say, for its own sake. At the same time they may strive hard to win a match or a league, and that striving will form part of their enjoyment. Furthermore it is the essence of the whole scientific endeavour that we look for ever more embracing explanations of what is happening. We might, for example, observe herds of animals in the bush moving from one place to another. We know there is some reason for this, some purpose, and we conclude that they are looking for new pastures, the old ones having been eaten or dried up. Beyond that, we know they are driven to do that by the evolutionary imperative to stay alive and reproduce. As beings with a rational intelligence we cannot help but look for further levels of explanation. Of course, at one level life is indeed to be lived for its own sake. But is there a wider purpose in which this is set? Religion is many things to different people. But for some of us it is not primarily about finding comfort or discovering a need for it within oneself, as John Diamond suggested. It is simply about posing a rational question and exploring possible answers.

A perfectly proper answer to the question is, 'We don't know', or even more strongly, 'I don't think it is possible to know.' But as rational beings we will continue to probe the issue to the end of our days. As was argued in Chapter 2, it remains a proper question.

For someone who lives life in the faith that there is a wise and loving power behind the universe, the question takes a particular form and is posed with a special intensity, for so much of what happens in life seems to contradict that faith, indeed to shake its very foundations. It is not surprising, therefore, that Jews and Christians, for example, have tried to find some rational meaning in such happenings.

After all the qualifications, traditional answers were of two types. Either God is punishing us for our sins or he is testing our faith that we might grow in character. Both answers are unacceptable. The plain fact is that it is often the innocent who suffer most – children, for example. Moreover as we would not think much of a friend who tripped us up and broke our leg to see if we would develop qualities of patience, no more can we think highly of a deity who acts in a similar way.

In 1755, Lisbon was struck by an earthquake that left 50,000 dead. It shook up optimists, Christians and satirists alike. Some Christians saw this event as a divine punishment. John Wesley, for example, suggested it was a punishment for the sins of the Inquisition, which had its origin in Spain. Sadly that strain of thought is still present today. It emerged again with the advent of HIV, from which 1.5

million people died in 2013 alone, and which some people blamed on homosexuality. Others at the time of the earthquake suggested that in God's great plan every event is specially designed so that it turns out for the best. This was brilliantly satirized by Voltaire in his novella *Candide*, in which Professor Pangloss argues after each calamity that all is for the best in this best of all possible worlds.[5]

An even fiercer critique of simplistic and insensitive attempts to see the hand of God in events was written by that intensely devout Christian, Samuel Johnson. Soame Jenyns had written a book on the nature of evil, and reviewing it in 1757 Johnson wrote:

> The only end of writing is to enable the readers better to enjoy life or better to endure it; and how will either of those be put more in our power by him who tells us we are puppets, of which some creature not much wiser than ourselves manages the wires? That a set of beings unseen and unheard are hovering about us, trying experiments on our sensibility, putting us in agonies to see our limbs quiver, torturing us to madness that they might laugh at our vagaries, sometimes obstructing the bile that they may see how a man looks when he is yellow; sometimes breaking a traveller's bones to try how he will get home; sometimes wasting a man to a skeleton, and sometimes killing him fat for the greater elegance of his hide?[6]

Johnson experienced much suffering personally through both the struggles of his life and the severe depressions he suffered. He was a passionate Christian believer but he also knew he had no final explanation for the existence of evil. Attempts to justify suffering such as that provided by Soame Jenyns struck him as facile and cruel and aroused his bitter scorn.

The great strength of the book of Job in the Bible lies in its main, central section, when Job refuses to accept any explanation that God is punishing or testing him. He protests against all such ideas. Earlier in the Bible the patriarch Jacob had to face the fact that his dearly loved son Joseph had been eaten by wild animals: 'Though his sons and daughters all tried to comfort him, he refused to be comforted' (Genesis 37.35). This kind of protest is a strong feature of Judaism, if a lesser one in Christianity.[7] It was well put by the former Chief

Rabbi, Jonathan Sacks. He argued that we should reject any philosophy that encourages an acceptance of the world as it is but should cry out against it and act to change what is happening. He writes:

> Abraham's protest, and Moses' and Jeremiah's, were not cries wasted in the wind. They were cries born in the cognitive dissonance between the world that is and the world that ought to be. The only way of resolving this dissonance is a deed. That is the difference between faith-as-acceptance and faith-as-protest. The only way to deal with slavery is to lead the people to freedom. The only way to confront the evils of the *polis* is to build a more just social order, with special emphasis on loving the stranger.[8]

This is a crucial point that must not be lost sight of, and I return to it later. However, it does not mean that nothing can be said or that what might be said should lead to acceptance. If we have accidents on our roads we can understand why: humans, being what they are, and cars being potentially lethal, there will be accidents. This does not and should not lead to an acceptance of the fact, rather to renewed efforts to make our roads safer. Similarly we might come to see that there are risks in the very idea of creation without this in any way leading us to be complacent about what happens in the world. So what we can and should do is to try to understand why the world is the way it is. Could the world be other than it is and we still be here with our special human capacities?

Could the world be other than it is?

In one sense, of course, God can make any kind of world he chooses. But could he make a world that produced us with our capacity for rational thought and choice if it had been fundamentally different from the one we know? The first obvious point, mentioned in Chapter 4, is that to exist at all is to exist with a life of one's own. This applies at every level of creation, the subatomic, amoebas, bananas, lobsters, monkeys and ourselves. From the simplest to the most complex structures, everything goes on being itself while at the same time forming part of other structures that go on being themselves. When God says 'Let there be', he lets things go. He gives them genuine autonomy, a freedom to go their own way. That is what is meant by creation. If we value being part of creation, that is what is involved. It cannot be any other way, for any other way would not give us the autonomy that is integral to the very concept of existence. A tiger is a tiger is a tiger. You are you and I am I.

Yet it could be asked: could not the forces of nature be kept in leading reins so that they always worked directly for our physical safety? This is a question that will be returned to. First, however, is the fact that the autonomy of creation has become conscious and self-conscious in us human beings. We know and know we know, we can choose and know that we are choosing. Again, there is an inescapable implication of this. If we are genuinely free, as was argued earlier, in however narrow limits, then there might be occasions when we deliberately choose what is wrong. If we can choose to do what is right, then we also have the option of doing the opposite.

Some scholars have argued that we could have been created in such a way that we always freely choose the good. If our choices arise out of us, then we could have been given a nature that always wants the best. The philosopher John Hick argued that while this might be a theoretical possibility in our relations with one another, there is a fatal flaw if we consider a possible relation to God. For we would in fact be like people who had been hypnotized. We would think we were freely doing something but in fact we would have been put under hypnosis and directed to do it. And God would be the hypnotist. He would know that our choices had not been freely chosen but that he himself had put them into us. So if his purpose was to create beings who were genuinely free to choose for themselves, then that purpose would have been contradicted. The fact remains that if we are free to do good we are also free to do evil, with all the consequences that follow from this. We have not been hypnotized, and we are not robots.

One of the implications of being able to choose is that we must be able to consider the consequences of our actions and assess them.

Choosing is much of the time a matter of weighing up one thing with another and, if there is a moral dimension, which set of consequences is likely to maximize good and minimize harm. This means we need a predictable, stable environment. We need to know the sun will rise and apples fall, water at a certain temperature and pressure will freeze and at another boil. We take these considerations into account and plan our lives accordingly. This has huge implications for the question raised just now about nature being kept in leading reins. Or, to change the metaphor, if nature were like a piece of clay being moulded in such a way as to keep us from physical hurt, then the world would be totally unpredictable and we would be incapable of making rational choices. Indeed because rational choice is essential to what it is to be a human being, we would no longer exist as such. Consciousness, with our ability to think and plan and choose, would simply not have developed.

What we call the laws of nature are observed regularities on the basis of which we make predictions about the future. Because of the law of gravity and other basic facts about the world, I walk and do not float to the ceiling; I sit on a chair and it holds me up. If these were treated as so much clay being moulded to stop us being hurt it would in fact be tantamount to a series of non-stop miracles. Miracles, events that cannot be accounted for in terms of known natural laws, need not be ruled out as a matter of principle but it is possible to see why, if there are any, they must be very few. For every event has repercussions over the whole globe. If I am driving a car and this is about to crash into the one in front of me but a miracle occurs to pull me up short in 10 feet rather than 20, that might be fine for me but what about the car just behind me and the one behind that? To stop a multiple pile-up there would have to be a succession of miracles. And if it were a world in which such suspensions of the ordinary laws of nature occurred every time there was the possibility of an accident, we could not make rational decisions about the future. It would be an Alice in Wonderland world in which rational minds could not have developed. The inescapable fact is that for rational minds to have developed, we need a stable, predictable environment, and that means that the laws of nature have to continue to operate even when their effect is to do me immediate harm. In real terms, this means that we have earthquakes that shake down houses, volcanoes that erupt and send their lava down into villages, tsunamis and whirlwinds. This is the hard reality of nature doing its own thing.

Those examples, however, do bring out another point. Life has evolved on a cooling star. We are told that if it was any colder and the earth was solid, life would not have emerged. We are also told that if it was any hotter, again, life as we know it could not exist. The earth has cooled enough to form a solid crust but remains warm enough to support life. But the maximal conditions for life also allow for the possibility of volcanoes and earthquakes. When these cause destruction and harm to us they are usually termed material evils. We also know that what has made evolution possible, as mentioned in Chapter 4, is the combination of random mutation with the principle that only organisms which adapt successfully to their environment can survive. It is this combination of fixity pro-vided by the latter, with the possibility of something new provided by the former, that allows ever more complex organisms to emerge. However, random mutation means that not every mutation is beneficial and copying errors cause disease.

But these material evils, which are simply the result of natural forces following their own course, take on a stronger moral dimension when we take into account that those who suffer most as a result of them are the poor and powerless. When, as a result of climate change, the sea levels rise, it will be above all the poor in places like Bangladesh who will be affected, for they live on land from which the better off have been able to move away. The rich are able to build concrete reinforced buildings to protect them from earthquakes; the poor are not. If the world were truly just and the earth's resources distributed equally, there would not be this imbalance. So although human beings are not directly responsible for material evils, the fact that the poor suffer disproportionately as a result of them is a consequence of human choice, our millions of individual decisions.

I believe, whatever final view a person comes to on these issues, we have to face the fact that if we value being able to take responsibility for our own lives and make our own decisions, this carries with it the risk we will sometimes choose wrongly. Furthermore I believe we similarly have to face the fact that this requires that we are born and grow up in a stable, predictable environment, for this is fundamental to being able to think about the future and make rational decisions. What is much more difficult to work out is why we should have been created as vulnerable bodies in a material world, moreover one that has evolved over billions of years. One traditional answer to this goes under the name of the principle of plenitude. God creates angels, archangels and the whole company of heaven, or so the story goes, and then continues to create every possible form of being, so that we are a kind of rock garden at the bottom of the divine estate in which the divine creator grows some things he has not grown elsewhere. The problem with this myth is that there is no limited garden God has to fill up; there are no pre-set limits on what God can or cannot do except those that contradict logic or his nature.

It may be that the answer lies in the nature of freedom of choice. Perhaps choice is inevitably something related to growth and development. Young children are very much at the mercy of their immediate requirements. What they want they want now, and they find it hard to think in terms of delayed gratification, of putting aside those wants in favour of other people or a long-term good. To grow up and mature is to be less at the mercy of our immediate desires. We take a wider, longer view. Of course, this often fails to happen, and to some extent it fails in all of us. But we recognize that genuine maturity means a greater width of choice, in the sense that we are less at the mercy of natural desires and can choose other options. This highlights one of the difficulties about belief in angels, especially a fallen angel, at least as conceived as beings with personalities. For personality, as we experience it, is a result of growth and development, and this includes the choices we make. For it is through our choices that we make ourselves into a particular kind of person.

It is difficult to conceive of a being conjured into existence fully formed and with a full capacity for choice. It would seem then that the capacity to make mature choices is not something that can come fully fledged but emerges, if it does, only as part of a process of growth and development. From this it follows that we have to be rooted in something like a biosphere whose essential characteristic is one of growth and development; in other words, a material world in evolution.

This is linked to another idea, once suggested by Austin Farrer, that we have been created at an epistemic distance from God – that is, a distance of knowing – and this distance is ensured by our being part of a material world that, as it were, acts as a screen between us and the divine. If we had been created in the immediate presence of God then we would have had no real freedom to respond or not. We would have been drawn as moths are to a candle or metal filings to a magnet. For this reason God creates us at a distance of knowing so that when we are born we have no immediate sense of God, and in so far as we do come to faith, it will be as part of a process of growing and developing. Now it is true that some people, according to their own account, are aware of being born with an immediate awareness of the divine. Notable examples are Thomas Traherne and to a lesser extent William Wordsworth, but they seem to be very much the exception. It is also true that many people witness to a dramatic conversion, when their lives are turned upside down. But those conversions, however sudden, will in fact come to people who have made many choices before that, some good, some bad. Their capacity for choice will have been enlarged.

So it is of the essence that we are growing, developing beings, able to enlarge the genuine area of choice in our lives and able to respond little by little to those intimations of immortality, as Wordsworth termed them. By enlarging the genuine area of choice I do not of course refer to the millions of possibilities we now have as consumers. In that market, we are still being addressed as a consumer. True enlargement of choice is when we are aware of the fact that we need not simply go along with all the enticements to consume, but we can do other things with our time and money. It also includes the capacity to recognize and respond to truth as it touches and takes hold of us. Blaise Pascal emphasized that the God of the Bible is not obviously present to us. He is *Deus absconditus,* a hidden God. We can find this God only if we seek him. The world both reveals and hides him, and in faith there is enough light for those who want to see but enough darkness for those who do not. As Pascal wrote:

> For it is not true that everything reveals God, and it is not true that everything conceals him. But it is at the same time true that he hides himself from those who ask him for miracles, and that he reveals himself only to those who seek him, because men are at the same time unworthy of God and capable of knowing him.[9]

So as we grow up we become aware that there are choices to be made, and some of these involve putting aside our immediate desires in favour of other people or a longer-term goal. From the perspective of faith, there will also be glimmers of light leading us on; always leaving us free, never forcing us, but offering a way forward into the life of God. There will be moments of illumination and as someone once put it, faith is life lived on the evidence of its highest moments.

Faced with the brutality and horror of the world it is natural to think that if God is omnipotent he could have created one that is less harsh than the one we have now. But it is meaningless to ask God to do what is illogical. So, summing up the argument to this point, first God cannot give us a life of our own with the capacity to make choices without it following that some of those choices might be badly wrong. Second, following on from this by a logical extension, although the basic constituents of the universe could in theory be different, for minds to develop at all there would have to be those observed regularities on the basis of which we can make reliable predictions about the future that we call laws of nature. There is an inevitable impersonality or indifference about all such laws whatever form they take or in whatever universe they might operate. Third, though this is much more speculative, for our freedom in relation to God to be genuine, creation must allow for a process of growth and development.

In the previous chapter and again later in this one, I refer to the Christian hope that in God there is an ultimate state of affairs in which death will be no more and divine love will fill and irradiate all things. It might therefore be argued that if God can create a new world, heaven, at that point, without pain and anguish, why has he created this one so differently? But a fundamental point about heaven is that as far as we are concerned there is continuity and well as discontinuity with the life we know now. From the human point of view, as opposed to that of angels, heaven is the consummation of a process. As a result of our finite, flesh-and-blood existence we have become a particular person. Physical existence has given us a medium in which to shape ourselves. Death has served its purpose in giving us a limited lifespan in which choices have to be made and a self fashioned. Heaven, from our point of view, takes up what has been wrought over time and achieved in space. After that process a further physical death would serve no purpose and although there will be further growth as a result of the fire of God's love, which brings with it the fire of painful self-knowledge, it is the person or self that has developed on earth that experiences this. To put this another way, heaven is only heaven because we are 'in Christ'. This is Christ incarnate, crucified, risen and drawing all people to himself. Again, it is a process, something achieved, which comes to its glorious consummation. God in his infinite power creates the stuff of glory, the medium in which eternity is lived out, but death and the laws of nature with their indifference to human well-being will have served their purpose and no longer have a rationale.

14

Refusing to be comforted

A person can be persuaded by what I have said so far and still be left with a fundamental problem. It was powerfully stated in Albert Camus' novel *The Plague*. A town is in the grip of a deadly plague and an agnostic doctor is working night and day to alleviate the suffering. Present too is the parish priest, Father Paneloux. They meet over the bedside of a dying child. All night they wait, both unutterably moved. The priest says to Dr Rieux: 'Why did you speak to me with such anger just now? . . . I too found that unbearable to watch.' The doctor replies that he can feel only outrage and revolt at what they are experiencing, to which the priest responds: 'I understand . . . It is outrageous because it is beyond us. But perhaps we should love what we cannot understand.' The doctor shakes his head:

> 'No, Father,' he said. 'I have a different notion of love; and to the day I die I shall refuse to love this creation in which children are tortured.'
>
> A shadow of profound distress passed across Paneloux's face.
>
> 'Ah, doctor,' he said sadly. 'I have just understood what is meant by God's grace.'[1]

It is the doctor's remark that stays in the mind, his refusal to love a scheme of things in which children are put to torture. The problem is that 'this scheme of things' is the world as we know it, and as far as we can understand the matter, for reasons explored above, it could not have been fundamentally different. Disease is just another expression of nature doing its own thing, going its own way. There may indeed have been an element of human culpability in the way the plague took hold and spread, but again that brings up the reality and seriousness of the choices we make, always with the risk of making the wrong ones.

The logical conclusion of the doctor's remark is that if a world in which children suffer so much is the only one available then it might have been better had there been no world at all. This was the conclusion drawn by Ivan Karamazov in Dostoyevsky's great novel referred to in Chapter 12. He tells some horrifying stories of children being hunted to death and says:

> If the sufferings of children go to make up the sum of sufferings which is necessary for the purchase of truth, then I say beforehand that the entire truth is not worth such a price . . . we cannot afford to pay so much for admission . . . It is not God I don't accept, Alyosha, I merely most respectfully return him the ticket.[2]

He was not prepared to have life under those conditions. When all that can be said has been said, here is the heart of the challenge. God was not justified in creating a world if an inevitable result was to produce situations when children die in agony from disease or human cruelty.

At this point it is not possible to continue the discussion without bringing into focus specifically Christian considerations discussed earlier in the book. First, there is the conviction, based on the picture of Jesus being tortured to death, that God shares our suffering to the full, even to the sense of total abandonment. As Simone Weil put it: '"My God, my God, why hast thou forsaken me?" There we have real proof that Christianity is something divine.'[3]

This is not just a once-for-all historical event, though it is grounded in what actually happened to Jesus on the cross. Rather, as Pascal put it in words later used by Georges Rouault for his painting of Jesus in the Garden of Gethsemane, 'Jesus is in agony until the end of time.' However, this claim, even if true, as I believe it to be, offers only limited comfort. It may indeed be a source of great strength for an adult believer going through a difficult period to know that God in Jesus shares his or her suffering, but it cannot be of much direct use to a sick child before the age of understanding. Genuine sympathy, which, in the Greek from which the word comes, means suffering with another person, is crucially important pastorally when offered by friends or priests. But this does not actually change the situation of the person. He or she may still be in agony, may still die prematurely.

However, the Christian conviction is that God in Christ not only shares our agony but in the resurrection has undone death. For this is a promise of an ultimate state of affairs when suffering and death will be no more and God's purpose of love will prevail over all things. I do not myself think that the challenge posed by Dr Rieux and Ivan Karamazov can be faced without taking into account this full spectrum of Christian belief. Yet this way of considering the issue is just the one that was subjected to such a fierce moral challenge by Ivan Karamazov, as was quoted in Chapter 12. He argued that no future state, however wonderful, could justify the kind of world in which cruelties of the kind he describes occur. This argument must be taken with the greatest moral seriousness.

I would suggest that the question whether life is worth living is one we can only answer for ourselves, not for anyone else. Sometimes when, for example, we see someone totally paralysed or afflicted in some hideous way, we think to ourselves that we could not cope in that situation, we would rather be dead. Yet the fact is that so many who are in that situation don't say that. Not all – but there are very many who would agree with what the journalist Malcolm Muggeridge once said: 'I believe that at all times and in all circumstances, life is a blessing.' The physicist Stephen Hawking would not perhaps use the word 'blessing' but he has remained remarkably positive about life even though he was diagnosed with a rare progressive form of motor neurone disease at the age of 21, so that his expectations for life then appeared to him zero. He reflected on this more than 50 years later and said that he had been fortunate in almost every other way. His work and sense of humour had kept his spirits up. The point is that the question whether, despite everything, life remains a blessing is one we can answer only for ourselves.

Then even in this life we know instances of how some terrible period in it can fade into oblivion in the light of some wonderful new experience. It may not have been forgotten but the pain has gone. A couple who have been separated for some time and as a result developed a number of misunderstandings that turned into quarrels are reunited, talk the issues through and find a new closeness as a result. In that new stage of the relationship, the previous painful months just drop away. So in the Christian vision of the future all will look different. 'There shall be an end to death, and to mourning and crying and pain, for the old order has passed away!' (Revelation 21.4). All will be able to bless the Lord for their being.[4]

The community of heaven is heaven not just because its inhabitants are at one with God but because they are at one with one another. It would not be heaven otherwise. And this means a mutual acceptance that is rooted in God's acceptance of us. When we think of some of the terrible things we do to one another it seems impossible and outrageous that a victim should come to have a positive relationship with the perpetrator of such appalling suffering. Yet as was argued in Chapter 12, if heaven is to be heaven, that has to be the case. As John Donne put it: 'In heaven, we shall have communion of joy and glory with all, always; *ubi non intrat inimicus, ned amicus exit*. Where never shall come any in that loves us not, nor go from us that does.'[5]

Even in this life there are some remarkable examples of victims developing a positive relationship with someone who tortured them. One of them was Leonard Wilson, later Bishop of Birmingham, who was tortured by the Japanese and later went back to confirm the person who had tortured him. Another was Eric Lomax, the author of *The Railway Man*.[6] He had joined the army at the age of 19, was captured in the fall of Singapore and sent to work on the notorious railway from Burma to what was then called Siam, where one in three allied prisoners died. After the war, traumatized by the event, he dreamed of getting his hands round the neck of his tormenter and beating him to death. Then, with the help of skilled medical help he worked through these memories and sought out the man who had tortured him. They arranged to meet on the bridge over the River Kwai, and although Lomax arrived in an unforgiving mood he was so overcome by the deep contrition of the Japanese veteran that after a few days they could even laugh and talk about their wartime experiences.

I do not think we should take this or similar stories as in any way detracting from the horror of what someone might have gone through. There is no easy forgetting or consolation. But there are people, like Leonard Wilson and Eric Lomax, who at great personal cost show us that what seems impossible, even morally repugnant, is achievable.

The Scottish poet and novelist Edwin Muir had an idyllic childhood in the Orkneys but his family fell on hard times, and he himself went to work in a bone factory in Glasgow. There he had a terrible vision of humans being nothing but animals. He did not have an easy life but in the course of it he recovered his sense of a spiritual dimension to existence and in particular of the immortality of the soul. From this came some wonderful poetry, including 'One Foot in Eden', which very much reflects his personal journey as well as the experience of the world as a whole. It begins:

> One foot in Eden still, I stand
> And look across the other land.
> The world's great day is growing late,
> Yet strange these fields that we have planted
> So long with crops of love and hate.

In terms of Muir's own experience, he still has part of him in that Orkney childhood Eden, 'One foot in Eden still, I stand'. The world about him now is so full of love and hate. Yet there is a strange paradox.

> But famished field and blackened tree
> Bear flowers in Eden never known.
> Blossoms of grief and charity
> Bloom in these darkened fields alone.
> What had Eden ever to say
> Of hope and faith and pity and love
> Until was buried all its day
> And memory found its treasure trove?
> Strange blessings never in Paradise
> Fall from these beclouded skies.[7]

Here we have to be very careful not to think in terms of a calculus with later blessings justifying earlier ills. I think Muir got it right when at the end of his autobiography he reflects on his own periods of depression:

> Now and then during the years I fell into the dumps for short or prolonged periods, was subject to fears which I did not understand, and passed through stretches of blankness and deprivation. From these, I learned things which I could not otherwise have learned, so that I cannot regard them as mere loss. Yet I believe that I would have been better without them.[8]

I love that statement – its understated pain and honesty. He wrote that out of the blankness and deprivation came things that otherwise he would not have learned, but nevertheless it would have been better to have been without them. Life was sometimes very difficult for him and in one poem he writes about his depression in terms of devastation. He knew what it was like to live with famished field and blackened tree. He would rather not have gone through all that yet he recognized that out of it came some of the aspects of life we most cherish. As he put it above: 'Strange blessings never in Paradise / Fall from these beclouded skies.'

As stated earlier, I reject the idea that God plans unpleasant things for us that we might grow in character. I also reject the idea that God planned this hard world full of suffering in order to bring about these 'strange blessings'. It is rather, as I also argued earlier, that we cannot have the kind of existence we value, as rational beings responsible for own lives, without living in an environment that has the kind of character of the world as we know it. According to the Christian faith, God wills to create free beings able to grow in wisdom and love, and we can understand how this might necessitate a world like ours. Within this tough environment it is the experience of many that God works to bring 'Blossoms of grief and charity . . . hope and faith and pity and love'; qualities that would have had no opportunity to emerge and show themselves in an innocent paradise. These are 'flowers in Eden never known.'

Again, it is important not to draw the wrong conclusions from this. I once ministered to a family whose daughter had been shot dead by a former fiancé. The mother said to me: 'I suppose God must have wanted Jennie[9] more in heaven than we did.' This is an understandable attempt by a devout soul to try to find some religious meaning in a terrible tragedy. But it is misconceived, as I tried gently to explain to her. Some happenings, indeed many happenings, are clean contrary to what God wants. Yet that family will have found some comfort and strength in the loving support of those who cared for them. They will have discovered themselves living at a deep level of existence, coming up against the grain of things where God is to be found.

What this means in practice is that in the experience of grief and charity we find a quality of existence that adds a new dimension, that makes everything else seem different; the cause of the grief is not forgotten or the pain of it underestimated, but it is taken up into a larger whole. We may not be able to see the meaning of that larger whole, indeed the attempt to do so at that point may be entirely inappropriate, but the charity is as real as the grief. The most frequent occurrence of this experience, of course, is when someone we love dies and family and friends are wonderfully supportive, but there are many other instances and many wonderful people and families who in different ways witness to this. There are those like the academics Frances Young and Margaret Spufford, mothers of very severely disabled children who need round-the-clock care, who are still able to testify to 'strange blessings'. Margaret Spufford used the image of a stunted oak. This does not have the majestic beauty of an oak full grown, but we have all seen trees that have not grown as they should, or have grown old, that have yet taken on a different, spare kind of beauty. As Andrew Brown wrote in his obituary about her book *Celebration*:[10]

> It is a tough, clear meditation on illness and suffering in the light of her faith in God. Margaret itemized without flinching the cruelties she had discovered in creation, in her daughter's life and on the wards at Great Ormond Street, where she once reached out to stroke a crying child's face and was stopped by a nurse who told her that the slightest touch could break the child's bones. She could reconcile

none of these things with the idea of a loving and benevolent God and she made no attempt to do so. Instead, she was convinced that God shared in the sufferings of his creation and that through the symbolic recreation of Jesus's acceptance of death in the eucharist it could somehow, sometimes, be made bearable.[11]

Then there is Jean Vanier, through his experience of L'Arche, the community for children with severe handicaps, who has witnessed across the world to the extraordinarily powerful effect such children have had on him and his whole understanding of God.

For some people, there can be a counterpart to this in the experience of the arts, especially music. This is suggested in Rebecca West's 1956 novel *The Fountain Overflows* when one of the characters, a musician, asks: 'What's the good of music . . . if there's all this cancer in the world?' to which someone else replies: 'What's the harm of cancer, if there's all this music in the world?'[12] This must not be taken too literally. There is a great deal of harm in cancer. But it hints at the truth that it is the quality of things that count, and that includes not just the loving support we can give one another but music or great literature, which can also take us into a deeper dimension of life.

When all this has been said, and whatever truth there is in it as a most wonderful and glorious hope, as I believe there is, a cry of protest still arises in our hearts. Life as we know it is, too often, simply intolerable. Nothing in the future can justify what is happening now. So we come back again to the words of Jonathan Sacks that there is a 'cognitive dissonance between the world that is and the world that ought to be. The only way of resolving this dissonance is a deed.'[13] Hope and protest do not exclude each other; rather they belong together. For as St Paul emphasizes, hope that is seen is not hope. Hope is for what is not yet seen, which from a human point of view still has to come about. This hope is not acceptance of things as they are but an active striving to make them different in the conviction that what is of God will not be lost but find an ultimate fulfilment.

15

Rebellion or acceptance?

Albert Camus and Simone Weil

The novelist Albert Camus had profound respect for the thought of the philosopher Simone Weil. This was not simply for her intellectual brilliance but because they had a shared dislike of purely abstract thought and a passionate desire to find an appropriate form of life in a world beset by suffering. Both were politically active. He called her 'the only great spirit of our times' and gave a laudatory review of her book *The Need for Roots*. He also played an important part in the posthumous publication of her writings. There is much too in Weil's thought with which he agreed, but there remains a funda-mental difference between them, one that goes to the very heart of my own book.[1] For Camus, the suffering in the world was such that the only possible response was one of protest, revolt and rebellion. This was vividly depicted in the character of Dr Rieux in *The Plague* quoted earlier. It is no less present in Camus' novel *The Outsider*, especially in the way the main character rails against the ministrations of the chaplain in prison. More generally it was the metaphysical view set out in his book *The Rebel*.

Simone Weil rejected this attitude of rebellion for three reasons. First, it presupposed a view of God in which she did not believe: 'To rebel against God because of man's affliction, after the manner of [Alfred de] Vigny or Ivan Karamazov, is to represent God to oneself as a sovereign.' In the same notebook entry, she had written: 'We have to *empty God of his divinity* in order to love him. He emptied himself of his divinity by becoming man, then of his humanity by becoming a corpse (bread and wine), matter.'[2] Second, she had a fear that what began as a protest against suffering would become just another form of self-assertion. For her, what was needed was attention to the suffering of the sufferer. It involved a self-emptying in contemplating the other. However, it could be pointed out that Dr Rieux is indeed fully attentive to the pain of his patients. His rebellion against a universe that allowed such suffering does not rule out a genuine self-transcendence for the other. The third reason she gives is that metaphysical rebellion like that of Camus and Ivan Karamazov detaches a person from reality. For her, reality means accepting the world as it is in all its destructiveness and horror: 'Not to accept some event taking place in the world is to desire that the world should not exist.'[3] This brings us to the crux of the issue. It was fundamental for Simone Weil that we love the order of the world in all its impersonality and everything within it, without however blurring the distinction of good and evil. Two points must be made, however, to avoid giving a misleading impression of Weil as either insensitive or passive in the face of evil. First, the suffering of others was literally agony to her. Her writings reveal a person who felt within herself the pain of the world in a more intense way than any other modern writer.[4] Second, it was for her an unconditional duty not just to attend to that suffering but to alleviate it in so far as it was in her power. But with those two important qualifications, it is fundamental to her thought that we have to accept and come to love the world in its totality. In order to see the importance of this for her, and the implications for living, it is necessary to try to see her thought as a whole.[5] For Weil's response to the kind of attitude expressed by Camus raises an acute challenge to most humane views, whether secular or religious.

Born in 1909 into an agnostic Jewish family, Simone Weil emerged from the French educational system as one of the intellectual elite of the time. She was politically active on the left, supporting trade unionists, and went to Spain with the anarchists in the civil war. At the same time she was opposed to totalitarianism of any kind, including Communism. What distinguished her from most of her contemporary intellectuals, however, was her deep desire to identify personally with all forms of suffering. This for her was the only way we could begin to think truthfully about the world. Truth for her was not abstract but reality in all its harshness. For that reason, she spent a year doing piece work in car factories despite the fact that then and later she suffered from excruciating headaches and was also physically clumsy, so it was always a desperate effort simply to go on. When war came she left France only reluctantly, because she knew her parents would not leave without her, and went to America, but she was always passionate in her desire to get back to Europe to take part in the struggle. She came to England and worked for General de Gaulle, all the time hoping to be sent to France in the front line of danger. While in England she refused to eat more than people in France at the time were eating, and partly as a result of this and partly as a result of TB, she died in a sanatorium in Ashford in 1943. She wrote a number of essays and books but the main key to her thought is in the 2,000 pages of notebooks she kept over the years. A brilliant intellectual, many of her pages are about abstruse maths, which she regarded as essential to clear thinking, and the history of science, in both of which she had a keen interest. But it is her reflections on philosophy and religion that are at once so fresh, startling and challenging. Many are so extreme that the first reaction is to disagree with them, but as T. S. Eliot wrote in his introduction to her book *The Need for Roots*,[6] what is important with Weil is not agreeing or disagreeing but trying to enter into what she is saying. This is difficult and complex and even 80 years later it remains an ongoing task.

The nub of the challenge presented by Weil is her passionate conviction that everything that happens in the world, including all that we call evil, is the will of God, and that to grow in the spiritual life means accepting this, even when what happens strips us of everything we regard as worthwhile. For her, the need to do this arises out of the very nature of creation, for creation is a world of necessity from which God has withdrawn his presence. There are resonances here with the thought of the cabbalist Isaac Luria (1575), for whom creation was an act of *tsimtsum*, of God withdrawing into himself leaving a space empty of the divine. There is, however, no evidence that Weil was influenced by Luria.

The dominant feature of our present sphere of existence is that it is a closed world of cause and effect. Its essential character is that of necessity, a key word for Weil. Because it is autonomous, which in the case of human beings emerges in the form of the self-determining 'I', it is also sinful because it is other than God, and this is the essence of sin. So for her, to use traditional language, creation and fall are one. Creation comes into being already sinful. At the same time God, through his eternal Word, enters into this creation, so there is a split within the Godhead itself, what she terms a crucifixion. The actual incarnation of God in Jesus and his crucifixion simply make explicit what is inherent in creation itself. So there is a fundamental paradox about God in being at once plenitude, and total absence or crucifixion.

Although in her scheme of things there seems no real role for human choices making a difference to the course of events, fundamental to her thought is the idea of grace, of which she had a powerful experience. Reading George Herbert's poem 'Love' one day and trying to concentrate despite her crippling headaches, she said: 'Christ himself came down and took possession of me'.[7] So although she deliberately chose not to be baptized because she did not want to distance herself from other religious and intellectual traditions that meant so much to her, especially Greek thought, the self-emptying of God in Christ, above all his crucifixion, became the controlling centre of her thought. Everything remains determined, but grace enables a person to accept everything as the divine will.

Life in the end strips us of everything, and to live truly means living on the basis of this truth. We are all born with a desire for what we think is our good. Little by little these goods are taken away from us until in death we are left with nothing. That is the point, what she termed the void, reaching out with nothing for nothing, at which we find God, for that absence is also a presence. That is the end point of human life, the point to which it is designed to lead. That is why she felt that to think truly, that is realistically, she had to identify with the most extreme forms of human suffering. She accepted the point of Ivan Karamazov that innocent suffering could not be justified by future compensation. Yet she still argued that such suffering had to be totally accepted.

> To say like Ivan Karamazov: nothing can possibly make up for a single tear from a single child. And yet to accept all tears, and the countless horrors which lie behind all tears. To accept such things not simply in so far as they may admit compensations but in themselves. To accept that they should exist, simply because they do exist.[8]

However startling and extreme some of her lapidary statements, there is a depth in her thought that not only resonates richly with a more orthodox Christian view but challenges it. So a critical assessment is necessary from a more traditional Christian standpoint.

First, contrary to Weil, creation is not sinful in itself. God created the world and 'Behold it was very good'. Blessing, not sin, is the original condition. The fact that the world contains independent centres of existence, and in the case of human beings, conscious selves, is not sinful but a freely given sphere of existence.

Second, human choice, within however narrow limits, makes a difference to the way the world goes – for good or evil. Grace not only enables one to accept the world, it enables one, in however small a degree, to change the world.

Third, life is full of good things and it is right that in the words of the Book of Common Prayer we should say 'We bless thee for our creation, preservation and all the blessings of life.' Simone Weil did in fact have a great capacity for appreciation of this world's goods. When she spent time in Italy her notebooks are full of joy over the natural and cultural treasures she is encountering. But it is difficult to avoid the conclusion that in her desire to identify personally with the worst that life offers she lost sight of this in her overall view. Here she stands in contrast to Camus and his great love of life in North Africa, which comes across especially in his notebooks.

The simple fact is that life consists of two parts, living and dying. Simone Weil so concentrated on the latter that she appears to neglect the former. It is said that when school inspectors visited Ampleforth, the Roman Catholic public school, they asked the headmaster what the purpose of education at the school was. He replied: 'To prepare pupils for death'. In a world obsessed by living, this reply came across as rather strange and shocking. Simone Weil would have strongly agreed with it, however. And it is indeed true that traditionally the Christian Church has tried to help people prepare for death and so to 'die daily'. Yet at its best it has done this while also helping them affirm life with its many blessings.

One person who kept the balance well was the Jesuit priest and palaeontologist Teilhard de Chardin. In one of his prayers, he first gives thanks for all that is strong and healthy within him and then goes on to pray that he may also see 'the forces of diminishment' as equally God's touch upon him.

> It was a joy to me, O God, in the midst of the struggle, to feel that in developing myself I was increasing the hold that you have upon me . . . Now that I have found the joy of utilising all forms of growth to make you, or let you, grow in me, grant that I may willingly consent to this last phase of communion in the course of which I shall possess you by diminishing in you.[9]

Another person who kept the balance well was D. H. Lawrence. Few have been more affirmative of life than Lawrence but he was also clear that if we are going to sing the song of life, we have to learn to sing the song of death as well: 'For without the song of death the song of life becomes pointless and silly.'[10]

Working for change

And so returning to the challenge presented by Simone Weil: the human spirit revolts against accepting that everything that happens is directly the will of God. We feel that something has gone wrong; things happen that God does not will, certainly in the case of wicked human choices. However, there is no escaping the conclusion that God, on any Christian view, in creating the universe knew what it would be like, knew we would be cruel as well as kind, knew the long toll of anguish that would ensue and yet chose to go ahead with it. According to the argument presented in earlier chapters, much of the suffering is due to the fact that we can have existence only as we know it in an environment akin to the one we have with its regular natural laws. So although God is ultimately responsible, because he created the world knowing what he was doing, suffering is not directly willed by him; it is an indirect, inevitable consequence of creating rational beings in the stable environment they need. Nevertheless we cannot escape the fact that God, if we believe in him in anything like a traditional form, is responsible for the world's being here, for our existing in the kind of world we have.

Also, according to the argument in Chapter 12 and further developed in Chapter 16, this life is not all there is. Christian hope looks to a consummation of God's loving purpose beyond time and space when 'All shall be well; and all manner of thing shall be well.'[11]

These arguments have three implications. First, far from accepting all that happens as the will of God, we should protest against what causes suffering and work to end it. Second, in the case of one's own life, when something appears inevitable and inescapable, say the limitations of old age or an incurable illness, we should look to the grace of God to bring some blessing from it, for oneself or others. Third, in the case of other people we have no locus or right to take the same attitude to their affliction as we do to our own. If some good is to come out of their situation, only they themselves can look for this. We can but live with a Christian hope that in the end all who live will be able to bless God for their being. So in terms of the words of Edwin Muir quoted earlier, all the goods of Eden – health, happiness and well-being – are to be cherished, and when they are threatened we will seek to protect them. At the same time we can hope that faith and pity and love, these blossoms of grief and charity that bloom in our darkened fields, will not only come to suffuse all things but be recognized by all as being of surpassing worth and joy. We may know that charity in our own grief and experience strange blessings of faith and pity and love falling from our own beclouded skies. But we cannot presume that this is so for others or in any way imply that it is, least of all with facile talk about clouds having silver linings. At the same time we can have a deeply rooted hope that what we might have begun to discover for ourselves will prove true in the end for humanity as a whole.

It was pointed out above that Weil's rejection of metaphysical rebellion on the grounds that it distracted us from paying attention to sufferers in their suffering did not apply in the case of Dr Rieux, nor does it in very many real-life examples. But is this sense of protest compatible with a religious spirit? Two considerations suggest it is. First, there is a powerful tradition in the Hebrew Scriptures from Abraham onwards of argument with God, of protests that challenge his justice. The Bible does not teach resignation to things as they are, even when God is worshipped as the supreme creator. Second, some kind of dualism has been either inherent in traditional accounts of the faith or a strong temptation even for serious believers. Dualism suggests that there is another power at work, antagonistic to God and his purposes. Within traditional orthodoxy there was the idea of a cosmic fall, Satan being responsible for the ills in nature and leading humans astray. That did not let God off the hook for Satan was a created entity, even though one that had gone wrong. But people who shared this myth had an obvious target to blame for what had gone wrong in life, namely Satan, and the question of who created Satan could be pushed one stage further back. Outside the traditional framework we can see how strong the appeal of dualism has been when we remember that the great St Augustine was, for many years before he became a Christian, a Manichaean, believing in a form of dualism widespread in the Roman world at the time, which suggested that matter itself was evil. Other forms of dualism held that matter had been created by a lesser god and was to be escaped from. The point is that in one way or another people were conscious of the difficulty of attributing to God responsibility for everything and sought ways of avoiding doing so. Although we cannot share such myths in either their Christian or sub-Christian form, I would suggest that they alert us to the need to keep the tension between protest and acceptance.

It is not necessary to get into vast and difficult subjects like God's alleged omnipotence and omniscience to live a life of faith. Believers will have a basic conviction that the one in whom they trust, the God made manifest in Jesus, in creating the world out of his goodness and wisdom knew what he was doing. They will also have a profound hope that what divine wisdom and goodness initiated will have a successful outcome.

What is being suggested is that we have to live with a proper tension between protest at the way the world is on the one hand, the attitude of Camus and Ivan Karamazov, and trust and hope on the other. We cannot resolve, nor should we try to resolve, that contradiction. For it can be resolved only in reality, not thought, when the divine purpose of love has won through. What this means in practice is that we should celebrate all that makes for human well-being, and when this is threatened or diminished by poverty, ill-health, unkindness or for any other reason, we should do what is in our power to remedy the situation. Our protest will take a practical form. With what is outside our power the sense of protest will still be there, even if helpless. If some good comes out of our efforts or those of others, that is precious but it should not take away from an implacable refusal to accept a world in which there is so much innocent suffering.

As so often, some words of Austin Farrer get the balance right:

> Good breeds more good than any evil can. It is a special revelation of God's divine power that he is able to bring some good even out of evil. But his use of evil for good ends does not immediately sterilise it; it continues to breed after its own kind.[12]

Part of the good that divine power brings out of evil is our greater awareness of evil and a desire to change the world for the better. As quoted in Chapter 2, on the grave of Karl Marx in Highgate Cemetery are carved the words 'The philosophers have only interpreted the world in various ways. The point however is to change it.' Christians will have a great deal of sympathy with that statement, for two reasons. First, because every interpretation of the world is limited by its time and place. History, it has been said, is a continuous interaction of the past with the present. Every historical period gets reinterpreted in the light of the changing present; philosophical interpretations of the world work under the same limitation. This means that the true meaning of the world can be fully seen only at the end. It is only in the light of the end that everything can be seen in its proper perspective. Even Christians, who believe that the heart of the matter has been disclosed to us in Christ, do not claim to know the meaning of the whole. As St Paul put it at the end of his hymn to love in 1 Corinthians 13.12: 'For now we see through a glass, darkly; but then face to face: now I know in part; but then shall I know even as also I am known.' That is the King James Version, or as a modern translation, the Revised English Bible, puts it: 'At present we see only puzzling reflections in a mirror.'

The central, all-important truth has been revealed, which is that three things last for ever: faith, hope and love, the greatest of these being love. But how this love finds its final triumphant form in God's everlasting kingdom we do not know. We know the heart of the universe to be the love made manifest in Jesus Christ and we put our trust in that now. This carries with it the hope that in the end that love will prevail over all things. But that hope is not a passive waiting for something to happen. It is an active expectation that God will work through us now towards that final goal.

So Christians should agree with Karl Marx's statement that the world has to be changed. We have to allow God to work through us to bring about that final state of affairs. It is action that is called for, not resignation; anger at the evils of the world, not acceptance. So I come back to what Jonathan Sacks said, quoted in Chapter 13. For Christians, like Jews, live not only rooted in faith but upheld by hope. This is not mere optimism and it comes at a price, for 'Those who hope *refuse to be comforted* while the hoped-for outcome is not yet reached.'

They are driven by:

the cognitive dissonance of a faith that sees the world as it is while refusing to let go of its vision of the world as it ought to be. In that world, contradiction is to be resolved not by philosophical thought but by redemptive deed.[13]

One implication of this is that the religious believer will never cease to be painfully aware of the suffering of existence and the challenge this poses to a belief in a wise and loving power behind human existence. The very nature of his or her belief may make this an acute problem in a way that it might not be, exactly, for the person without faith. This is because for believers it will be an existential one, a threat to what is most fundamental to them as people, namely their faith. Furthermore it will be a challenge that never goes away and may indeed become more intense as the years go by. Austin Farrer wrote:

An overmastering sense of human ills can be taken as the world's invitation to deny her maker, or it can be taken as God's invitation to succour his world. Which is it to be? Those who take the practical alternative become more closely and more widely acquainted with misery than the onlookers; but they feel the grain of existence, and the movement of the purposes of God. They do not argue, they love; and what is loved is always known as good. The more we love, the more we feel the evils besetting or corrupting the object of our love. But the more we feel the force of the besetting harms, the more certain we are of the value residing in what they attack; and in resisting them are identified with the action of God, whose mercy is over all flesh.[14]

16

Beyond tragedy

Sad but still affirming life

To celebrate World Book Day on 2 March 2006, a poll was commissioned among readers of various kinds about the kind of ending they preferred. Some 41 per cent wanted a happy ending. Only 2.2 per cent chose a sad one. The author Adele Parks made her own position quite clear: 'I think my readers deserve happy endings: there's enough grimness to deal with without adding to it.' William Boyd took a totally contrary point of view, arguing that serious literature has to reflect the grimness of life. Happy endings lead us into the realm of fantasy, romance and fairy tale, as he put it, which he disliked.

One of the interesting questions is whether the Christian faith offers a happy ending or not. Clearly many people think it does and this is one of the reasons they dismiss it as so much fantasy, romance and fairy tale, to use William Boyd's terms. Whether it does or does not offer a happy ending is one of the underlying questions of this chapter, and if so, what kind of happy ending that might be. Closely related to this is whether it is possible to have happy endings, in novels or in religion, that have integrity; that is, endings that take the tragic dimension of life with all seriousness, that don't pretend that suffering is other than it is and that offer a conclusion that comes across as real as the tragedy. The challenge, both in relation to novels and from the standpoint of religious faith, is essentially the same: how to convey a deep continuity, a hard core of integrity running right through both the suffering and its resolution, without the latter being open to rejection on the grounds of fantasy, romance and fairy tale.

In *The Story of Lucy Gault* by William Trevor, the Gaults are an old Protestant family living in Cork. As a result of a series of terrible mishaps, Lucy loses all touch with her parents and lives an unfulfilled, solitary life. When old she is visited by nuns. They were amazed that despite the fact that calamity had shaped her whole life story, she was tranquil, and towards the end Lucy reflects on her years alone, her years of visiting a man in an asylum, in these words:

> What happened simply did. The cow parsley was white every month of May when she drove away from the high spiked gates, the fuchsia bright in autumn at the cottage where the greyhound was always on the wall. Her visits were the joy in that inmate's life, an old keeper said years later, before they pulled the place down. A flicker in the dark, he said, even though the inmate never knew who she was.
>
> She should have died as a child; she knows that but has never said it to the nuns, has never included in the story of herself the days that felt like years when she lay among the fallen stones. It would have lowered their spirits, although it lifts her own because instead of nothing there is what there is.[1]

It is difficult to imagine a more calamitous, tragic, sad story. Yet her spirits are lifted when she reflects that she did not in fact die, 'because instead of nothing there is what there is.' In Auden's words, considered in Chapter 12, she can bless God for being.

A novel that goes beyond this in not only affirming life as such but in celebrating what can be achieved, despite the tragic dimension, is *Stoner* by John Williams. The reception history of this novel is interesting in itself. First published in 1965, it was appreciated but not raved about. It was then forgotten and its author died. Then suddenly at the end of 2013 a number of reviewers recommended it as one of the best novels of recent decades and it began to gather a wide range of readers who came to agree with this judgement. It is a simple story of a man from a very humble rural American background who educates himself and obtains a position as a university lecturer. After some initial success a colleague turns against him and conducts a vendetta against him for the rest of Stoner's career. Not only is he denied a justified promotion, he is forced to teach the most elementary courses rather than the more demanding ones for which he was suited – certainly enough to make a person bitter and twisted. As he is dying, Stoner 'contemplated the failure that his life must appear to be'. He reflects on his failures in friendship, love and marriage in the words:

> And he had wanted to be a teacher, and he had become one; yet he knew, he had always known, that for most of his life he had been an indifferent one. He had dreamed of a kind of integrity, of a kind of purity that was entire; he had found compromise and the assaulting diversion of triviality. He had conceived wisdom, and at the end of the long years he had found ignorance. And what else? He thought. What else?
>
> What did you expect? He thought again.[2]

Then as he continues to reflect on the theme of 'What did you expect?' something shifts inside him. He becomes aware of the world outside, the sound of laughter, the beauty of students walking across the grass:

> A kind of joy came upon him, as if borne in upon a summer breeze. He dimly recalled that he had been thinking of failure – as if it mattered. It seemed to him now that such thoughts were mean, unworthy of what life had been . . . a sense of his own identity came upon him with a sudden force and he felt the power of it. He was himself and he knew what he had been.[3]

Neither Lucy Gault nor Stoner are heroic figures. They are characterized rather by a certain stoicism and endurance when life went against them so badly. But in their different ways they are grateful for the life they have been given. At the end of her life Lucy Gault's spirits are lifted 'because instead of nothing there is what there is.' William Stoner experiences a kind of joy because 'He was himself and he knew what he had been.'

The vindication of value

There are other novels that emphasize the moral dimension more strongly than these but still have unresolved failure and devastation as their theme. This raises again the question of the nature of tragedy, raised in Chapter 5 in relation to Nietzsche. I use the word to indicate not just a particular form of drama but the large number of novels today that have a story that seems irredeemably tragic.

In popular usage, the word 'tragedy' indicates serious loss and destruction; something that cannot be put right, which brings grief and lasting sadness. For Rowan Williams, the key word is 'unresolved'. We may say, for example, about a car crash in which a mother and her children are killed, leaving a grief-stricken husband, that it is really tragic. There is no consolation to be found. It was suggested in Chapter 5 that tragedy on the stage usually suggests larger forces at work that are involved in that destruction – fate or the gods or economic or social factors. This does not mean that human choices do not matter. They do, but very often they seem the weaker element in a wider, inexorable drama. Then, as F. R. Leavis stressed, the value of what is destroyed is heightened by its destruction, indeed may only have been brought into sight by its loss.

Literature that has these marks of the tragic is crucially important from a Christian point of view for a number of reasons. First, it is a healthy antidote to all superficial optimism, a Pollyanna or Panglossian approach to life. Second, because a tragedy highlights and reinforces the value of what is destroyed, and we can find something in this that is deeply satisfying, there is a hint that there might be a meaning to life that goes beyond a simple calculus of pain and pleasure. We sense that something big is at stake. Philip Roth's novel *The Human Stain*,[4] which reflects a strong set of values, sets out a tragic history. The central character, Coleman Silk, has been a highly successful dean in a university, but an innocent remark of his was interpreted as racist and he was hounded out of his teaching post by a highly ambitious French woman whom he had appointed. What only gradually emerges in the story is that Coleman had himself been born into a black family, but because his skin was quite fair he had deliberately recreated himself as a white person and sundered all ties with his past, including his parents. After his humiliation in the university he finds himself in a powerful sexual relationship with Faunia Farley, who all her life had been a victim, first of child abuse and then of a violent husband. Her ex-husband, thrown off balance by his service in Vietnam, kills Coleman and Faunia. The story is told as a modern tragedy, as indicated by the opening quotation from *Oedipus the King*. Coleman, who by talent and a superb effort of the will has recreated himself as a successful white man, is tripped up by wider forces at work in society. So, incidentally, in a different way, is the ambitious young French woman who brings about his downfall. *The Human Stain* is a good title. But it could equally have been 'Human Sin' – for we are conscious of the racism of American society, the brutality of the Vietnam War, pretentious scholarship and academic infighting. These are forces that make victims of some and stain everyone involved in one way or another.

In this novel, as in a good number of modern novels, however much they reveal of human brutality and sadness, there is an affirmation, explicit or implicit, of important values; values that may in fact be starkly outlined just by their apparent denial, by the way events unfold. In *The Human Stain*, for example, it is the racism in society and the brutality of the Vietnam War that have stained the individuals. But there is also one character depicted who exhibits a genuine integrity – Coleman's sister. She retained her black identity and remained in her original environment, working as a nurse. Furthermore she refused to go along with the rest of the family who vowed to have nothing more to do with Coleman because he had said he would cut himself off from them. She kept in touch with him over the telephone but never revealed his secret to anyone. At the same time she made it clear that she strongly disapproved of what he had done. She is a woman of strength and integrity, who remains true to her strong values. Though not a central character, she points up the falsity and hubris of the world to which the others are conforming.

As suggested earlier, there are a number of reasons why we are deeply suspicious of happy endings, much though we may enjoy them on occasions. First, life, at least for a great many people, is indeed grim. This sense of the grimness of life was sharply accentuated during the cruel twentieth century with the Holocaust and other genocides, two world wars, Stalin's purges in the Soviet Union, the millions of deaths under Mao in China and numerous other atrocities. The fundamental shift in consciousness brought about by the twentieth century is vividly illustrated by the reception history of the German fifteenth-century artist Matthias Grünewald's *Isenheim Altarpiece*. This is a painting of the crucifixion that more vividly than any other depicts Christ in his pain and agony. It was hardly discussed in the nineteenth century but the turning point came when it was shown in Munich for a year during 1918–19. It suddenly promulgated and reinforced a German self-image as a martyred angst-ridden people, and then later in the century came to express the self-image of an anguished European people as a whole.

Second, as discussed earlier, at the same time as this reappraisal, Sigmund Freud was imbuing Western culture with the notion of wishful thinking. It is not surprising, therefore, that the dominant Christian image in painting in the twentieth century is Christ crucified, and attempts to convey the resurrection of Christ or anything hopeful are very few. In his draft notes on religion and theology, W. H. Auden wrote: 'Today, we find Good Friday easy to accept: what scandalizes us is Easter: modern man finds a happy ending, a final victory of love over the Prince of this World, very hard to swallow.'[5]

But does Christianity offer a happy ending? Is it perhaps better read as a tragedy? There are the wider forces at work bringing about the death of Jesus, with the sense of everything being predestined. There is Jesus himself wanting to confront the powers that be. There is his denial and betrayal. The traditional view does of course affirm the reality of the resurrection as a pledge of the final victory of God's love over all that is evil, including death. But on that ancient view heaven was reserved for true believers; the fate of millions of others was more sombre – not a happy ending for them. In fact Christianity has never offered a happy ending in any straightforward sense; rather it has emphasized the inescapable tragic dimension to life. Sin has seeped into every aspect of human existence. Christ was rejected and crucified and God remains implacably opposed to our wickedness and smugness. Yet even without a traditional view of the resurrection or a belief in the afterlife, people have been able to see something victorious in the life of Jesus. They have wanted to affirm the values he stood for, values sharply highlighted by the very fact that he was spurned and killed. It is that paradoxical tragic experience that gives us an insight into the true value of things, even when life is devastating. On this view the resurrection of Jesus is a shift in consciousness in the minds of his followers. From defeated abject disciples contemplating the total failure of his mission, they come to see that mission, and in particular his life of total commitment to the concept of a divine kingdom of love, as something worth committing their lives to; as something victorious however the world goes. This is a view of the resurrection held by some theologians. The earliest manuscripts of the earliest Gospel, St Mark, break off rather abruptly with no resurrection appearances. They end with the women finding the tomb empty and the words: 'They said nothing to anyone, for they were afraid' (16.8). The reason for this is disputed but for some people this lack of a conclusive ending has held a profound moral and spiritual appeal. I am not arguing the truth of this view of the resurrection; indeed it is not an adequate account and not one I share. It is mentioned now in order to highlight the point that Christianity does not necessarily offer a happy ending in any conventional sense. It can be understood in a way that is congruous with the deepest insights of morally serious people who sense the tragic character of existence. A character in an Iris Murdoch novel is asked his view of Christ and he replies:

> I have to think of him in a certain way, not resurrected, as it were mistaken, disappointed – well, who knows what he thought. He has to mean pure affliction, pointless suffering, the deep and awful and irremediable things that happen to people.[6]

That is a powerful but characteristic approach of a modern novelist to Christ. But a writer might also want to suggest that in the values that Christ taught and represented there shines out something of abiding worth; and that these shine out all the more clearly against the dark background of his rejection and death. Further, we could say that it was this that changed the hearts and minds of his first followers to the extent that they gave up their own lives to follow him. Christ was resurrected in and through them.

To understand the resurrection of Christ in this way, in terms of a change in the hearts and minds of the first followers of Jesus, has great moral and spiritual appeal. But is it enough? Is it enough to give hope that life is not finally tragic? And if it's not finally tragic, is it possible to talk about resurrection, about redemption, about things coming right, in a way that doesn't immediately come across as a happy ending that is simply tacked on; one which fails in artistic and moral integrity, which lacks the kind of moral and spiritual grittiness we discern in a tragic view of existence? The rest of this chapter will discuss four works that suggest a stronger view of resurrection might be possible.

He is always beside us

Shusaku Endo, who has been called the Japanese Graham Greene, is best known for his two novels about Christians in Japan in the sixteenth and early seventeenth centuries. Christianity was brought to Japan in the middle of the sixteenth century and by 1614 there were 300,000 Christians in a population of 20 million. However, Japanese rulers turned against them and thousands were tortured and crucified to force them to renounce their faith. *Silence* deals with this terrible period of persecution, the title of Endo's novel referring to the apparent silence of God at this time. *Samurai* is his other novel, set in the early seventeenth century when things were just beginning to look ominous. It follows the fortunes of four Samurai, or minor gentry, on a diplomatic mission to Mexico and Europe to explore the possibilities of trade. Travelling with them as an interpreter is a Jesuit priest. As the politics change, the Samurai first embrace the Christian faith then abandon it. Because they had embraced it, they went back to Japan knowing that torture and death awaited them. The novel brings out powerfully not only the universal self-seeking and misery of humanity but the difficulty that

Japanese culture finds in seeing anything admirable in Christianity, especially the figure of someone crucified.

In Mexico, the mission came across a strange man, a Japanese living with the Indians. It turned out he had been brought up in Japan by a Christian priest and himself had become a believer, indeed a monk. But he had become disillusioned with the institutional Church both in Japan and Mexico and now lived with the Indians trying to help them. As he says:

> Wherever the Indians go, I shall go; where they stay, I shall stay. They need someone like me to wipe off their sweat when they are ill, to hold their hands at the moment of death. The Indians and I – we are both without a home.[7]

When the Samurai go home one of them pulls out a piece of paper given him by that strange Japanese. Written on it were the words

> He is always beside us.
> He listens to our agony and grief.
> He weeps with us.
> And says to us,
> 'Blessed are they who weep in this life, for in the Kingdom
>   of Heaven they shall smile.'

Then he reflects:

> 'He' was that man with the drooping head, that man as scrawny as a pin, that man whose arms stretched lifelessly out, nailed to a cross . . . for some reason he did not feel the same contempt for him he had felt before. In fact, it seemed as though that wretched man was much like himself as he sat abstractly by the hearth.[8]

Later he speaks to his servant Yoso, a Christian who had followed his master through thick and thin.

> I suppose that somewhere in the hearts of men, there is a yearning for someone who will be with you throughout your life, someone who will never betray you, never leave you – even if that someone is just a sick, mangy dog. That man became just such a miserable dog for the sake of mankind.[9]

Then the Samurai leaves his home for virtually certain death.

> The swirling flakes seemed like the white swans of the marshlands. Birds of passage which came to the marshland from a distant country and then departed for a distant country. Birds which had seen many countries, many cities. They were himself. And now, he was setting off for another unknown land . . .
>
> 'From now on . . . he will be beside you.'
> Suddenly he heard Yoso's strained voice behind him.
> 'From now on he will attend you.'[10]

It is a novel that powerfully reinforces the point that in our time it is Christ crucified to whom we respond. In Japan, of course, in addition to the catalogue of horrors mentioned earlier by Endo there was the bombing not only of Hiroshima but Nagasaki, the traditional centre of Christianity in Japan. But the novel is not just about universal suffering and the failure of every human endeavour. In all this, a voice is heard: 'From now on . . . he will be beside you . . . From now on he will attend you.'

The next novel to be discussed is Patrick White's *Riders in the Chariot*. In an Australian suburb Himmelfarb, a Jewish refugee from Germany, is strung up in a mock crucifixion. After his death strange things happen to the four main characters, the four riders in the mystical chariot of the title. Two ladies talking together after the event were at pains to emphasize that there was no miracle: 'Only, there was no miracle. Definitely no miracle!',[11] Mrs Colquhoun shouted. But she and Alf Dubbo, who trusted in fate, Mrs Godbold, a solid washerwoman, and Miss Hare all have mystic visions of one kind or another and their lives are changed. In worldly terms, all are marginal, all failures, yet in their different ways they have all been given a glimpse into the truth of things through Himmelfarb's death. Through that death they have all, in different ways, been taken up into another dimension.

William Golding's *Darkness Visible* is the least known and least understood of his major works. The central character is Matty, who emerges out of a fire in London's Blitz most terribly disfigured. From his earliest days and throughout his life, people cannot bear even to look at him. Matty's mind is a strange one, scarred as it is by his terrible experience, but it keeps formulating a pressing question: 'Who am I?' The question is never answered but Matty comes to reformulate it as: 'What am I for?' and begins to feel he exists for something. When he is working as an odd-job man in a smart prep school there is a terrorist attack as part of an attempt to kidnap some of the boys and he is killed. But he seems to become one of the flames in the fire, fire being a key image in the book. The flames of fire force one of the terrorists who is fleeing with a boy to let him go. Even more remarkable is what happens next. While a child, Matty had met Mr Pedigree, a paedophile, who had been revolted by Matty; but Matty through some strange misreading of the relationship had become devoted to Mr Pedigree. At the time of Matty's death Mr Pedigree is in the grip of one of his compulsive cycles and is waiting outside a public lavatory to seduce some children. Matty appears to him in a vision of gold to free him from his enslavement.

> He came and stood before Pedigree and looked down at him. Pedigree understood that they were in a park of mutuality and closeness where the sunlight lay right on the skin.
> 'You know it was all your fault Matty.'
> Matty seemed to agree; and really the boy was quite pleasant to look at![12]

As in *Riders in the Chariot* there is a contrast between two worlds. When the terrorists attack the school in order to kidnap the children the media is focused on all the outward events, with television camera crews and reporters rushing everywhere. The death of an obscure, strange odd-job man is not noticed. But while the world watches these dramatic outward happenings another plot is all the time being worked out. Matty is an agent of redemption. He knows his life exists for something and his death releases him from the constraints of time and space for the redemption of Mr Pedigree. I am not arguing the merits or the demerits of these novels, though both Patrick White and William Golding won the Nobel Prize for

Literature. The point is that they are examples of serious attempts, which in no way shy away from the most appalling features of human existence, to think about resurrection and redemption in a way that is 'real' and has artistic integrity.

Flannery O'Connor was born in 1925 and died at the age of 39 after years of a painful, incapacitating illness. Two facts are fundamental to her writing. She was a practising Catholic and she lived in and wrote about the American Protestant Bible Belt that she knew well – usually poor whites, uneducated, bizarre and caught up in fundamentalist religion. Flannery O'Connor wrote very definite things about the challenge of being a believing Christian novelist in a largely secular Western world. She said, for example, that one of the reasons she wrote about the unfashionable people she did is because their faith and passion reveal truths hidden from politer society. More deeply, at a time when Christian truth is ignored or rejected, to believe in the Incarnation and redemption makes a total difference to the way one sees things. As she put it, the Christian novelist 'will have, in these times, the sharpest eyes for the grotesque, for the perverse, and for the unacceptable'.[13]

This is certainly borne out by *Darkness Visible*, just discussed. O'Connor has also written:

> The Christian novelist is distinguished from his pagan colleagues by recognizing sin as sin. According to this heritage he sees it not as sickness or an accident of environment, but as a responsible choice of offence against God, which involves his eternal future. Either one is serious about salvation or one is not. And it is well to realize that the maximum amount of seriousness admits the maximum amount of comedy. Only if we are secure in our beliefs can we see the comical side of the universe.[14]

She believed that the Deep South of the United States still reflected the sense that our human condition is a broken one: that sin is a reality. And though the South was not Christ-centred it was certainly Christ-haunted.

No less important to her is the working of grace in her characters. As she put it: 'My subject in fiction is the action of grace in territory held largely by the devil.'[15] So even when the central character of a story is what she terms a freak, she is trying to show what we have in us to become and what we could become. There is in her stories, she says, an action that is totally unexpected yet totally believable. Such an action indicates that grace has been offered. Frequently it is an action in which the devil has been the unwilling instrument of grace.

Flannery O'Connor wrote both novels and short stories. One of her short stories, which illustrates this attitude, is called 'Parker's Back'.[16] It is only 20 pages but she worked on it over many years and finished it as she was dying in hospital.

Parker had left school early and ran away to join the navy, but one leave had failed to return, so after nine months' punishment was discharged. He did odd jobs to earn a living and had married Ruth, whom he thought ugly but somehow wanted to attract. Parker's obsession in life was tattooing. His whole body, except his back, is covered in tattoos. One day after an accident on a tractor he went to a local town and had his whole back tattooed as well, with a Christ Pantocrator in mosaic design – the rather stern figure usually found on the inside of the dome of an Orthodox church – which he just happened to see in a book of designs and about which he knew nothing. Parker goes home and, in expectation that his wife, who is religious, will be pleased, shows her his back. She does not recognize the Christ of the Orthodox tradition, beats him over the back with a broom and Parker goes into the yard to weep.

Parker was too stunned to resist. He sat there and let her beat him until she had nearly knocked him senseless and large welts had formed on the face of the tattooed Christ. Then he staggered up and made for the door. His wife looks out and sees him crying like a baby. Suddenly the reader sees the longing and suffering of Parker; and the longing and suffering of Christ in him. Parker is an ordinary, uneducated, unattractive, rather useless man with a futile obsession, caught up in an apparently loveless marriage. Yet he is also a man who, almost totally uncomprehendingly, knows that God is ceaselessly searching him out and who senses the glory of God to be revealed in him.

We can see how well this story fits in with Flannery O'Connor's philosophy that a Christian writer in a time of indifference and unbelief has to have a narrative that is totally surprising and shocking. It is hardly a happy ending in any straightforward sense of the term. But of course it all depends on of what the end, in the sense of the *telos* or goal of human existence, consists. If it is that the glory of God might be revealed in and through us, then this is what the author sees in even such an unlikely person as Parker.

This chapter has suggested that the Christian faith takes the tragic dimension of life with utter seriousness and does not try to evade or gloss over it in any way. At the same time it has been argued that some outstanding writers have been able to show how it is possible to take that tragic dimension fully into account and at the same time to affirm life; indeed to go beyond that to celebrate the worthwhileness of an achieved life even in the face of outrageous fortune. Furthermore tragedy can actually make more luminous the values that apparently lose out in the world of events. Most ambitiously of all, certain writers, such as Endo, White, Golding and O'Connor, are able to convey how such values, incarnate in Jesus Christ, are not just kept alive in the imagination for future generations but have a transcendent dimension. They are able to do this in such a way that the story holds together as a whole, with no loss of integrity when it moves beyond tragedy to a hopeful consummation. There is no Panglossian optimism and at the same time no artificial happy ending in ordinary terms. Tragedy and an imaginative grasp of what might lie beyond tragedy occupy the same moral universe. Christians will want to remain alert and sensitive to the tragic nature of existence. At the same time their faith enables them to go beyond tragedy: not to a happy ending in any ordinary sense of the word but to participation in a new kind of life that has no end. These novels suggest how this might be possible, in particular to believe in the resurrection of Jesus Christ and the hope of everlasting life in a way that has both moral and aesthetic integrity.

If the wonderful truth of the Christian faith is difficult to convey in a way that rings true in literature, it is even more difficult in the visual arts. It is easy to depict the crucifixion and it is not surprising that artists so often used it as a symbol for the terrible suffering of the twentieth century. But visualizing Christian hope in a way that is as real as the suffering is very difficult and not often achieved. A rare example in the visual arts is *The Golden Crucifixion* by Norman Adams. In this painting, the suffering is all there: the three crucified figures, the wailing women, the sinister soldiers. But all this is against the background of the yellow and gold of the butterfly wings, suggesting a transcendent glory going out to the world.[17]

17

Towards a true humanism

Faith and scepticism

Humanism is a debated notion and terms like 'secular humanism' and 'Christian humanism' are contentious.[1] However, a definition of humanism accepted by the humanist organizations of more than 40 countries reads:

> Humanism is a democratic and ethical life stance, which affirms that human beings have the right and responsibility to give meaning and shape to their own lives. It stands for the building of a more humane society through an ethic based on human and other natural values in the spirit of reason and free inquiry through human capabilities. It is not theistic, and it does not accept supernatural views of reality.[2]

Any Western definition of humanism is likely to be criticized from the perspective of the Dharmic religions of India and South East Asia as being speciesist, for they would see humans as bound up with the whole of creation. The position taken here is that human beings do have a special role and responsibility within creation as a whole and that from the standpoint of Christian faith the icon or model of this is Jesus, the true human being. This can, however, coexist with radical questioning. More than this, genuine questioning implies an openness to the force of the objection, if there is one, and the persuasive appeal of a position different from one's own. Moreover as a person grows in faith the capacity to take on board even the most fundamental objections increases. For T. S. Eliot, scepticism was not an alternative to faith but an essential element of it. One of the reasons Eliot was drawn to Pascal was that he 'faced unflinchingly the demon of doubt which is inseparable from the spirit of belief'.[3] As Eliot himself wrote: 'the more conscious becomes the belief, so the more conscious becomes unbelief: indifference, doubt and scepticism appear . . . A higher religion imposes a conflict, a division, torment and struggle within the individual.'[4]

Indeed what made Eliot's Christian faith different from that of many was that in contrast to his family's Unitarianism, for example, it incorporated so much radical doubt. Often when someone is first converted, whether to the Christian or another faith, he or she becomes less open to other points of view. But the opposite of doubt is not faith but certainty, for doubt can coexist with faith. What comes across in the letters of Eliot at the time of his conversion is how undefensive he was about his new faith. When his new stance was criticized, he was remarkably unfazed and continued to have good relations even with people who had sharply, and for the wrong reasons, attacked his work. He remained friends with people who had very different views of life from his own (nearly all the people he knew), continuing to offer objective literary judgements about the literary worth of their writing. There was no insecure defensiveness about him. This was because he had first faced in himself all the worst things others might say. Conrad Aiken, for example, had criticized Eliot's essay *For Lancelot Andrewes* as showing 'A thin and vinegarish hostility to the modern world . . . a complete abdication of intelligence' and so on, to which Eliot replied:

> You may be right. Most of these criticisms I had anticipated, or made myself. Thrice armed is he who knows what a humbug he is. My progress, if I ever make any, will be purging myself of a large number of impure motives.[5]

More widely, he welcomed the new hostile situation in which Christians now found themselves, for it released the Christian faith from what had burdened it since the eighteenth century, namely being a badge of respectability for the English middle classes. Eliot showed the zeal of a new convert not in closing his mind, which remained wide open, but in the adoption of a strict Christian discipline for his new lifestyle. So a Christian will not be separated from a secular humanist by a closure of mind to radical questioning. Such questions will always remain to be faced.

Atheism takes many forms. Christians, for example, were once called atheists because they did not believe in the gods of the Roman world. Atheism in the modern Western world, with its Christian heritage, takes the form of denying that there is a wise and loving power behind the universe. It goes beyond agnosticism in being a settled conviction that the universe is indifferent to human life and human values. Yet, paradoxically, it may be important for Christians to take on board this apparent denial of the core of Christian faith. This means actually feeling the power, the persuasive pull, of the arguments for atheism and sometimes sharing them. It is true that one reason Eliot moved towards faith was, he said, the thinness of Bertrand Russell's arguments. He wrote to Russell, who was an old friend, about his pamphlet on Christianity to say that it was a piece of childish folly and that the arguments in it had been familiar to him at the age of six or eight. Nevertheless he took serious atheism with the utmost seriousness and said that 'Atheism should always be encouraged for the sake of the Faith.'[6]

Eliot did not elaborate on what he meant by that but I suspect it relates to his line of Julian of Norwich in *Four Quartets* about 'the purification of the motive / In the ground of our beseeching'[7] as well as Simone Weil's reflections on what she called 'the purification of atheism'. Weil said that God both did and did not exist. He did not exist in the sense that 'nothing real can be anything like what I am able to conceive when I pronounce this word [God]. But that which I cannot conceive is not an illusion.'[8] Here we come up again against the limitations of human language to convey the transcendent that was discussed in Chapter 3. It reinforces the point that even if an image or metaphor can point to God it will at the same time be limited and misleading. Atheism is important in driving this point home. But Weil, like Eliot, goes beyond this warning in affirming the necessity of atheism for the believer. 'Religion in so far as it is a source of consolation is a hindrance to true faith: in this sense atheism is a purification. I have to be atheistic with the part of myself which is not made for God.'[9]

She does not define what might count as consolation. I take it to refer to the illusion that believers will be spared the ills of life because of their faith, or that things will turn out all right for them. She gives the example of people being badly tortured and says: 'Such men if they had previously believed in the mercy of God would either believe in it no longer or else they would conceive of it quite differently from before.' Although she said she had not personally been through such an experience, she knows that is the reality of many and that therefore she herself 'must move towards an abiding conception of the divine mercy, a conception which does not change whatever event destiny may send'.[10] So under the heading of consolation she does not rule out a conviction of divine mercy, the experience of grace that was so fundamental to her, or the touch of Christ upon her. However, she would certainly have regarded as false consolation any hugging of religious emotion for its own sake, or even placing an undue emphasis on it, when what was so fundamental for her was simply waiting on God.

Flourishing even in failure

What this means in practice is that if God is to be found, it must not just be when things go well, in all that makes for human flourishing, but especially in the midst of weakness and failure and when the world seems in the grip of evil. One remarkable testimony to the possibility of this is provided by Etty Hillesum, who died in Auschwitz in 1943 and who kept a journal for the two years before her deportation and death. Of Jewish background and very much the product of modern European culture, she and her psychotherapist Julius Spier found themselves shyly using the word 'God' even though it sounded ridiculous.[11] In particular, Etty found herself beginning to kneel and pray.[12] As the political situation became worse she found herself ever more attentive to the God dwelling within her, and she quoted Rilke: 'Even if we don't want it: God ripens'.[13] About her mentor Spier she wrote that his stature lay in having 'given shelter' in his person to 'a portion of life and suffering and God'.[14]

Even more remarkable is the prayer she wrote to God:

You cannot help us . . . we must help You to help ourselves. And that
is all we can manage these days and also all that really matters: that
we safeguard that little piece of You, God, in ourselves.[15]

Then summing up how she felt: 'There must be someone to live
through it all and bear witness to the fact that God lived, even in
these times. And why should I not be that witness.'[16] Although Etty
Hillesum was Jewish, what she writes brings to mind what St Paul
wrote in 2 Corinthians 4 about being handed over to death that the
life of Jesus might live in and through us.

Another remarkable witness to where we should and should not
look for God was provided by the late Rabbi Hugo Gryn. One day
in Auschwitz he saw jet streams in the sky, possibly from 'experimental V2 bombs',[17] and he believed that God himself was about
to intervene to put a stop to the terrible evil that was happening.
Then, trying to keep Yom Kippur, the Day of Atonement, as best
he could in the camp, he found himself sobbing for hours. As
he wrote:

Never before or since have I cried with such intensity and then I
seemed to be granted a curious inner peace. Something of it is still
with me. I believe God was also crying . . . I would like you to understand that in the builder's yard on that Day of Atonement, I found
God. But not the God I had churlishly hung to until those jet streams
dissolved over Auschwitz. People sometimes ask me 'Where was God
in Auschwitz?' I believe that God was there Himself – violated and
blasphemed. The real question is 'Where was man in Auschwitz?'[18]

The challenge presented by the title of the present book is how
we live in a world characterized by both beauty and horror and
how we might find God within such a world. The witness of both
Christians, and Jews like Etty Hillesum and Hugo Gryn, is that the
only way we can retain a consistent and truthful understanding of
God is by seeing him in the midst of the horror. We look to those who
are caught up by the evil of the world but who refuse to succumb
to it; to those who witness to the God who is with them and within

them at such times. If we see him there, we see an iridescent beauty that radiates the beauty of life as such.

Christian humanism like secular humanism affirms all that makes for human flourishing, personal and political; at the same time it believes that we are called to grow in love for God and one another through Jesus Christ, crucified and risen. This means that even in weakness and failure and when beset by evil, human flourishing can come to a fulfilment that death cannot diminish.

What this understanding establishes is that there is clear common ground with secular humanists on the goal of human flourishing in this world. Christians and secularists ought to be able to work together on a range of issues towards this end. After that, however, there is an equally clear distinction between the two approaches. First of all, the one Christians believe to be the true and fully perfect human being, Jesus the Word made flesh, was crucified. This raises a big question mark against all purely secular understandings of what it is to flourish. We live in a world steeped in evil and there is bound to be a clash between a world organized along the lines of ruthless self-interest and those committed to the flourishing of humanity as a whole. Does secular humanism in our society fully reckon with this? The criticisms of John Gray on this issue were mentioned in Chapter 10. He has argued that liberal humanism has a too facile and optimistic view of human nature and it assumes that progress towards a more human society is inevitable. On the contrary, the situation in the future could be worse than it is now, there is no guarantee things will get better, and human beings will continue to do unspeakable things to one another. He finds himself more at home with the tough-minded philosophers of ancient Rome than modern humanism.[19]

There is clearly a great deal of truth in what Gray asserts, at least in relation to some forms of secular humanism. Whether it can be disassociated from that kind of optimistic liberal progressivism is obviously up to those who call themselves secular humanists. But from a Christian point of view it can be argued that whatever else may be said against Christianity, it has at least taken evil seriously.

There have been exceptions, for example the kind of Social Gospel that was preached in the 1930s, which met such a fierce critique from Reinhold Niebuhr, but for the most part where the Church has erred is in stressing humanity's propensity to sin at the expense of our equally real capacity to care about justice.

The final part of the definition of Christian humanism marks a further clear point of difference with secularists. For it makes the bold claim, based on its understanding of God's purpose for humanity, that our vocation and destiny cannot finally be thwarted by whatever life throws at us. There is a richer, deeper concept of human flourishing that includes – but goes beyond – all that makes for our material and psychological flourishing, which has to do with our capacity to transcend the ego in attention to the other and the other's good. For a Christian, this is made possible through life in Christ, in whom God and humanity are joined never to be unjoined. Through this union the divine life comes to live and work through us. This work is not thwarted by apparent failure and this union is not broken by death.

18

'Keep your mind in hell and do not despair'

One of William Golding's less well-known novels concerns a woman who acted as the oracle of Delphi.[1] In reality, her job was simply to pass on the interpretation given by the high priest, who was manipulating her for his own political ends. However, she does sometimes go into genuine prophetic trances and eventually at the end of her long service the authorities want to erect a statue to her on one of the altars of the Field of Mars. She declines and asks instead for a simple altar inscribed with the words: 'To the unknown God', words with which the novel ends.

Gustave Flaubert once wrote a letter containing the words: 'Just when the gods had ceased to be, and the Christ had not yet come, there was a moment in history, between Cicero and Marcus Aurelius, when man stood alone.'[2] In 1927, the Belgian-born writer Marguerite Yourcenar came across these words and was haunted by them for the rest of her life. One result was her book *Memoirs of Hadrian*, in which she incarnates the idea of a human standing utterly alone. As he is dying, Hadrian reflects on how he has no confidence in the gods or their justice, nor in human wisdom.

> Life is atrocious, we know. But precisely because I expect little of the human condition, man's periods of felicity, his partial progress, his efforts to begin over again and to continue, all seem to me like so many prodigies which nearly compensate for the monstrous mass of ills and defeats, of indifference and error.[3]

It is a brave statement of a human being standing alone, aware of the brutal reality of existence yet cherishing what might survive of art and learning.

The books by Golding and Yourcenar are illuminating fictions. In reality, Jesus had lived and died by the time of Hadrian; and Paul, drawing attention in Athens to the altar erected to the unknown God, as recounted in Acts 17, had preached Christ crucified and risen. The unknown God had made himself known. Humanity was no longer alone. It is true that in the time of the emperor Hadrian in the second century the community of Christians was still a tiny persecuted sect. Yet by the end of the third century they had succeeded in winning the imagination and heart of a great part of the Roman world. The conversion of Constantine to the Christian faith in the fourth century, with the consequence that Christianity became first legalized and then the official religion of the empire, had huge consequences of course, but it is important to note that by the time of the last and fiercest of the persecutions under the emperor Diocletian, which lasted from 303 to 313, the defenceless and for the most part powerless Christian faith had won over vast numbers of people simply by the attractive power of what it proclaimed and the witness to this by Christians in acts of charity and self-sacrifice. Without armies, without conquests it had captured the imagination and won the loyalty of the Roman world. This is still a fact worth pondering, standing as it does in striking contrast to so many religions, including Christianity itself later, which have been spread by force of arms.

My book has been written from that Christian position. It is I believe an orthodox Christian perspective. I am well aware of revisionist versions of the faith but in my view they raise more difficulties than they solve. More crucially, it is the Christian faith in its fullness that I find so interesting and compelling. Whatever one makes of its claims to be true, the Christian story must be one of the most sublime told by human beings and not surprisingly has been the inspiration for so much art, music and literature.

Francis Spufford, in his book *Unapologetic*, explained 'Why, despite everything, Christianity can still make surprising emotional sense',[4] which is the subtitle of his book. The emotions I am concerned with

are above all our sense of wonder at existence and our protest at
its horrors, our relish in the gift of life and our despair about it.
I seek to set these emotions in an intellectual framework that
may make it more bearable for us to live with them. It is not a
polemical book, because debates on these issues have been very
badly served in recent years by the public mauling of believers
and their defensive response; the oversimplified, aggressive and
fundamentally untruthful nature of so much of that discussion
has not done justice to the seriousness of the subject. I have written
with an awareness that most intelligent people these days do not
believe what I believe, and they do not believe for perfectly understandable reasons.[5] Like Francis Spufford, I am acutely aware of
the case that can be made against what the Christian faith claims.
Indeed the situation has been well likened to one in a good detective
story. All the clues seem to point in a particular direction but the
good detective is struck by a small piece of evidence that suggests
it is not quite so simple and that the truth lies elsewhere. The
case against the possibility of a wise and loving power behind the
universe is massive, and it is easy to sympathize with people
like Stephen Fry who explode against the idea of God, calling him
an 'evil, capricious, monstrous maniac'. But there is a piece of
evidence almost totally overlooked by the world at the time and
largely hidden today, which suggests that the truth is stranger
and more astonishing than that; and that is Jesus crucified and risen.
It is said that fact is stranger than fiction. I have, however, drawn
on a number of novels because today it is often in imaginative
literature rather than philosophy or theology that we can best
feel the astonishing beauty of what is being claimed. But it is of
course real life that in the end we are dealing with. In that con-
nection, what Géza Röhri says sums up so much of what a believer
will want to say.

Röhri, a teacher, poet and actor, took the lead role in a harrowing
film about Auschwitz, *Son of Saul*. He stresses that it was not God
who rounded up the Jews, Gypsies and others but the human
family. This does not let God off the hook, he thinks,

But I would not be able to get up from my bed in the morning, let alone pray, if I didn't fully believe that God somehow was there holding the hands of each and every Jew in the gas chamber – each and every Tutsi, Armenian, Kurd, Israeli, Palestinian who suffers unjustly.

It isn't the right of survivors to say God was not present, he thinks, given that those who died are not available for testimony.

So I think there is room for me to believe, as irrational as it sounds, that since God is all capable, in some mysterious way, he suffered and was there. If I wasn't able to believe this, I don't know why I'd take my next breath.[6]

The horror Röhri refers to can lead people to the edge of despair. Here some words of Staretz Silouan (1866–1938) are at once startling and salutary. Silouan was a Russian monk who after military service joined a monastery on Mount Athos. After much spiritual struggle he achieved an inner peace and wisdom that led him to be much sought out as a guide and counsellor. Thomas Merton called him the most authentic monk of the twentieth century and he was canonized by the Ecumenical Patriarch in 1987. He is reported to have heard the words from God: 'Keep your mind in hell and do not despair.' They are words that bring to mind the teaching of Simone Weil discussed earlier in the book, for whom the suffering of others, even those unknown to her or perhaps especially those unknown to her, was an agony that continually rent her apart. At the same time she believed that it was not possible for any of us to think truly about life without putting themselves in the position of someone tortured and utterly humiliated. She did indeed keep her mind in hell. Yet she did not despair. She did not despair because she saw in this affliction an identification with Christ in his abandonment on the cross. For her, this was the true destiny of human beings, for in this way we are one with God in both his self-emptying and plenitude.

Beauty and horror, hope and despair. *The Fine Balance*, by Rohinton Mistry, is a gut-wrenching novel about the degrading effect of the

Indian caste system, set in the time when Mrs Gandhi declared a state of emergency in the mid-1970s. Amid poverty, cruelty and humiliation, the main characters struggle somehow to survive. As one said: 'You have to maintain a fine balance between hope and despair.'[7]

From the standpoint of Christian faith, that hope is not just whistling in the dark or wistful longing. It is the blessed hope of which Thomas Hardy's 'darkling thrush' seemed to know and of which he himself was unaware.[8] It is a hope grounded in trust and expressed in love. At the end of a Eucharist in 1993, Brother Roger of Taizé said: 'You are there beneath our despair, and in the beauty of our hope.'

I referred above to a crime novel in which all the evidence seems to point in one direction but a good detective picks up a clue that suggests the true story is somewhat different. The case against the possibility of a wise and loving power behind creation does often seem overwhelming as we listen to or read the news about the daily hells people find themselves in. Its seriousness cannot be over-emphasized. From a Christian point of view, however, there is a clue that is all too easily overlooked in the endless human struggles for power and prestige with their consequent cruelty and suffering. This is, as I said above, Jesus crucified and risen, in whom is seen the self-emptying of God in creation, and his identification with the whole of humanity in their travail. From the standpoint of ordinary day-by-day existence, this seems an absurd claim. But day-by-day existence is not so ordinary. What could be more astonishing than the fact that each of us exists? We can be brought up short by the sheer marvel of it. The meaning, if there is one, cannot be anything ordinary. Against that background the Christian claim, outrageous though it may seem to be, is congruous with that mystery and marvel.

I have not argued that the contradiction between the beauty and horror of life can be fully resolved, or that in our search for God all the answers can be found, only that in the light of the Christian faith a faith-based way of living can be discovered. There is a final mystery that we cannot penetrate. The eminent New Testament scholar G. B. Caird, commenting on Ephesians 3.19, wrote:

> The attempt *to know* the unknowable is a paradox which is at the heart of all true religion. *Omnia exeunt in mysteria* ('all things run out into mystery'). Man must know God or perish; but unless he knows him as ultimate mystery, he does not know him at all.[9]

Part of that mystery lies in the hope of what lies beyond death, when the contradiction will be finally resolved. I have argued that this hope is a fundamental element in a Christian world view that cannot be dislodged without bringing the whole edifice down. Nevertheless that hope can be given substance even now, in however an oblique and fragmentary way. The most accomplished literary attempt in recent years that I am aware of to depict a Christian vision of human existence is the trilogy by Marilynne Robinson, *Gilead*, *Home* and *Lila*.[10] The theological vision is that there is redemption not just after affliction but in it. A visionary moment occurs when a church is struck by lightning and burns down. Rain is falling and all is blackened, but the congregation are still singing hymns. John's father breaks a biscuit in two and gives it to the young boy. It seemed like Holy Communion, and 'much of my life was comprehended in that moment'.

If the purpose of life were simply to maximize pleasure and minimize pain, then it would be difficult to claim that the former outweighs the latter. But if the great goal is rather to draw us into the very life of God, it puts a totally different perspective on the sadness and failure that characterizes so much of life. Christians claim that purpose is being achieved by the God who comes among us in Christ to draw our lives into union with him and who through the power of the Spirit enables us to live at one with the Father. This is no passive union but an openness to let God work through us for his good purpose. This is indeed a holy union, or communion of love.

Within the wider context of 'unknowing', this way of living is beautifully summed up in 1 Corinthians 13 quoted earlier:

For now we see through a glass, darkly; but then face to face: now I know
in part; but then shall I know even as also I am known. And now abideth
faith, hope, charity, these three; but the greatest of these is charity.

(AV)

Faith here and elsewhere in the New Testament means trust; trust
in God through all difficulties. It is a trust that in all circumstances,
and despite all appearances to the contrary, there is a wise and
good purpose behind our life. It goes along with a hope that this
will indeed be revealed to be the case, and this good purpose will
be fully known and vindicated. This hope is not that life on this
earth will get better and better, the kind of optimism so savagely
criticized by John Gray and which Terry Eagleton categorizes as the
banality of hope. Rather it is a hope that survives the destruction
of all earthly hopes. This is 'hope against hope'. As Eagleton puts it,
Christianity is a creed that breaks the link with progress: 'Hope,
then, is what survives the general ruin.'[11] This hope is not passive
or quiescent. It is the active hope expressed in the words of Jesus:
'Blessed are those who hunger and thirst to see right prevail' (Matthew
5.6). Although there can be progress from time to time, this is not
to be confused with redemption. As Eagleton well puts it:

> The relation between history and the *eschaton* is not simply disjunct-
> ive. There is indeed a continuity between them but it is not in the
> manner of some stately teleology. In irrupting apocalyptically into
> historical time, the kingdom of God brings to fruition a pattern of
> transfigurative moments immanent within it, a fractured narrative
> of justice and comradeship which runs against the grain of what one
> might call its central plot.[12]

He suggests it is as though there were a coded pattern of hope woven
into history, a subtext that will be known only at the end when there
is a fully decipherable script. It is the kind of history within history
implicit in Augustine's *City of God* and which is a theme of some
of Golding's novels.

And this points up the fact that the three marks or defining features
of the Christian life, faith, hope and love, are integrally linked. For

the faith and hope are expressed in the striving for God's justice in an unjust world. Taking up the theme of Chapter 14, 'Refusing to be comforted', in this striving we are acutely aware of a dissonance between the world as it is and the world as it ought to be and work to make the one closer to the other. In words that are very much in the spirit of the teaching of Jesus quoted earlier, the playwright Tennessee Williams once said:

> I've met many people that seemed well-adjusted, but I'm not sure that to be well-adjusted to things as they are is . . . to be desired . . . I'm not sure that I would want to be well-adjusted to things as they are. I would prefer to be racked by desire for things better than they are, even for things which are unattainable, than to be satisfied with things as they are.[13]

Rooted in the way of love, this refusal to be satisfied with things as they are carries with it the hope that in God's good time that love will be vindicated. In the light of that hope, we put our trust in the source of that love now. Within the wider mystery in which we continue to ask questions, protest and rebel, it is commitment to a way of life within a living community, a way of life that, facing the hells we make of the world, remains racked with desire and striving for a better world.

Notes

1 Life – so astonishing and so appalling

1 C. S. Lewis analysed this feeling brilliantly in his book *Surprised by Joy* (London: Fontana, 1959).
2 Quoted by Ara H. Merjian in the *Times Literary Supplement*, 4 September 2015, p. 5.
3 Stanley Spencer, in *Sermons by Artists* (London: Golden Cockerel Press, 1934), p. 50.
4 Kenneth Pople, *Stanley Spencer: A Biography* (London: Collins, 1991), p. 195.
5 Deirdre Bair, *Samuel Beckett: A Biography* (London: Jonathan Cape, 1978), p. 528.
6 Joseph Conrad, *Heart of Darkness* (Harmondsworth: Penguin, 1973), p. 100.
7 John Carey, *The Unexpected Professor: An Oxford Life in Books* (London: Faber & Faber, 2014), p. 70.
8 Brian R. Clack, *Love, Drugs, Art, Religion: The Pains and Consolations of Existence* (Farnham: Ashgate, 2014). For a critique, see Richard Harries, *Theology* 118(3), May/June 2015, p. 222.
9 *Church Times*, 1 January 2016.
10 Terri Roberts, *Forgiven: The Amish School Shooting, A Mother's Love, and a Story of Remarkable Grace* (Minneapolis, MN: Bethany House, 2015).
11 Nel mezzo del cammin di nostra vita, mi ritrovai per una selva oscura, ché la diritta vie era smaritta.

2 Asking the right questions

1 George Eliot, *Middlemarch* (Harmondsworth: Penguin, 1965), p. 349.
2 George Eliot herself was an agnostic with a very strong set of moral beliefs that had been shaped by her early adult life as a Christian. No doubt Mary Garth, in the social setting of the time, was a churchgoer. So the question arises about how a society will sustain its set of moral values when its earlier religious inspiration is no longer widely shared. But that is another question. See Richard Harries, *The Re-enchantment of Morality: Wisdom for a Troubled World* (London: SPCK, 2008).
3 Ronald Dworkin, *Justice for Hedgehogs* (Cambridge, MA: Belknap Press, 2011), p. 196.
4 Dworkin's position that moral values are objective, even though he does not believe in God, is not widely shared today, but his main point is that you do not need a religious faith to give meaning to life.
5 Ronald Dworkin, *Religion without God* (Cambridge, MA: Harvard University Press, 2013), p. 423.

6 Interview in *Third Way* 39(3), April 2015.
7 Dworkin sets out a unified view that encompasses morality, legal philosophy and political philosophy. Without suggesting that it amounts to a proof, I argue that his view lends itself to an even more encompassing theological perspective. See Richard Harries, 'God, Goodness and Contemporary Society', in *The Runcie Lectures, 2000–2012*, intro. John H. Morgan (Mishawaka, IN: Graduate Theological Foundation, 2012).
8 Karl Marx, 'Contribution to the Critique of Hegel's Philosophy of Right', *Essential Writings of Karl Marx*, ed. D. Caute (London: Panther, 1967), p. 93; emphasis in original.
9 *The Middle Length Discourses of the Buddha: A New Translation of the Majjhima Nikaya*, trans., ed. and revised B. Bodhi (Boston: Wisdom Publications, 2001), p. 524. I am grateful to Dipli Saikia for directing me to this translation and for pointing out its original context: the criticism of the status quo in which certain groups were privileged with knowledge.
10 *Middle Length Discourses of the Buddha*, p. 535.
11 *Middle Length Discourses of the Buddha*, p. 535.
12 Sarah Bakewell, *How to Live: A Life of Montaigne in One Question and Twenty Attempts at an Answer* (London: Vintage, 2011), p. 146.
13 'What we discover here for the first time, and what Screech alone could have made us discover, is quite simply the religious dimension of the *Essays*, the spirituality contained in Montaigne's wisdom' – Marc Fumaroli, in M. A. Screech, *Montaigne and Melancholy: The Wisdom of the Essays* (Harmondsworth: Penguin, 1991), p. xiv.
14 Terry Eagleton, *Culture and the Death of God* (New Haven, CT: Yale University Press, 2014).
15 Eagleton, *Culture and the Death of God*, p. 186.
16 Eagleton, *Culture and the Death of God*, p. 190.
17 Eagleton, *Culture and the Death of God*, p. 188.
18 Eagleton, *Culture and the Death of God*, p. 191.
19 Gerard Manley Hopkins, *Selected Letters*, ed. C. Phillips (Oxford: Oxford University Press, 1990), p. 225.
20 Hopkins, *Selected Letters*, p. 169.
21 Ray Monk, *Ludwig Wittgenstein: The Duty of Genius* (London: Vintage, 1991), p. 214.

3 Knowing and unknowing

1 Maximus the Confessor, 'The Four Hundred Chapters on Love', Third Century, no. 99, *Maximus Confessor: Selected Writings*, trans. and notes G. C. Berthold (New York: Paulist Press, 1995), p. 75.

2 John of Damascus, 'Exposition of the Orthodox Faith', I, 4, *Nicene and Post Nicene Fathers, Volume 4* (Grand Rapids, MI: Eerdmans, 1983).

3 *New Essays in Philosophical Theology*, edited by Antony Flew and Alasdair MacIntyre (London: SCM Press, 1955), was the seminal text. MacIntyre, one of the most influential philosophers of our time, has fluctuated in his beliefs but has basically held to a combination of Marxism and Catholicism. Antony Flew, towards the end of his life, converted to belief in a strange, limited god, not unlike that caricatured in Philip Pullman's *Dark Materials* trilogy. The phrase of Antony Flew's is on page 97.

4 Letter to his brother and sister, 14 February 1819.

5 Eberhard Bethge, in Dietrich Bonhoeffer, *Letters and Papers from Prison* (London: Fontana, 1959), p. 11.

6 Kenneth Pople, *Stanley Spencer: A Biography* (London: Collins, 1991), p. 205.

7 R. S. Thomas, 'Perhaps', in *Collected Poems, 1945–1990* (London: Dent, 1993), p. 353.

8 David Jones, *The Anathemata: Fragments of an Attempted Writing* (London: Faber & Faber, 1952), p. 15.

9 David Jones, 'Religion and the Muses' (1941), in *Epoch and Artist: Selected Writings*, ed. H. Grisewood (London: Faber & Faber, 2008), p. 98.

10 Jones, 'Religion and the Muses', p. 103; emphasis in original.

11 Sir Roy Strong, Commemoration of Founders and Benefactors Address, 25 November 2001.

12 R. S. Thomas, 'The Absence', in *Frequencies* (London: Macmillan, 1978), p. 48.

13 W. H. Auden, 'Epistle to a Godson', in *Collected Poems of W. H. Auden*, ed. E. Mendelson (London: Faber & Faber, 1976), p. 626.

14 Samuel Beckett, *Worstward Ho*, in *Company, Ill Seen Ill Said, Worstward Ho, Stirrings Still* (London: Faber & Faber, 2009), p. 81.

15 T. S. Eliot, 'East Coker', in *Four Quartets* (London: Faber & Faber, 1959), Part III.

16 Simone Weil, *Waiting on God*, trans. E. Craufurd (London: Fontana, 1959), esp. p. 149.

17 R. S. Thomas, 'Kneeling', in *Collected Poems*, p. 199.

18 *The Cloud of Unknowing*, trans. C. Wolters (Harmondsworth: Penguin, 1961), p. 59.

19 Rowan Williams, *The Wound of Knowledge: Christian Spirituality from the New Testament to St John of the Cross* (London: Darton, Longman & Todd, 1979).

20 Philip Pullman, *The Good Man Jesus and the Scoundrel Christ* (Edinburgh: Canongate, 2010), p. 195.

21 Simone Weil, *Gravity and Grace*, trans. E. Craufurd (London: Routledge & Kegan Paul, 1963), p. 99.

22 T. S. Eliot, 'The Dry Salvages', in *Four Quartets* (London: Faber & Faber, 1959), Part V.

23 This silence is not a blank, for it is always related to the linguistic context in which it occurs. 'To talk about silence is always to talk about *what specifically* we are not hearing; or what we decide not to listen to in order to hear differently; or what specifically we find we cannot say.' At this point we may find ourselves looking for a new kind of language altogether, one in a different register that shifts our whole understanding. It is here that Dr Williams locates the point at which natural theology, the use of our ordinary reason to know God and revealed theology, what God has disclosed to us of himself, meet. The traditional arguments for the existence of God, a staple of natural theology, for example, do not work as proofs but they indicate the point at which the nexus of cause and effect no longer applies, and if there is anything to be said it will be in a different mode altogether. 'Revelation does not fill a gap, but shows why the gap is there, not resolving the difficulty but offering a perspective in which difficulty is what makes sense and what we must become accustomed to' – *The Edge of Words: God and the Habits of Language* (London: Bloomsbury, 2014), pp. 157, 180.

24 Marilynne Robinson, *Lila* (London: Virago, 2014), p. 24; see also pp. 22, 77.

25 Bertrand Russell, *The Autobiography of Bertrand Russell* (London: Allen & Unwin, 1961), ch. 2; see esp. p. 303. 'The centre of me is always and eternally a terrible pain – a curious wild pain – a searching for something beyond what the world contains, something transfigured and infinite – the beatific vision – God – I do not find it, I do not think it is to be found – but the love of it is my life.'

4 Pursuing the truth

1 The story is told in Richard Harries, 'Evolution and Christian Faith in the Nineteenth Century', in *Intelligent Faith: A Celebration of 150 Years of Darwinian Evolution*, ed. J. Quenby and J. MacDonald Smith (Ropley: O Books, 2009). Acknowledgements to the extensive research on this episode appear in the article.

2 From the essay 'The Natural Theology of the Future' in Kingsley's *Westminster Sermons* (London: Macmillan, 1874), pp. v–xxxiii, on p. xxv. Frederick Temple (1821–1902) said much the same thing in his 1884 Bampton Lectures at Oxford University, when he remarked that God 'did not make the things, we may say; no, but He made them make themselves' – Frederick Temple, *The Relations between Religion and Science* (London: Macmillan, 1885), p. 115.

3 Rowan Williams, *The Edge of Words: God and the Habits of Language* (London: Bloomsbury, 2014), p. 180.

4 Dag Hammarskjöld, *Markings* (London: Faber & Faber, 1964), p. 169.

5 John Henry Newman, *Apologia pro Vita Sua* (London: Fontana, 1959), p. 225.

6 Austin Farrer, *The One Genius: Readings through the Year with Austin Farrer*, selected by Richard Harries (London: SPCK, 1987), p. 50. For ease of reference, quotations from Austin Farrer are sometimes given from this anthology. References to his writings are given there.

7 Pascal, *Pensées*, ed. and trans. R. Ariew (Indianapolis, IN: Hackett, 2004), S751/ L919, p. 276.

8 St Bernard of Clairvaux, *On Loving God and Selections from Sermons*, ed. H. Martin (London: SCM Press, 1959), p. 41.

9 This is a view of the role of reasoning in faith that is set out by, for example, Michael J. Langford in *The Tradition of Liberal Theology* (Grand Rapids, MI: Eerdmans, 2014), esp. pp. 24–32.

10 St Augustine, *Confessions*, trans. H. Chadwick (Oxford: Oxford University Press, 1992), pp. 183–4.

11 C. S. Lewis, *Surprised by Joy* (London: Fontana, 1959), p. 172.

12 This is best seen in his wonderful essay 'The Weight of Glory' but it is also a theme in his spiritual autobiography up to the time of his conversion, *Surprised by Joy*. See also Richard Harries, *C. S. Lewis: The Man and His God* (London: Collins, 1987).

13 T. S. Eliot, 'Little Gidding', in *Four Quartets* (London: Faber & Faber, 1959), Part V.

14 Lewis, *Surprised by Joy*, p. 182.

15 From 'Bishop Blougram's Apology', in *Browning: Poetical Works 1833–1864*, ed. I. Jack (Oxford: Oxford University Press, 1970), p. 650.

16 Farrer, *The One Genius*, p. 153.

17 Alec Vidler, *The Church in an Age of Revolution: 1789 to the Present Day* (Harmondsworth: Penguin, 1961), p. 113.

18 I have explored this in *God Outside the Box: Why Spiritual People Object to Christianity* (London: SPCK, 2002).

19 Austin Farrer, *A Celebration of Faith*, ed. L. Houlden (London: Hodder & Stoughton, 1970), p. 61.

20 Austin Farrer, *Saving Belief: A Discussion of Essentials* (London: Hodder & Stoughton, 1967), p. 30.

21 For the whole argument, see that remarkable little book by Austin Farrer, *A Science of God?* (London: Geoffrey Bles, 1966).

5 Truth in its beauty

1 Václav Havel, *Living in Truth: Twenty-two Essays Published on the Occasion of the Award of the Erasmus Prize to Václav Havel*, ed. J. Vladislav (London: Faber & Faber, 1986), p. 131.

2 Hilary Spurling, *The Unknown Matisse: Man of the North: 1869–1908* (London: Penguin, 2000), p. 278.

3 Simone Weil, *Waiting on God*, trans. E. Craufurd (London: Fontana, 1959), p. 36.

4 John Masefield, 'Truth', in *The Collected Poems of John Masefield* (London: Heinemann, 1923), p. 367.

5 Hans Urs von Balthasar, *The Glory of the Lord: A Theological Aesthetics, Volume 1: Seeing the Form*, trans. E. Leiva-Merikakis (Edinburgh: T. & T. Clark, 1982), p. 18.

6 See Roger Wagner and Andrew Briggs, *The Penultimate Curiosity: How Science Swims in the Slipstream of Ultimate Questions* (Oxford: Oxford University Press, 2016). This shows how scientific explorations of the world have arisen out of and been shaped by views about ultimate reality.

7 This is the theme of Richard Harries, *Art and the Beauty of God* (London: Mowbray, 1993).

8 Review by Ian Ground in the *Times Literary Supplement*, 27 February 2015, p. 13, of Paul Guyer, *A History of Modern Aesthetics*, 3 vols (Cambridge: Cambridge University Press, 2014).

9 F. Nietzsche, *The Will to Power*, trans. W. Kaufmann and R. J. Hollingdale (London: Weidenfeld & Nicholson, 1968), pp. 434–5; emphasis in original.

10 F. Nietzsche, *The Birth of Tragedy and The Case of Wagner*, trans. W. Kaufmann (New York: Vintage, 1967), p. 59. Both this and the previous quotation are discussed by Anthony Storr in *Music and the Mind* (New York: Free Press, 1992), pp. 157–8, in which he argues that art, especially music, gives a reason for living.

11 Arthur Miller, *A View from the Bridge* (Harmondsworth: Penguin, 1961), p. 85.

12 F. R. Leavis, 'Tragedy and the "Medium"', in *The Common Pursuit* (Harmondsworth: Penguin, 1962), pp. 127, 132.

13 Albert Camus, *The Myth of Sisyphus*, trans. J. O'Brien (Harmondsworth: Penguin, 1975), p. 11.

14 Graham Greene, *The Power and the Glory* (London: Reader's Union Ltd and Heinemann, 1941), p. 31.

15 See, for example, the last pages of Samuel Beckett's novel *The Unnamable*, with its repeated refrain 'where I am, I don't know, I'll never know, in the silence you don't know, you must go on, I can't go on, I'll go on.' *The Beckett Trilogy* (London: Picador, 1979), p. 382.

6 A living tradition

1 See Richard Harries, *The Authority of Divine Love* (Oxford: Blackwell, 1983).

2 A. M. Allchin, *The Dynamic of Tradition* (London: Darton, Longman & Todd, 1981), p. 28.

3 T. S. Eliot, 'Tradition and the Individual Talent', in *Selected Prose of T. S. Eliot*, ed. F. Kermode (London: Faber & Faber, 1975), p. 38.

4 'The state ought not to be considered as nothing better than a partnership agreement in a trade . . . it is a partnership not only between those who are

living, but between those who are living, those who are dead, and those who are to be born' – Edmund Burke, *Reflections on the Revolution in France: And on the Proceedings in Certain Societies in London Relative to That Event* (Harmondsworth: Penguin, 1968), p. 195.

7 What do we know about Jesus and why does it matter?

1 The opening sentence of L. P. Hartley's novel *The Go-Between* (London: Hamish Hamilton, 1953).
2 A. N. Wilson, *The Book of the People: How to Read the Bible* (London: Atlantic Books, 2015). Despite his scepticism about recovering the figure of Jesus behind successive layers of interpretation, Wilson suggests the Gospels are in the end based on eyewitnesses. A book of massive scholarship that supports this claim is Richard Bauckham, *Jesus and the Eyewitnesses: The Gospels as Eyewitness Testimony* (Grand Rapids, MI: Eerdmans, 2006).
3 Richard Harries, *Christ Is Risen* (Oxford: Mowbray, 1988).
4 This is the view I argued for in *Christ Is Risen*.
5 Dietrich Bonhoeffer, *Letters and Papers from Prison*, ed. E. Bethge, trans. R. H. Fuller (London: Fontana, 1959), p. 173.
6 In *Browning: Poetical Works 1833–1864*, ed. I. Jack (Oxford: Oxford University Press, 1970), p. 822.
7 For a highly accessible account of the main teaching of St Paul, see Rowan Williams, *Meeting God in Paul* (London: SPCK, 2015).
8 Wilson, *Book of the People*, p. 116.
9 Gerard Manley Hopkins, *The Poems of Gerard Manley Hopkins*, 4th edn, ed. W. H. Gardner and N. H. Mackenzie (London: Oxford University Press, 1970), p. 90.

8 One religion among many

1 Towards the end of the group we decided to draw together our reflections with the publication of *Dialogue with a Difference: The Manor House Group Experience*, ed. T. Bayfield and M. Braybrooke (London: SCM Press, 1992).
2 The fruit of our work appeared in *Abraham's Children: Jews, Christians and Muslims in Conversation*, ed. N. Solomon, R. Harries and T. Winter (Edinburgh: T. & T. Clark, 2005).
3 The first sentence of the 'Conclusion' of Kant's *Critique of Practical Reason*, trans. T. K. Abbott (London: Longmans, Green, 1954), p. 260.
4 The relationship of Christianity to Judaism has been a tortured, tragic one but is now being rethought. See Richard Harries, *After the Evil: Christianity and Judaism in the Shadow of the Holocaust* (Oxford and New York: Oxford University Press, 2003).

9 Why did it all begin?

1 Evelyn Waugh, *Decline and Fall* (London: Penguin, 1980), p. 33; emphasis in original.

2 For the doctrine of the Trinity, see Keith Ward, *Christ and the Cosmos: A Reformulation of Trinitarian Doctrine* (Cambridge: Cambridge University Press, 2015).

3 See the article on 'Theosis' in *The Oxford Dictionary of Byzantium, Volume 3* (Oxford: Oxford University Press, 1991), p. 2069. Also Timothy Ware, *The Orthodox Church* (London: Penguin, 1963), pp. 236ff.

4 *Sermons by Artists* (London: Golden Cockerel Press, 1934), p. 51; emphasis in original.

5 In *The Complete Works of W. H. Auden: Prose, Volume 2: 1939–1948*, ed. E. Mendelson (Princeton, NJ: Princeton University Press, 2002), p. 339.

10 The mystery of good and evil

1 John Gray, 'The Evil Within', *The Guardian*, 21 October 2014, p. 25.

2 Gray, 'Evil Within', p. 25.

3 Reinhold Niebuhr, *Moral Man and Immoral Society: A Study in Ethics and Politics* (New York: Scribner, 1960).

4 Cormac McCarthy, *The Road* (London: Picador, 2006).

5 Rowan Williams, *New Statesman*, 1–6 May 2015, p. 43.

6 William Golding, *Free Fall* (Harmondsworth: Penguin, in assoc. with Faber & Faber, 1963), p. 5.

7 Golding, *Free Fall*, p. 68.

8 Rowan Williams, *The Edge of Words: God and the Habits of Language* (London: Bloomsbury, 2014), p. 170; emphasis in original.

9 Quoted in Williams, *Edge of Words*, p. 45.

10 For the evidence, see Martin Gilbert, *The Righteous: The Unsung Heroes of the Holocaust* (London: Doubleday, 2002).

11 See <www.churchofengland.org/prayer-worship/worship/texts/principal-services/holy-communion/orderone.aspx>.

12 John Hick, *Evil and the God of Love* (London: Macmillan, 1966).

13 Professor John Carey in his analysis of *Paradise Lost* argues that Milton intended to show that the fallen angels fell freely and could, had they chosen, not have fallen. One angel, Abdiel, refuses to be stirred up to revolt by Satan and goes back to join the heavenly host. (A personal note from the author. See also his article 'Milton's Satan', in *The Cambridge Companion to Milton*, 2nd edn, ed. D. Danielson (Cambridge: Cambridge University Press, 1999).)

14 A partial exception to this is the Benedictine Community, founded in the sixth century, which is based on a rule that takes our egoism seriously but applies

sanctified common sense within a disciplined structure and way of life to manage this.

15 William Golding, *The Inheritors* (London: Faber & Faber, 1961).

16 A. E. Housman, 'The Laws of God, the Laws of Man', in *The Works of A. E. Housman* (London: Wordsworth Editions, 1994), p. 91.

17 Reinhold Niebuhr, *The Nature and Destiny of Man: A Christian Interpretation, Volume 1: Human Nature* (London: Nisbet, 1941), p. 213.

18 Niebuhr, *Nature and Destiny of Man*, p. 191.

19 Helmut Thielicke, *Theological Ethics, Volume 2: Politics* (London: A. & C. Black, 1969).

20 John Milton, *Paradise Lost*, ed. J. Leonard (London: Penguin, 2000), Book 1, lines 38–41.

21 C. S. Lewis, *A Preface to Paradise Lost* (London: Oxford University Press, 1960), p. 101.

22 Rowan Williams, *On Augustine* (London: Bloomsbury, 2016), p. 79. St Augustine had a long struggle to free himself from the view that the material world itself was evil. See Robin Lane Fox, *Augustine: Conversions and Confessions* (London: Allen Lane, 2015).

11 Overcoming evil

1 D. H. Lawrence, 'Pax', in *The Complete Poems of D. H. Lawrence, Volume 2*, ed. V. de Sola Pinto and W. Roberts (London: Heinemann, 1964), p. 700.

2 Austin Farrer, *Saving Belief: A Discussion of Essentials* (London: Hodder & Stoughton, 1964), p. 99.

3 'My song is love unknown', in *Ancient and Modern: Hymns and Songs for Refreshing Worship* (London: Hymns Ancient & Modern, 2013).

4 L. N. Tolstoy, *War and Peace, Volume 1*, trans. R. Edmonds (Harmondsworth: Penguin, 1957), p. 403.

5 Reinhold Niebuhr, *Justice and Mercy*, ed. U. M. Niebuhr (New York: Harper & Row, 1974), pp. 99–100.

6 Thomas Hardy, 'Surview', in *The Complete Poems*, ed. J. Gibson (London: Macmillan, 1976), p. 698.

7 Simone Weil, *Gravity and Grace*, trans. E. Craufurd (London: Routledge & Kegan Paul, 1963), p. 65.

8 Samuel Beckett, *Waiting for Godot: A Tragicomedy in Two Acts* (London: Faber & Faber, 1965), p. 52.

9 The Icon of the Anastasis is discussed in Richard Harries, *The Passion in Art* (Aldershot: Ashgate, 2004), p. 81.

10 William Langland, *Piers Plowman*, trans. A. V. C. Schmidt (Oxford: Oxford University Press, 2000), p. 223.

11 Julian of Norwich, *The Revelations of Divine Love of Julian Norwich*, trans. J. Walsh (London: Burns & Oates, 1961), p. 142.

12 The 26th, 38th and 23rd Lamentations of the First Stasis, from the service of Matins of Great Saturday in Holy Week (just three of very many Lamentations sung in three sections (Stasis)). From *The Lenten Triodion*, trans. Mother Mary and Archimandrite Kallistos Ware (London: Faber & Faber, 1978).

13 Cited in Leonard Sweet, *What Matters Most: How We Got the Point but Missed the Person* (Colorado Springs, CO: WaterBrook Press, 2004), p. 129, n. 28.

12 Hope in the face of death

1 Poll carried out by the think tank Theos in April 2009.

2 Iris Murdoch, *The Sovereignty of Good* (London: Routledge, 1970), p. 59.

3 Anton Chekhov, *Plays: The Seagull and Other Plays*, trans. E. Fen (Harmondsworth: Penguin, 1954), p. 245.

4 Karl Marx, 'Contribution to the Critique of Hegel's Philosophy of Right', in *Essential Writings of Karl Marx*, ed. D. Caute (London: Panther, 1967), p. 93.

5 Austin Farrer, *A Celebration of Faith*, ed. L. Houlden (London: Hodder & Stoughton, 1970), p. 119.

6 Wilfred Owen, 'Last Words', in *War Poems and Others*, ed. D. Hibberd (London: Chatto & Windus, 1973), p. 88.

7 Gerard Manley Hopkins, 'That Nature Is a Heraclitean Fire and of the Comfort of the Resurrection', in *The Poems of Gerard Manley Hopkins*, 4th edn, ed. W. H. Gardner and N. H. MacKenzie (London: Oxford University Press, 1970), p. 105.

8 John Donne, Devotion XVII, *Complete Poetry and Selected Prose*, ed. J. D. Hayward (London: Nonesuch Press, 1962), p. 537.

9 See <www.vatican.va/roman_curia/congregations/cfaith/documents/rc_con_cfaith_doc_19860322_freedom-liberation_en.html>.

10 St Augustine, Letter XC11, *The Nicene and Ante-Nicene Fathers, Volume 1: St Augustine* (Grand Rapids, MI: Eerdmans, 1886 and 1983), p. 390.

11 C. S. Lewis, 'The Weight of Glory', in *Screwtape Proposes a Toast, and Other Pieces* (London: Fontana, 1965), pp. 106ff.; emphasis in original. See Richard Harries, *C. S. Lewis: The Man and His God* (London: Collins, 1987), ch. 9.

12 The New Testament reports Jesus using the imagery of hell. This was part of the culture of his time, which he drew on to bring home to people the seriousness of their choices.

13 Richard Harries, 'On the Brink of Universalism', in *Julian: Woman of Our Day*, ed. R. Llewelyn (London: Darton, Longman & Todd, 1985), pp. 41ff.

14 *The Letters of T. S. Eliot, Volume 5: 1930–1931*, ed. V. Eliot and J. Haffenden (London: Faber & Faber, 2014), p. 210.

15 William Golding, *Pincher Martin* (London: Faber & Faber, 1962), p. 184.

16 R. C. Hutchinson, *Johanna at Daybreak* (London: Michael Joseph, 1980), p. 314.

17 T. S. Eliot, 'Little Gidding', in *Four Quartets* (London: Faber & Faber, 1959), Part IV.

18 The challenge is discussed in 'Ivan Karamazov's argument', in Richard Harries, *Questioning Belief* (London: SPCK, 1995), pp. 20ff.

19 F. Dostoyevsky, *The Brothers Karamazov, Volume 1*, trans. D. Magarshack (Harmondsworth: Penguin, 1958), p. 287; emphasis in original.

20 See Richard Harries, *After the Evil: Christianity and Judaism in the Shadow of the Holocaust* (Oxford and New York: Oxford University Press, 2003), ch. 4.

21 W. H. Auden, 'Precious Five', in *Collected Poems of W. H. Auden*, ed. E. Mendelson (London: Faber & Faber, 1976), p. 447.

22 Ann Ridler, in Charles Williams, *The Image of the City and Other Essays*, ed. A. Ridler (Oxford: Oxford University Press, 1958), p. xxxi; emphasis in original.

23 Charles Williams, *He Came Down from Heaven* (London: Heinemann, 1938), p. 55. For the life of Williams, see Grevel Lindop, *Charles Williams: The Third Inkling* (Oxford: Oxford University Press, 2015).

24 Williams, *He Came Down from Heaven*, p. 57.

13 Why suffering?

1 Letter to Lady Georgiana Morpeth, 16 February 1820, in *Selected Letters of Sydney Smith*, ed. N. C. Smith (Oxford: Oxford University Press, 1981), p. 94.

2 From *The Unnamable*, in Samuel Beckett, *The Grove Centenary Edition, Volume II: Novels* (New York: Grove Press, 2006), p. 304.

3 John Diamond, *The Guardian*, 1 January 2000.

4 John Diamond, *The Observer*, 31 December 2000.

5 Voltaire was not in fact an atheist. On his large estate at Ferney he built a church. He dedicated this to God, who he thought was more important than the saints to which churches were usually dedicated. He strongly combated atheism and was more than a deist who believed God simply wound up the world and then let it go. He believed in a compassionate God who sustains relations with human beings. I owe this information to the late Dr T. F. Glasson.

6 Samuel Johnson, 'Review of Soame Jenyns, A Free Enquiry into the Nature and Origin of Evil', 1757, in *Samuel Johnson*, ed. D. Greene (Oxford: Oxford University Press, 1984), p. 522.

7 Richard Harries, *After the Evil: Christianity and Judaism in the Shadow of the Holocaust* (Oxford and New York: Oxford University Press, 2003), ch. 3.

8 Jonathan Sacks, *The Great Partnership: God, Science and the Search for Meaning* (London: Hodder & Stoughton, 2011), p. 245.

9 Blaise Pascal, *Pensées*, trans. A. J. Krailsheimer (Harmondsworth: Penguin, 1961), 603, on p. 222.

14 Refusing to be comforted

1 Albert Camus, *The Plague*, trans. R. Buss (London: Penguin, 2001), p. 168. An earlier translation had 'this scheme of things' instead of 'this creation'.
2 F. Dostoyevsky, *The Brothers Karamazov, Volume 1*, trans. D. Magarshack (Harmondsworth: Penguin, 1958), p. 287.
3 Simone Weil, *Gravity and Grace*, trans. E. Craufurd (London: Routledge & Kegan Paul, 1963), p. 79.
4 I debated some of these issues with Stewart Sutherland in 'Stewart Sutherland on Suffering' and 'A Reply to Richard Harries', *Theology* 91(742), July 1988, pp. 308, 317.
5 John Donne, 'Sermon on Easter Day in the Evening', 28 March 1624, *Complete Poetry and Selected Prose*, ed. J. D. Hayward (London: Nonesuch Press, 1962), p. 607.
6 Eric Lomax, *The Railway Man* (London: Jonathan Cape, 1995).
7 Edwin Muir, 'One Foot in Eden', in *Collected Poems, 1921–1958*, ed. W. Muir and J. C. Hall (London: Faber & Faber, 1960), p. 227.
8 Edwin Muir, *An Autobiography* (London: Chatto & Windus, 1987), p. 280.
9 I have changed the name.
10 Margaret Spufford, *Celebration* (London: Fount, 1989).
11 Andrew Brown, 'Margaret Spufford Obituary', *The Guardian*, 17 April 2014.
12 Rebecca West, *The Fountain Overflows* (London: Virago, 2011), p. 336.
13 Jonathan Sacks, *The Great Partnership: God, Science and the Search for Meaning* (London: Hodder & Stoughton, 2011), p. 245.

15 Rebellion or acceptance?

1 The commonalities and differences are well set out by Stewart R. Sutherland in *Faith and Ambiguity* (London: SCM Press, 1984), ch. 4. The quotation about Weil is on p. 81.
2 Simone Weil, *The Notebooks of Simone Weil, Volume 1*, trans. A. Wills (London: Routledge & Kegan Paul, 1956), p. 283; emphasis in original.
3 Weil, *Notebooks, Volume 1*, p. 297.
4 Simone Weil, *Waiting on God*, trans. E. Craufurd (London: Fontana, 1959), p. 55.
5 This has been brilliantly done by Lissa McCullough in her *The Religious Philosophy of Simone Weil: An Introduction* (London and New York: I. B. Tauris, 2014).
6 Simone Weil, *The Need for Roots: Prelude to a Declaration of Duties towards Mankind*, trans. A. F. Wills (London and New York: Ark, 1987). Eliot wrote: 'We must simply expose ourselves to the personality of a woman of genius, of a kind of genius akin to that of the saints' (p. vi).

7   Weil, *Waiting on God*, p. 35.

8   Weil, *Notebooks, Volume 1*, p. 288.

9   Teilhard de Chardin, *Le Milieu Divin: An Essay on the Interior Life*, trans. B. J. Wall (London: Collins, 1960), pp. 69–70.

10 D. H. Lawrence, 'Song of Death', in *The Complete Poems of D. H. Lawrence, Volume 2*, ed. V. de Sola Pinto and W. Roberts (London: Heinemann, 1964), pp. 723, 980; discussed in Richard Harries, 'Attitudes to Death in the Twentieth Century', reprinted in Richard Harries, *Questioning Belief* (London: SPCK, 1995), pp. 32ff.

11 *The Revelations of Divine Love of Julian Norwich*, trans. J. Walsh (London: Burns & Oates, 1961), p. 91 – words made famous by T. S. Eliot in 'Little Gidding'.

12 Austin Farrer, *Love Almighty and Ills Unlimited* (London: Collins, 1966), pp. 177–8.

13 Jonathan Sacks, *The Great Partnership: God, Science and the Search for Meaning* (London: Hodder & Stoughton), pp. 242, 248.

14 Farrer, *Love Almighty*, p. 188.

16 Beyond tragedy

1   William Trevor, *The Story of Lucy Gault* (London: Penguin, 2003), p. 227.

2   John Williams, *Stoner* (London: Vintage, 1965 and 2003), pp. 284–5.

3   Williams, *Stoner*, p. 287.

4   Philip Roth, *The Human Stain* (London: Jonathan Cape, 2000).

5   Notes on Religion and Theology, 1966–7, Holograph Notebook in the Henry W. and Albert A. Berg Collection, New York Public Library.

6   Iris Murdoch, *The Good Apprentice* (London: Chatto & Windus, 1985), p. 147.

7   Shusaku Endo, *The Samurai* (London: Peter Owen, 2004), p. 121.

8   Endo, *Samurai*, p. 242.

9   Endo, *Samurai*, p. 245.

10 Endo, *Samurai*, p. 262.

11 Patrick White, *Riders in the Chariot* (Harmondsworth: Penguin, 1974), p. 484.

12 William Golding, *Darkness Visible* (London: Faber & Faber, 1979), p. 263.

13 Flannery O'Connor, *Mystery and Manners: Occasional Prose* (London: Faber & Faber, 1984), p. 33.

14 O'Connor, *Mystery and Manners*, p. 167.

15 O'Connor, *Mystery and Manners*, p. 108.

16 Flannery O'Connor, 'Parker's Back', in *Everything That Rises Must Converge* (London: Faber & Faber, 1985), p. 219.

17 For Norman Adams, see Richard Harries, *The Image of Christ in Modern Art* (Farnham: Ashgate, 2013), pp. 111–16.

17 Towards a true humanism

1 See *The Wiley Blackwell Handbook of Humanism*, ed. A. Copson and A. C. Grayling (Chichester: Wiley, 2015).

2 Byelaw 5.1 of the International Humanist and Ethical Union.

3 Barry Spurr, *Anglo-Catholic in Religion: T. S. Eliot and Christianity* (Cambridge: Lutterworth Press, 2010), p. 8, quoting T. S. Eliot, 'The Pensées of Pascal', in *Selected Essays* (London: Faber & Faber, 1972), p. 411.

4 T. S. Eliot, *Notes towards the Definition of Culture* (London: Faber & Faber, 1948, 1962), p. 67.

5 *The Letters of T. S. Eliot, Volume 4: 1928–1929*, ed. V. Eliot and J. Haffenden (London: Faber & Faber, 2013), p. 572.

6 *The Letters of T. S. Eliot, Volume 3: 1926–1927*, ed. V. Eliot and J. Haffenden (London: Faber & Faber, 2012), p. 424. But about Russell (and to Russell), he said 'What I dislike is the smell of the corpse of Protestantism passing down the river' – *Letters, Volume 3*, p. 739.

7 T. S. Eliot, 'Little Gidding', in *Four Quartets* (London: Faber & Faber, 1959), final lines of Part III.

8 Simone Weil, *Gravity and Grace*, trans. E. Craufurd (London: Routledge & Kegan Paul, 1963), p. 103.

9 Weil, *Gravity and Grace*, p. 104.

10 Weil, *Gravity and Grace*, p. 104.

11 Etty Hillesum, *Etty: The Letters and Diaries of Etty Hillesum, 1941–1943*, ed. K. A. D. Smelik, trans. A. J. Pomerans (Grand Rapids, MI: Eerdmans, 2002), p. 181.

12 Hillesum, *Etty*, p. 148. Rowan Williams delivered a characteristically brilliant Romanes Lecture on this theme on 18 November 2004, 'Religious Lives', reproduced in *Faith in the Public Square* (London: Bloomsbury, 2012), pp. 313–26.

13 Hillesum, *Etty*, p. 192.

14 Hillesum, *Etty*, p. 564.

15 Hillesum, *Etty*, p. 488.

16 Hillesum, *Etty*, p. 506.

17 Hugo Gryn, *Chasing Shadows* (London: Penguin, 2001), p. 248.

18 Gryn, *Chasing Shadows*, p. 251.

19 Another good example of his approach is his dialogue with Laurie Taylor, who describes himself as a liberal humanist; see 'A Conversation between . . . Professor John Gray and Professor Laurie Taylor', *Public Policy Research* 12(4) (2005–6), pp. 239–45.

18 'Keep your mind in hell and do not despair'

1 William Golding, *The Double Tongue* (London: Faber & Faber, 1993).
2 Quoted in Marguerite Yourcenar, *Memoirs of Hadrian* (London: Penguin, 1959, 2000), p. 269.
3 Yourcenar, *Memoirs of Hadrian*, p. 245.
4 Francis Spufford, *Unapologetic: Why, Despite Everything, Christianity Can Still Make Surprising Emotional Sense* (London: Faber & Faber, 2012).
5 There is, however, a lovely piece of divine irony here, in that two of the most outstanding public intellectuals of our time are the former Chief Rabbi, Dr Jonathan Sacks and the former Archbishop of Canterbury, Dr Rowan Williams.
6 Interview with Catherine Shoard, *The Guardian*, 20 May 2015.
7 Rohinton Mistry, *A Fine Balance* (London: Faber & Faber, 2006), p. 231.
8 Thomas Hardy, 'The Darkling Thrush', in *The Complete Poems*, ed. J. Gibson (London: Macmillan, 1976), p. 150.
9 G. B. Caird, *Paul's Letters from Prison* (Oxford: Oxford University Press, 1984), p. 70.
10 A number of key themes in my own book find consummate expression in Marilynne Robinson's trilogy. Stating them briefly they are as follows. First, the sheer difficulty, if not impossibility, of putting religious conviction into words; yet the necessity of doing so. At the same time, however necessary this may be, words can only seem inadequate and hollow to the one who uses them. Second, the hardship and horror of human existence, which is focused in Lila, one of the central characters. Her face contains sorrow and anger. Third, at the same time there is the sheer beauty of the world and of life itself. One of the clergymen, John Ames, lives with a sense of astonished rapture. Fourth, the mystery of how someone surrounded by love can act perversely. Fifth, how good and evil are intertwined so that an apparently feckless person can show courageous love and respectable good people be blind to manifest social evils. Sixth, how much of life, particularly when people get old, is simply struggling on. Seventh, a firm hope in an afterlife in which God's redeeming love holds sway over all that has existed. The incident referred to is in *Gilead*, pp. 109, 117. (Marilynne Robinson, *Gilead* (London: Virago, 2005); *Home* (London: Virago, 2008); *Lila* (London: Virago, 2014).)
11 Terry Eagleton, *Hope without Optimism* (New Haven, CT and London: Yale University Press, 2015), p. 115.
12 Eagleton, *Hope without Optimism*, p. 28.
13 *Conversations with Tennessee Williams*, ed. A. J. Devlin (Jackson, MS: University Press of Mississippi, 1986), p. 90.

Copyright acknowledgements

Copyright acknowledgements

Index

Index

Index

Index

Did you know that SPCK is a registered charity?

As well as publishing great books by leading Christian authors, we also . . .

. . . make assemblies meaningful and fun for over a million children by running www.assemblies.org.uk, a popular website that provides free assembly scripts for teachers. For many children, school assembly is the only contact they have with Christian faith and culture, and the only time in their week for spiritual reflection.

. . . help prisoners to become confident readers with our easy-to-read stories. Poor literacy is a huge barrier to re-habilitation. Prisoners identify with the believable heroes of our gritty fiction. At the same time, questions at the end of each chapter help them to examine their choices from a moral perspective and to build their reading confidence.

. . . support student ministers overseas in their training. We give them free, specially written theology books, the International Study Guides. These books really do make a difference, not just to students but to ministers and, through them, to a whole community.

Please support these great schemes: visit www.spck.org.uk/support-us to find out more.